D0899115

Three Queer Lives

Three Queer Lives

*An Alternative Biography of Fred Barnes,
Naomi Jacob and Arthur Marshall*

PAUL BAILEY

HAMISH HAMILTON
an imprint of
PENGUIN BOOKS

HAMISH HAMILTON

Published by the Penguin Group
Penguin Books Ltd, 80 Strand, London WC2R 0RL, England
Penguin Putnam Inc., 375 Hudson Street, New York, New York 10014, USA
Penguin Books Australia Ltd, Ringwood, Victoria, Australia
Penguin Books Canada Ltd, 10 Alcorn Avenue, Toronto, Ontario, Canada M4V 3B2
Penguin Books India (P) Ltd, 11 Community Centre,
Panchsheel Park, New Delhi – 110 017, India
Penguin Books (NZ) Ltd, Cnr Rosedale and Airborne Roads,
Albany, Auckland, New Zealand
Penguin Books (South Africa) (Pty) Ltd, 24 Sturdee Avenue,
Rosebank 2196, South Africa

Penguin Books Ltd, Registered Offices: 80 Strand, London WC2R 0RL, England

www.penguin.com

First published 2001
1

Copyright © Paul Bailey, 2001

The moral right of the author has been asserted

The publishers wish to thank the following copyright-holders for permission to quote copyrighted material:

The Estate of Naomi Jacob and the Deborah Owen Literary Agency for extracts from *Me* (1933), *Robert Nana and – Me* (1952), *Me – Likes and Dislikes* (1954), *Me – Looking Back* (1950), *Me – In the Kitchen* (1935), and *That Wild Lie* (1930); Peter Kelland and the Estate of Arthur Marshall for extracts from *Girls Will Be Girls* (1974), *Life's Rich Pageant* (1984), and *Nineteen to the Dozen* (1953) and private correspondence; Polly Muir and Rogers, Coleridge and White Ltd for private correspondence of Frank Muir; IMP for the extract from Ira Gershwin's 'The Man That Got Away'. Words by Ira Gershwin. Music by Harold Arlen. © 1954 Harwin Music Corp, USA, Chappell Morris Ltd, London W6 8BS. Lyrics reproduced by permission of IMP Ltd. All rights reserved; and David Wheeler for the photographs of Arthur Marshall in Somerset Maugham's *The Circle*, ADC, June 1929.

Every effort has been made to trace or contact all copyright-holders. The publishers will be pleased to make good any omissions and rectify any mistakes brought to their attention at the earliest opportunity.

All rights reserved.
Without limiting the rights under copyright
reserved above, no part of this publication may be
reproduced, stored in or introduced into a retrieval system,
or transmitted, in any form or by any means (electronic, mechanical,
photocopying, recording or otherwise), without the prior
written permission of both the copyright owner and
the above publisher of this book

Set in 12/14.75 pt Monotype Bembo
Typeset by Intype London Ltd
Printed in Great Britain by Clays Ltd, St Ives plc

A CIP catalogue record for this book is available from the British Library

ISBN 0241–13455–2

FOR OFFICER M. HAMBLING
(South London Corps)
AND HER PRIVATES

Contents

Acknowledgements

My special thanks are due to the late Lord Annan, who entrusted me with the M'Bonga letters; to Tony Barker, for his essay on Fred Barnes in *Music Hall*, the magazine he edits, and to John Harper, for introducing me to Micky's surviving friends in Sirmione.

I should also like to express my sincere gratitude to the following people who gave me advice, information and help: Adam, Ionas and Theodosis Adamos; Nicholas Amer; Dame Beryl Bainbridge; James Bernard; Jack Boyce; Gilbert Bradley; Jonathan Croall; Maureen Duffy; Allan Hailstone; Georgina Hammick; Ronald Harwood; Joyce Hewitt; Ahmet Kaplan; Miriam Karlin; Pat Keen; Peter Kelland; Francis King; Charles Laurence; John McLay; David Miller; Polly Muir; Chris Neill; Patrick O'Connor; Keith Parker; Peter Parker; Bill Pashley; Kim Patel; Deborah Rogers; Michael Sells; Diana Souhami; Ann and Anthony Thwaite; Max Tyler; David Wheeler; Francis Wheen and Natalie Wheen.

I am grateful to Carlo Pagiaro and his enchanting mother, Angiolina, for sharing their memories of Signora Micky.

The staff of the London Library and the Mander and Mitchenson Collection gave me invaluable assistance.

My editor, Tony Lacey, exhibited stoicism and extraordinary patience in the face of permanent non-delivery, and I thank him warmly. My deep gratitude, as ever, goes to Jeremy Trevathan for his constant support and encouragement.

Prologue: 'A Wicked Mischief'

One Sunday in the spring of 1953, when I was sixteen, there was a family gathering at our home in Battersea. It seemed, at first, like any other Sunday, with my mother in a physical and mental sweat in the kitchen, preparing the customary mountainous lunch. Then, as noon approached, I noticed that my sister was covering the highly polished front-room table with the lace-fringed damask tablecloth that had last been used on the afternoon of my father's funeral, in November 1948. I grew suspicious, and asked my mother what was going on.

'We've got guests today,' she revealed, dabbing at her glistening face with a towel.

'Who?'

'You'll find out soon enough.'

It was my mother's habit never to give simple answers to her younger son's simple questions. The identity of the guests would remain her secret for the moment, only to be disclosed when she started to panic, as she invariably did, shortly before their anticipated arrival.

'I hope they haven't met with an accident.'

'Who?'

'Harry and Floss. They're honouring us with a visit.'

Harry was my mother's beloved elder brother, and Floss his wife. He ran a successful haulage business and owned a butcher's shop in Hornchurch in Essex. He was a man of some considerable means, and Floss a lady of leisure. Their house was a chintzy suburban haven, with antimacassars on the chairs and sofas, and the inevitable barometer in the hallway. Harry had 'come up in the world through sheer honest toil', my mother was constantly reminding me. His head, unlike mine, wasn't in the clouds.

God was thanked when Harry's substantial car drew up outside. Harry and Floss were not the kind to come empty-handed, and that day they brought presents of meat and fruit and flowers and a large box of chocolates.

There were seven of us around the table, for my brother and sister-in-law had been invited too. The best china was in service and the cutlery gleamed. This was an occasion, and my mother had risen to it, as usual, by roasting a large joint and surrounding it with every vegetable that was currently in season.

'You shouldn't have gone to all this trouble, Maud,' said Floss, a notoriously dainty eater, as the 'spread' kept on growing. 'You're not feeding the troops.'

'She thinks she is,' Harry remarked. 'She always does.'

The adults drank sherry or beer, and I was allowed a single glass of shandy.

The dessert was a gigantic trifle, lovingly assembled the previous day. 'I hope there's no lumps in the custard,' said my mother, who was perfectly confident there wouldn't be. 'I can't abide lumpy custard.'

After lunch – or dinner, as the family still called it – the conversation, hitherto light and humorous in tone, suddenly turned serious. My future was under discussion. Earlier in the year I had won a scholarship to study acting at the prestigious Central School of Speech and Drama, and none of my relatives appeared to share my delight in the achievement. They had gathered now, it transpired, to warn me of the dangers ahead.

My uncle was not of the type who make pronouncements and offer ill-considered considered opinions, so he was behaving completely out of character when he pronounced that the theatre was a 'breeding ground for pansies and prosti-tutes' and that 'theatricals' were 'all tarred with the same filthy brush'. The voice he adopted to convey this information sounded melodramatic, stagey even. Perhaps he had rehearsed his speech, or practised it in the mirror, because his features were set in a grim expression, as false to his genial nature as was the booming noise coming from his mouth.

'Actors are the sort of people who interfere with boys like you.'

I was desperate to be interfered with, aching to be seduced, but I could not admit to my peculiar need. I observed calmly that Dame Edith Evans, a great actress and a committed Christian Scientist, wasn't my idea of a prostitute, and my uncle conceded that there was always the exception who proved the rule.

'They'll have you in their cesspit, if you don't watch out.'

I was advised to think again. It was an honour, of course, to be awarded a scholarship, but a lad with brains like mine shouldn't be wasting them on the stage. I could find respectable employment in a bank – my uncle mentioned 'connections' – or in a solicitor's office, if I put my mind to it.

'I want to be an actor and nothing else.'

(I had already made my professional debut, as Baby Bear and Gnome in the children's musical *Buckie's Bears* at the Leatherhead Repertory Theatre. This twee affair had been a big hit in the 1930s. Its author was the ten-year-old son of the famous sexologist Dr Marie Stopes, who established the first birth-control clinic in Britain in 1921. The elderly pioneer, who had improved the lives of thousands of men and women, attended the dress rehearsal with the now grown-up playwright. I was introduced to Dr Stopes and shook her hand, not realizing what an important person she was. She told the cast that her clever child had dictated the play to her over several months and that she had written it down for him. She had been his happy amanuensis.)

Their next tactic was to remind me of my origins. I must

not forget that I came from working stock, and that my
ancestors – on both sides of the family – had toiled long and
hard to make a humble living.

I answered, reasonably, that there were plenty of working-
class actors. They could be seen in films concerned with the
Second World War, playing forelock-touching privates or naval
ratings, or – if they were women – chirpy Cockneys merrily
dispensing limitless cups of tea. I had no wish to play such
parts, since it was my intention to excel in Shakespeare.

The pansies were invoked again, before my uncle and aunt's
departure. It was common knowledge they were the sons of
the idle rich, who had nothing better to do than be waited on,
hand and foot. You wouldn't find a pansy where people had
to work. In Chelsea, yes, or Kensington – where, it was
sombrely pointed out to me, the Central School of Speech
and Drama was situated.

I had been a drama student for a matter of weeks when my
hero John Gielgud – whom I had seen as a schoolboy as
Benedick in *Much Ado About Nothing* and Leontes in *The
Winter's Tale* – was arrested, and subsequently fined, for importuning in a public lavatory. An over-diligent reporter from the
London *Evening Standard* had noticed that a certain Arthur
John Gielgud, described as a clerk resident in the Westminster
area, was listed to appear in court on a charge of soliciting, and
alerted a photographer to take a picture of the 'clerk' as he left
the building. The photograph of Gielgud, accompanied by an
account of his court appearance, made front-page news, and a
Conservative peer, Earl Winterton, a virulent anti-Semite and
bigot, called for the actor to be stripped of his knighthood
and horsewhipped in the street.

In a debate in the House of Lords, the earl announced that
he belonged to a club whose members had once included such

actors of the Edwardian era as Sir Herbert Beerbohm Tree, Sir John Hare and Cyril Maude. 'It is inconceivable that they would have been guilty of the disgusting offence of male importuning.'

Earl Winterton's splenetic speech received uncritical attention in the popular newspapers. An editorial in the *Sunday Express* echoed my uncle's ideas relating to wealth and privilege:

Perversion is very largely a practice of the too idle and the too rich. It does not flourish in lands where men work hard and brows sweat with honest labour. It is a wicked mischief, destructive not only of men but of nations.

In October 1953, Gielgud returned to the London stage in a play by N. C. Hunter – middle England's inadequate substitute for Chekhov – entitled *A Day by the Sea*. (It was renamed *A Day by the WC* within the theatrical profession.) I went with a fellow student to the first Saturday-evening performance at the Haymarket Theatre, which was packed. We sat in the gallery, feeling apprehensive. The lights dimmed, the curtain rose, and Gielgud walked on. The audience stood up as one person and applauded vigorously. The clapping continued for what seemed like several minutes and then gradually subsided. Everyone sat down, in the awareness that they had issued an unspoken statement to the intolerant hordes outside. The people in the theatre that night were exhibiting affection and admiration. Gielgud's little sexual peccadillo was of no importance whatsoever.

I was an adolescent when I first heard the word 'cottage' used to describe a public urinal. 'To cottage' meant visiting such a place with an intention other than simply urinating. An habitué of cottages was called, logically, a 'cottager'. This alternative definition, employed by male homosexuals over many decades, finally appeared in print in 1977, with the posthumous publication of the unfinished memoirs of the maverick Labour MP and journalist Tom Driberg. In *Ruling Passions*, Driberg regrets the official destruction in the 1960s and 70s of the London cottages – in 'the alley by the Astoria, the dog-leg lane opposite the Garrick Club, the one near the Ivy, the one off Wardour Street, the narrow passage by the Coliseum' – he had frequented as a young man. He recalls reviewing a guide to the West End cottages in the books pages of the *New Statesman*. Its title was 'For Your Convenience', and it was written by Thomas Burke under the pseudonym 'Paul Pry':

I carried this book about with me at night for some weeks: the fact that I was reviewing it professionally provided a perfect excuse for spending some time in a cottage, making notes on its *décor, ambiance,* security, graffiti, and general flavour; and very pretty some of those pierced metal Victorian ones, usually painted green, were.

'The one off Wardour Street' was the most famous, and notorious, London cottage of them all. It was located in Dansey Place, near Shaftesbury Avenue, in the very heart of theatreland. During the Second World War it became a favourite haunt for American servicemen, to the amazed gratification of the regular cottagers. When a certain leading actor was not in his dressing room fifteen minutes before the play was due to begin, a messenger was dispatched to Dansey Place to collect him. The legend persists that a former marine, who happened to be in England when it was announced that the *pissoir* was to be demolished, approached Westminster Council and asked if he could buy it. He had a taste for Victoriana, of which the green-painted urinal was a particularly fine specimen. His request was acceded to, and the once public lavatory became his private property. He paid for it to be transported to his ranch in

Arizona, but on unpacking it he was crestfallen to see it had been scrubbed clean. Its character was all but gone; its years-old graffiti expunged. He sent off a furious letter to the leader of the Council, accusing his staff of vandalism.

I was a timid cottager in my youth. Caution was necessary, because the police were intent on convicting as many hapless men as possible. A good-looking policeman, acting as an agent provocateur, would smile or stare at the person standing next to him, and when the smile or stare was returned an arrest was made. A second policeman was always in attendance, to perform the role of witness. Dozens of cases of 'gross indecency' that often ended in suicide or public disgrace amounted to no more than a misjudged smile, a hasty stare. The victims were invariably young and inexperienced, whereas seasoned cottagers had developed the gift of identifying the plain-clothes plotters at first sight. 'It's the haircut that gives them away,' I was told by someone who was never arrested in a lifetime of cottaging. 'The haircut and the jawline – they're both so *rigid*.'

I was cautious to the point of terror each time I entered a cottage. The urinal adjacent to the Pier Hotel, a pub on Chelsea Embankment, was a reader's paradise, its walls bedecked with inventive, scurrilous graffiti, mostly involving the sexual escapades of the Royal Family. These obscene court circulars were stylishly phrased and boldly displayed in large letters. The spelling and syntax were exemplary, indicating that the anonymous scribe had benefited from a good education. I pictured him working in isolation, in the middle of the night perhaps, with no fear of interruption. I wondered if the police had ever questioned him about his colourfully expressed Republican sympathies.

Fear kept me innocent – in cottages, at least. I was possessed occasionally of the vain hope that I would awake one morning with a burning passion for girls, but that bright day, alas, was not to dawn. I continued to wander in what the beetroot-complexioned hacks of the popular press, acting as the nation's moral arbiters, labelled the 'twilight world' – a dark and eerie region inhabited exclusively by men who lusted after each other. Terrible things were said to happen in this 'half-world', which was sometimes invaded by a brave investigative journalist, who returned from the shadows with predictable findings: 'A well-dressed man with an effete way of speaking emerged from the darkness on Hampstead Heath and invited me to engage in an unnatural practice. I spurned his offer and his money.' The tone was always censorious, and not a little prurient.

When I came of age, there were clubs and bars to go to – the Calabash, the Rouge et Noir, the Golden Guitar, the Flying Fountain. None of them functioned for very long. The police would wait until the newly opened joint had attracted a sizable clientele, and then they would raid it. A more discreet establishment, the Rockingham in Soho, was allowed to continue in business after these livelier places had all closed down. One approached the Rockingham up a flight of dingy stairs, and entered a room filled with men in pinstriped suits, or blazers and slacks with perfect creases. The atmosphere was of a rather solemn respectability. The membership of the club was composed of lawyers, doctors, accountants, and the kind of actors who played the officer class in films celebrating Britain's glorious achievements in the Second World War. The noticeably effeminate were refused entry, and boys from the poorer districts of London – the real objects of desire on most nights – were expected to honour the dress code. Open-necked shirts and jeans were frowned upon. A club very like the Rockingham is featured in *Victim*, the pioneering film starring Dirk Bogarde as a barrister who is being blackmailed for a supposed relationship with a younger man. *Victim* was released in 1961, four years after the publication of the

Wolfenden Report, and six years before the principal recommendation of the committee chaired by Sir John Wolfenden – to legalize homosexual acts by consenting adults in private – was accepted by the British Parliament. I ceased being a criminal in 1967, along with thousands of others, when the 'buggers' charter', as its voluble detractors deemed it, became law.

If *Victim* has an overall message, beyond the more obvious one that making homosexuality a crime encourages blackmail, it is that homosexual feelings need to be repressed. Dirk Bogarde's character is married to a trusting, but bewildered, woman, acted by Sylvia Syms. It was Pauline Kael, in a perceptive review of the film, who detected the 'terribly self-conscious and unconvincing attempt to distinguish between the "love" the barrister feels for his wife and the physical desire – presumably some lower order of emotion – that he felt for a boy who is more interesting in every way than his wife'. She also noted that the 'lesser characters make out; they don't have the hero's steel will, and they are very pathetic indeed, given to such self-illuminating expressions as "Nature played me a dirty trick"'. Kael concluded:

In *Victim* there is so much effort to make us feel sympathetic to the homosexuals that they are never even allowed to be *gay*. The dreadful irony involved is that Dirk Bogarde looks so pained, so anguished from the self-sacrifice of repressing his homosexuality, that the film seems to give rather a black eye to the heterosexual life.

Dirk Bogarde was among the celebrated bachelors who contributed an article to a newspaper series with the general title 'Why I Never Married'. Bogarde revealed that he was still searching for his ideal woman, while Noël Coward declared undying devotion to his mother, Violet, who put other women (his leading ladies excepted) in the shade. Other contributors deplored the restraints of domesticity, hinting that a brief, passionate affair with a woman was preferable to a long-term commitment. No one stated the obvious truth, because it would have taken unusual courage, not to say recklessness, to do so.

I was, of course, confused. My schoolfriends and I had received no education in sexual matters. If we were told anything, it was that marriage would solve our problems. Although I never said 'Nature played me a dirty trick', I often thought it, in one form or another. I turned to books for consolation and enlightenment. Someone recommended André Gide's *Corydon*, which I read in English. I left it open on the kitchen table at a chapter in which Gide argues that homosexuality is not confined to the human species. I hoped that my mother, who was constantly informing me that I wasn't 'natural', thanks to my interest in poetry and music, might be intrigued to learn that certain animals, who were nothing if not natural, were occasionally attracted to their own sex. The book was closed when I returned home that evening. 'There's a proper place for books,' my mother snapped, 'and the kitchen table isn't one of them.'

I read fiction – the gay novels of the period before the acceptable 'gay' replaced the unacceptable 'queer' in common usage. There was *A Room in Chelsea Square*, published anony-mously, in which a delicate young man struggles with his overpowering feelings, and *Finistère* by Fritz Peters, from which I learnt that gay men pee on the side of the toilet bowl rather than straight into the water, like their brash and self-confident heterosexual counterparts. The protagonists in such stories of doomed and thwarted love were usually 'sensitive', to the extent that the word was frequently employed to suggest a homosexual man. 'He is very sensitive' could be decoded to mean 'He's queer'. Previous generations had appropriated 'so' and 'musical', as in 'Is he *so*?' and 'They say he's *musical*.'

Suicide was a staple ingredient in many of the novels, good and bad, that came out in the years when every homosexual act was illegal. It was almost as if the authors were taking heed of King George V's observation: 'One expects men like that to shoot themselves.' The tormented and essentially noble hero would battle against his fate for 200 anguished pages before doing what was sometimes called the 'decent thing' and disposing of the flesh that was the cause of his torment. With the support of the World Health Organization, homosexuality was portrayed as a fatal disease with no known cure. Nature's 'dirty trick', indeed.

The homosexual man as tragic victim was a theme explored by dramatists, too. In Julian Green's *South*, which is set during the American Civil War, an army officer shoots himself in the final act because of his unrequited longing for another soldier; and Brick, the unhappy husband of Maggie the Cat in Tennessee Williams's *Cat on a Hot Tin Roof* is unhappy because he can't confront the truth about himself. Julian Green and Tennessee Williams were gay, the latter famously so. Green was a devout Roman Catholic who somehow managed to reconcile the spiritual with the physical. He died, contentedly, in his nineties, his younger companion at his side. Williams, by contrast, never stopped fighting his demons. Williams is the greater artist. *A Streetcar Named Desire* remains a masterpiece, even if the recollection by Blanche Du Bois of the 'sensitive' young poet who was too fragile for this brutal world now sounds dated.

Like *South* and *Cat on a Hot Tin Roof*, Arthur Miller's *A View from the Bridge* was staged in London in the late 1950s in theatres that were briefly transformed into private clubs for adult members. This creaky melodrama uses homosexuality as a plot device. A longshoreman from Brooklyn, Eddie Carbone, has an unnatural passion, repressed of course, for his wife's niece. What is unnatural about lusting after your wife's niece?

It doesn't constitute incest; so if the girl is attractive, as she is meant to be, Eddie's lust seems perfectly natural. It is when the girl falls in love with one of his wife's cousins, who has entered America illegally, that Eddie goes crazy with jealousy. He accuses the Italian boy, who is also intended to be attractive, of being homosexual. He kisses him fiercely on the lips. The scene rings hollow, since the accusation is hollow and only resorted to for dramatic effect. Is Eddie bisexual? Miller does not say. This bogus piece, with its laboured borrowings from Greek tragedy, tells us nothing of the plight of the homosexual man in a country run largely by God-fearing bigots. And to think that critics and playgoers considered it bold and daring at the time.

The short stories and early novels of Angus Wilson are not concerned with the nobility of suffering. The characters in his first novel, *Hemlock and After*, include a flamboyantly queeny theatrical producer; a gormless male prostitute; a suburban brothel keeper who procures young girls for mature gentlemen; and a willowy, sensitive youth who has caught the eye of the book's protagonist, a bisexual, middle-aged writer. They are recognizable people, functioning in a believable milieu, and none of them is especially pleasant or likeable. For me, at the age of nineteen, it was a revelation, and also a relief, to encounter such flawed human beings in an ostensibly gay novel. It was courageous of Wilson to depict some homosexual men as seedy and scheming at a time when other writers were busy ennobling them and, more importantly, isolating them from the everyday world. Wilson understood that there was fun to be had, and happiness too, in those dark years when homosexual acts between men were criminalized. A book like Rodney Garland's *The Heart in Exile*, which is now deservedly forgotten, was a typical example of the genre Wilson was reacting against. According to Rodney Garland (was this the author's real name, or is it an act of homage to Judy?), to be queer was to be marked out for suffering. This was an accepted point of view, shared by defenders and a few of the more liberal bigots. It was anathema to Wilson. Yet the fictional queer as tortured hero/victim has taken a long while to vanish, if indeed he has entirely.

I bought my copy of A. E. Housman's *A Shropshire Lad* in 1954, when I was a tortured seventeen-year-old, drawn by a strange compulsion into London's cottages, where I returned no one's beckoning look. Housman's poems, which were easy to learn by heart because of their steady Latinate metre, speak of doomed love, of lads who are unattainable, for the dreadful reason that they tend to be dead:

> The time you won your town the race
> We chaired you through the market-place;
> Man and boy stood cheering by,
> And home we brought you shoulder-high.
>
> To-day, the road all runners come,
> Shoulder-high we bring you home,
> And set you at your threshold down,
> Townsman of a stiller town.

These are the opening stanzas of 'To an Athlete Dying Young', one of his more overt declarations of homosexual longing. Housman's biographers have revealed that his abiding love for the handsome Moses Jackson remained unrequited, and that he regularly patronized a male brothel in Venice. Abroad was where you did such things. There is a mordant wit subtly buried in the poetry, but nothing of the exuberance, the relish for a literary scrap, that informs the essays and lectures on the Greek and Latin writers he studied so carefully. The author of *A Shropshire Lad* and *Last Poems* is the masochistic occupant of a living hell. Housman's frustrations are given finely tuned expression, and that expression held much appeal to a bewildered teenage boy who ached for the loving embrace of a sturdy lad of the kind the poet is perpetually killing off. It's ironic that Housman, along with many other queers of his class and background, had to satisfy his pent-up sexual appetites in a Catholic country where homosexuality was, and is, regarded as a sin, an abomination.

I have to thank two people for guiding me out of the darkness of guilt and shame. One of them is dead, and the other has disappeared completely from my life. The first was a middle-aged actor who plied me with wine and invited me to join him in bed. We undressed in the dark, to the smell of burning incense. He had no desire to kiss me, he declared – he simply wanted to play. Playing, it transpired, meant that my right hand was occupied for the number of minutes it took for him to achieve orgasm. He feigned sleep after that, and so did I.

The actor was a convert to Roman Catholicism. During the night he slid out of bed stealthily. When I heard him begging forgiveness from Jesus and the Virgin Mary for spilling his seed, I opened my eyes and saw that he was on his knees in front of a crucifix.

In the morning, he invited me to play again. I refused, but thanked him for his hospitality. What I couldn't thank him for, then, was the gift of his abjectness, which would help in some measure to release me from mine.

A few weeks before this unusual experience, I had attempted to make love to a congenial girl on a friend's divan. We kissed and cuddled. She began to giggle. I persevered. 'What's the matter?' I asked when her giggling became uncontrollable. 'You are,' she answered, pushing me off. 'You're the matter. You're soft where you shouldn't be. You want a man, don't you?'

'Yes,' I astonished myself by admitting.

'So do I,' she said, without malice. 'Let's go and get drunk.'

She was to marry and leave London, and our friendship of years slowly petered out. Yet the kindness and honesty she exhibited that evening were of a lasting benefit to the young pretender who had hoped to find sexual bliss in her arms. It was a doomed enterprise, but she had converted it into a comic one, a cause for salutary laughter.

The most quoted piece of gay graffiti from the 1950s was composed of a bold statement followed by an urgent request. 'My mother made me a homosexual' invariably appeared in large letters, while underneath it, in a different hand, was written 'If I buy her the wool, will she make me one?'

It was a commonly held belief that homosexual men were the sons of overprotective or domineering mothers. That was the reason for their effeminacy. Deprived of a father's influence, an impressionable boy could easily develop a liking for feminine things – like poetry, my family maintained – instead of such natural, masculine pursuits as boxing or football. My own perverse behaviour was attributed to the fact that my father was dead.

He had been dead for six months or so when my mother surprised me with an invitation to the theatre. She had been given tickets for a matinée performance of the musical *King's Rhapsody*, written by, and starring, Ivor Novello, and I was to be her guest. It was an unforgettable occasion. The audience seemed to consist entirely of middle-aged or elderly women with blue-rinsed hair. I was the only boy in the stalls, I took pains to notice. The show itself was a preposterous Ruritanian extravaganza, with the men in brilliant uniforms and the women in ball gowns and evening dresses. Novello, playing King Nikki of Murania, did not look effeminate as he strode about the stage, but his handsomeness was not of the kind you saw in the streets. His falcon-like profile singled him out from men with everyday noses. A tall soprano sang 'Someday My Heart Will Awake' and a plump contralto 'Fly Home, Little Heart' and a happy band of fiddling gypsies joined in the nuptials for King Nikki and Queen Cristian, whose heart he had awoken.

In the interval, eating an ice cream, I found myself staring at two men with lightly pancaked faces. In the days before the permanent suntan, a few brave spirits could be sighted in the capital wearing discreet make-up. The two men I stared at – until my mother told me off for being rude – were perfectly at ease among the blue-rinsed matrons in their tasteful summer outfits. They were sissies beyond a doubt, and I did not credit them with courage at the time, but I think I do now.

For my mother, *King's Rhapsody* was a wonderful treat, an escape from the daily round of drudgery. Once we were home again, she revealed that Ivor Novello had given her the tickets, in person. Some evenings earlier, she had waited at table and helped cook the meal at a dinner party hosted by Lady Juliet Duff, and Novello was there, along with Somerset Maugham, who was not polite to the staff. When the dinner was over, and the guests departing, Ivor Novello had come into the kitchen to thank everyone concerned for the delicious food. From that gracious moment onwards, my mother considered him a lovely man, and she wept when he died the next year.

Many of the women who flocked to see *King's Rhapsody* had been Ivor Novello's fans since they were teenagers. He was their heart-throb in the 1920s. They had married, raised families, but still went on worshipping him. They knew he was gay, but the fact didn't worry them. The subject of his sexual life was probably never discussed. He was their beloved, unattainable Ivor – the very epitome of the romantic leading man – and that was all that mattered. The day of his funeral was bitterly cold and windy, but the weather did not deter them. They turned up at Golders Green crematorium in their hundreds to express their devotion and say their tearful goodbyes.

Novello's very last musical, in which he did not appear, was called *Gay's the Word*. He was well aware that 'gay' was then a code word, as was Noël Coward when he wrote the line 'Let our affair be a gay thing'. Novello, it is said, provided his own alternative titles to two of his most successful shows – *The Dancing Years* was known to actors and singers as *The Prancing Queers*, and *Perchance to Dream* became *Perchance to Scream*. He neither pranced nor screamed himself, but he was certainly acquainted with those who did – such as Fred Barnes, perhaps, the debonair song-and-dance man of the music halls, who was already famous in 1920 when Novello was beginning to make his name. In his heyday, Barnes was the generous patron of innumerable working-class men, who regarded his ap-proaching Rolls-Royce as a welcome sight at a time of severe unemployment and social inequality. Sailors and guardsmen also benefited from his largesse. He was proud of his pretty features, which he flaunted in public.

Queers met in clubs, bars and cottages, but there was one event that brought them together en masse. If anyone could lure them out of the dark recesses of the twilight world, it was Judy Garland. Whenever she appeared at the London Palladium, they came to pay homage from all points of the compass. Hours before the performance was due to begin, the streets near the theatre were crammed with her ardent fans, chatting to each other in happy anticipation of an exciting evening. Telephone numbers and addresses were exchanged, and there were promises to visit Glasgow or Manchester or Aberystwyth. The police were present, too, but only to ensure that the crowd didn't get out of control. No one was arrested for gross indecency.

The atmosphere inside the Palladium was always electric on Garland nights. The term 'drama queen' might have been invented for her alone. The curtain was late rising, and the inevitable question was asked: 'Where is she?' It was feared that the manager would step forward and announce that, owing to an accident, an illness, any possible excuse, Miss Garland was unable to perform tonight. We crossed our fingers and waited, and waited. She couldn't let us down. It would be as heartless and wicked as shooing pilgrims away from Mecca or allowing the holy water to run dry at Lourdes. She wouldn't dare.

Then, just as we were imagining the worst, the orchestra suddenly struck up with a medley of her greatest songs. We smiled. What fools we were to have worried. She was here with us at last, somewhere in the building.

Or was she? The curtain rose, revealing a bare stage. A single spotlight was ready to be trained on our heroine. We waited, in silence. It was then that she fell into view, thanks to the considerate individual in the wings who had the forethought to push her. She tottered in the direction of the microphone as we yelled our greetings and applauded wildly. She began to sing, her voice hoarse with nervousness. The hoarseness soon went. Between songs, she told us how glad she was to be in London, and how very, very much she loved us. 'We love you, too, Judy,' several people shouted back, some of them women.

It was the same ritual, year after year. She loved us, and we loved her; we knew of her sufferings, and she knew of ours. When, late in the show, she started to sing Ira Gershwin and Harold Arlen's 'The Man That Got Away' –

> The night is bitter,
> The stars have lost their glitter,

The winds grow colder,
Suddenly you're older,
And all because of
The man that got away –

we understood what she was going through, even those of us
– like myself – for whom *the* man had yet to arrive. There
seemed to be nothing studiedly musical about her singing.
The sentiments were of prime importance, coming straight at
us from her damaged heart.

At the end of the evening, with the tune of 'Somewhere
Over the Rainbow' echoing in our ears, we emerged from the
theatre both elated and exhausted. She had put us through
the emotional mill yet again. In the morning, we would
return to a life of secrecy and deception, our feelings hidden
behind a carapace of ordinariness. She had promised us that
she would be coming back, and we would be there to welcome
her.

On one occasion, she coaxed an embarrassed Dirk Bogarde
out of his seat in the stalls and led him by the hand on to the
stage, where she serenaded him with 'You Made Me Love
You'. He kept his smile in place as she warbled 'I didn't wanna
do it, I didn't wanna do it', and the audience applauded him
for being such a good sport. Bogarde must have been aware
that everyone with a functioning intelligence understood that
he was gay, yet this awareness didn't stop him threatening
journalists with libel action if they even so much as hinted at
the obvious fact. Bogarde's lover, Anthony Forwood, whom
he nursed through a terrible last illness, was either referred to
as 'my manager' or by his surname alone. The word 'homosexual', or any of its variants, was not to be mentioned.

This kind of extreme discretion was practised by the majority
of homosexual men in Britain before 1967. Many still see fit
to practise it thirty years on. Gays of Bogarde's generation and

earlier had been of necessity secretive for so long that the idea
of 'coming out of the closet' filled them with terror. I recall
the poet William Plomer telling me how shocked and saddened
he was by the revelations in J. R. Ackerley's memoir *My Father
and Myself*, which was published posthumously in 1968.
William remembered Joe as a happier, funnier man than the
dissatisfied and frustrated narrator of that chillingly comic
masterpiece. Joe, in William's view, was 'letting the side down'
by spilling his miserable beans from beyond the grave. Private
lives should remain private, even if they sometimes ventured
into the public arena. Joe's desperate quest for the 'ideal companion' should have remained his own concern. E. M. Forster,
Joe's closest friend, was appalled by the book. 'It seems so ill-
tempered, and such a reproach to all his friends. I wish I could
give him a good smack!'

Forster and Plomer were too attached to the Joe they had
known and admired to appreciate the self-deprecating irony
that informs his catalogue of doomed affairs. Ackerley was a
romantic, and in the manner of romantics he tended to place
the working-class boys he was attracted to on pedestals that
quickly began to shake. He loved, in his fashion, a succession
of fallen idols. Heterosexual romantics experience similar dis-
enchantment with the lovers they idolize.

William was a considerable gossip, but even when regaling
me with stories involving the hilarious sexual misadventures
of the famous, he would purposely omit their names. It was
So-and-So who had to hide in a dustbin for several hours, and
Such-and-Such who jumped from a first-floor window, naked,
on hearing the voice of an outraged husband. The question
'Who is it, William?' elicited the reply 'Ah, that would be
telling.'

Plomer's gay friends were the recipients of useful information, especially when the poet was travelling outside
London. In his dependable biography, Peter Alexander

describes how Plomer, on a trip to Portsmouth, drew a map of that part of the city of most interest to homosexuals, with the initials HQ indicating the exact location of the liveliest cottage. He made copies of it, which he posted to Ackerley and others. Because of William's wiliness, it resembled a military map, and thus would not have invited suspicion if it had fallen into the wrong hands.

A joke dating from the 1950s has two rich women discussing male homosexuality. It was a popular topic of conversation in that especially repressive decade, when one gay scandal after another hit the front pages of the newspapers. Draconian prison sentences were meted out to men who had committed acts of gross indecency, often in the privacy of their homes. The term 'gross indecency' covered everything from a furtive grope in a cottage to sodomy in a bedroom. Blackmailers thrived as the witch-hunt, which was given the blessing of the Home Secretary, Sir David Maxwell-Fyffe, progressed. And one of the two rich women, sipping her first gin and tonic of the day, is moved to join the thunderous chorus of self-righteous disapproval:

'I think men like that should be shot. Or horsewhipped at least. Or put away where they can't do any harm.'

Her companion, a woman of the world, brings her firmly back to earth.

'Oh, don't be so silly, darling. We don't want Harrods to become self-service, do we?'

No, we didn't. I worked in Harrods, on and off, for eight years, when I was resting between theatrical engagements. The innumerable gay shop assistants were well-dressed and well-spoken. They were everywhere in the store – in the Food Hall, in Men's Wear, in Antiques, in Soft Furnishings – and very discreet and subdued they were. Only one of them achieved notoriety – a tall, willowy man with a startling gap in his front teeth who was in charge of Gentlemen's Dressing Gowns and nicknamed 'Magda'. What took place in the fitting room remains Magda's secret, but it certainly intrigued a large number of American and Japanese tourists. 'Where can I find your famous dressing gowns?' was a question the doorman on duty at the main entrance was accustomed to answering throughout the summer. 'He's a character, that one they call Magda,' this doorman remarked to me one morning in the canteen. 'You can't help wondering why he's so popular.'

I was alone in Foreign Books on the day I thought I was serving J. B. Priestley, the dramatist noted for his blunt opinions. I was on the point of addressing him as Mr Priestley when I realized that the individual with a Yorkshire accent was a northerner of a wholly different persuasion. This strange personage was wearing a tweed jacket, a shirt with a starched collar, a tie held in place with a gold pin, and a pork pie hat. A momentary glance at the matching tweed skirt completing the outfit rescued the pair of us from embarrassment and possible distress. The fruity baritone voice was similar to Priestley's, and the face not unlike his, but it was now clear to me that I had to address her as Madam, which I duly did. As soon as she had stomped out of the book department in her sensible brogues, I rushed across to another, older assistant and inquired after the identity of the masculine woman in tweeds. I was told that she was Naomi Jacob, the celebrated popular novelist.

There was always abroad, if you had the money to get there. Amsterdam was only an hour away. The hotels were cheap and clean, and what I wanted to do in Holland was not a criminal offence.

It was the open friendliness of the queers in Amsterdam that startled me at first. I was accustomed to furtiveness, to quick sidelong glances, so I was pleasantly disconcerted when an attractive man came up to me in the street and introduced himself. How easy, how absolutely natural, it seemed, to meet Kurt in the middle of the day, with passers-by going about their own business. We drank beer outside a café, and went to bed in the late afternoon. This was an occasion of mutual pleasure, not to be repeated – he was on the point of leaving for America, where he would find work and settle down – and not to be forgotten.

On a second visit to Amsterdam, I stayed in a small family hotel on Singel, run by a jolly, pink-cheeked married couple with a passion for tortoiseshell cats, one of which slept alongside me at night. In a bar one evening I met Rudi, who lived with his parents in Rotterdam. I was apprehensive about taking him back to the cat-strewn *pension*, and since a trip to Rotterdam was impracticable, it looked as if we had nowhere to go. Then Rudi said that he'd heard of a place in the dockland area of the city, owned by a nice old man. The place turned out to be a former warehouse, dimly lit, and the owner an elderly queen in a beret, who sat behind a reception desk. On the wall above him was a large, blown-up photograph of another man in a beret, whose face I recognized, bearing the inscription *A mon ami Eric, André Gide*. 'We were good friends,' Eric muttered, without removing the cigarette from his mouth. 'A long time ago.'

Eric relieved me of twenty pounds worth of guilders, and produced a threadbare towel from beneath the desk. He pressed a bell, and a pimply boy emerged out of the dimness. 'Take the gentlemen to their *chambre*,' Eric ordered with a smile, adding something in Dutch that Rudi said was too vulgar to translate.

The boy led us up a flight of stairs and showed us into a

cubicle with walls made of cardboard. It seemed to be one of many hastily built cubicles in an enormous dormitory. So much for our *chambre*. Groans and whispers and sudden cries of ecstasy greeted our arrival, and persisted until dawn. There were loud snores, and somebody's fart inspired derisive laughter. Rudi and I made love very, very quietly.

In the morning, we washed ourselves in icy water, and walked back to the centre of Amsterdam, where we had coffee and croissants at the American Hotel. We were never to meet again, but we corresponded regularly, and exchanged Christmas cards for twelve years. When I checked out of the hotel on Singel, I saw that the kindly couple had not charged me for the night I had spent in Eric's cardboard *chambre* down by the docks.

I discovered the poetry of Constantine Cavafy in 1961, in the translations by Rae Dalven. This edition has an Introduction by W. H. Auden, whose *Collected Shorter Poems 1930–44* I had been carrying about with me for seven years. Through one literary hero, I became familiar with another. Auden says of Cavafy:

The erotic world he depicts is one of casual pickups and short-lived affairs. Love, there, is rarely more than physical passion, and when tenderer emotions do exist, they are almost always one-sided. At the same time, he refuses to pretend that his memories of moments of sensual pleasure are unhappy or spoiled by feelings of guilt. One can feel guilty about one's relation to other persons – one has treated them badly or made them unhappy – but nobody, whatever his moral convictions, can honestly regret a moment of physical pleasure as such.

Cavafy's poetic voice always sounds honest. There is no

rhetoric, no overstatement. The boys with whom he found pleasure in the lodging houses and cheap hotels of Alexandria are remembered with gratitude. It's clear that some of them were prostitutes. Cavafy doesn't emphasize the fact, nor does he encourage his readers to giggle at his naughtiness. He is too thoughtful, too properly serious for that. His tone is measured, even when he is invoking states of ecstasy.

He is the most colloquial of the great modern poets. His Greek travels easily. He is the same Cavafy in the French of Marguerite Yourcenar, the Italian of Margherita Dalmàti and Nelo Risi, and the other English versions by John Mavrogordato and, best of all, Edmond Keeley and Philip Sherrard. Cavafy, in one version or another, has been my companion for virtually forty years. I like his ironic cast of mind, the way in which he rewrites and reimagines history. But, mostly, I like what Auden – who acknowledged him as a beneficial influence – liked: his freedom from misguided shame and guilt; his enjoyment of the passing moment, and the genuine nature of his gratefulness.

It's with this last in my thoughts that I recall my partners in crime from the 1950s and early 60s. A favourite place of assignation was Speakers' Corner in Hyde Park, where I delighted in the rantings of such eccentrics as Aggie, the toothless Bible-thumper who ignored the incessant cruel gibes of the hecklers, and the heavily tattooed man who boasted that he'd escaped from Sing Sing, the Santé in Paris, Wormwood Scrubs and every noted prison in the world. Maximum security meant nothing to him, he declared as he twisted his multicoloured body out of the bulky chains an accomplice had tied him in. A furious atheist talked of mumbo-jumbo, while Donald Soper, the head of the Methodist Church in Britain, observed that Jesus Christ was the first effective socialist.

The orator who attracted the biggest audience of queers was a weasel-faced man who denounced the residents of

Sodom and Gomorrah, threatening them with everlasting punishment. 'The cities of the plain are right here in London,' he shrieked, to occasional cries of 'You bet.' Weasel was testing his vocal cords to the limit when a smiling Jamaican lured me out of the crowd and invited me to 'come back for a coffee' – the regulation phrase gay men used to pick someone up. (It was the age of the coffee bar, and Londoners felt very European as they consumed espresso and cappuccino after decades of suffering the bitter taste of coffee-and-chicory essence, which came in thin bottles labelled 'Bev' or 'Camp'.) Yes, I responded, I would love to come back for a coffee. In the two years of our friendship, I never drank a single cup.

There was an international flavour to Speakers' Corner in midsummer, with visitors from the Continent and Scandinavia as well as America. Weasel was on the verge of something like happiness when his prophecies of hellfire and damnation were echoed by Mormons and Baptists with crew-cuts. I once asked Weasel to explain in simple language what actually happened, if anything, to the two angels who put up for the night in Lot's house, but he couldn't oblige. The scribe responsible for Chapter 19 of the Book of Genesis cannot be praised for his powers of detailed description, I remarked, and Weasel responded with the message 'Read and heed. Read and heed.' I departed with a young Corsican, who inspired me to learn Italian because he spoke it so beautifully.

Of all the chance encounters I had in that period, one in particular looms in my memory. I was in a telephone box on the corner of the street in Bayswater where I was living when a vision of male loveliness arose slowly, head first, from beneath the pavement. I stared in admiration as the overalled figure gradually appeared before me. The youth blinked as he greeted the daylight, and I watched as he replaced the cover on the manhole from which he had emerged. He caught my look of wonderment and smiled. I came out of the box and he said hello. I said hello, too, with a nervous tremor in my voice. 'My name's Mick. I'm a sewerman's apprentice. I could do with a wash.'

I told the smelly Adonis that I lived a minute's walk away. We descended the steps to the basement flat I shared, platonically, with a friend called John. Mick apologized for his stink, and I said I'd run him a bath. Since John was a house-painter and decorator, the bathroom cabinet contained several bars of carbolic soap. Mick scrubbed himself clean of sewage, with my incredulous assistance, and carbolic soap has never had a sweeter scent or taste than it had that far-off afternoon. Hours later, he thanked me for his 'last fling with a bloke' and confessed he was getting married the following Saturday. I declined his offer to attend the wedding, but wished him the best of luck. We kissed goodbye, and Mick ran up the steps and out of my life. Or so I imagined.

A year passed. I was in the tiny kitchen when the doorbell rang, unexpectedly. 'Who is it?' I called out, and the answer came 'It's me. Mick. I'm clean.' I opened the front door and there he stood, in a dark blue suit. He was on holiday and he just happened to be in the area and he'd wondered if his mate was still at the same address. He'd already had a bath, he went on to say, and if I was in the mood for a bit of fun, he was too. This repeated 'last fling' was indeed the last, and more subtly fragrant than the first. He now had his wife's name tattooed on his right arm, as a 'mark of respect'.

Mick was just one of several married men from my own background that I slept with in my twenties. Working-class boys were expected to marry young, and were subjected to a good deal of suspicious questioning if they failed to do so. 'I tied the knot to shut them up,' said Bob, in a sentence worthy of the T. S. Eliot of *Sweeney Agonistes*. It was Bob who left ten pound notes on the bedside table, under the impression, perhaps, that a man who hadn't married and enjoyed gay sex must be nothing but a tart.

It is only Johnny I recollect with sadness. He was a spirited and inventive lover, who changed character immediately after love-making. He would light a cigarette, puff on it, and proceed to call me a filthy, disgusting queer. I was too frightened the first time I received this abuse to remind him that, minutes earlier, he'd been as filthy and disgusting a queer as I was. 'If I ever see you again, I'll kill you,' he threatened, slamming himself out of the flat with the information that he was going home to the wife.

He kept on phoning me, and I kept on inviting him over. I willed myself not to respond to his insults, which became ever more virulent. It's his game, I thought, his terrible game, and I have to let him play it. I returned his glare, and remained silent. He promised to cut my cock off, to beat the shit out of me, to do to me what all dirty queers deserve. I reasoned that the abusive words were enough for him; that he would not, could not, progress beyond threats. It was his tortuous way of asserting his challenged masculinity. And then I realized that the day might come when words alone would no longer be an adequate substitute for violence. His self-loathing was immense. The next time he phoned, eager for the illicit sex he relished, I announced with strained confidence that I had decided to marry a girl I had fallen in love with, and to my relief and regret he offered me his congratulations.

My mother was overjoyed when I told her that I had abandoned acting. I neglected to tell her that I was writing plays which no one wanted to produce or direct. One of these ended up on the desk of Arthur Marshall, who was reading scripts for a television company. He wrote me a friendly letter, in which he said what pleasure my dialogue had given him. He added that *The Almshouses*, as my piece was called, would be impossible to broadcast, for two reasons: a) it lacked a conventional plot, and b) its characters were in their seventies and eighties. This was in 1965, when youth was in vogue and senility set in at the age of thirty.

The letter included an invitation to elevenses, if I cared to take it up. As a result, I met Arthur Marshall for the one and only time, in his office above the Queen's Theatre. We drank tea and chatted about my play. He advised me to persevere. I said that I loved his reviews of appalling books in the back pages of the *New Statesman*, and he accepted the compliment with a chuckle. I basked in his jolly company for an hour or more. 'Back to business, alas,' he sighed, pointing to a pile of typescripts. 'Dear me, what an *ordeal*.'

I knew nothing then of his brilliant, and affectionate, impersonations of schoolmistresses and other women in authority. It wasn't until I mentioned him to William Plomer, who was one of his many friends, that I learned how he had rechristened Montgomery of Alamein 'Brenda' and General Gort 'Gladys'. His fellow officers were each given appropriate names. Life, even in wartime, afforded him much to laugh about.

I'd guessed that day that Arthur Marshall was queer, although his behaviour was courteous and discreet. He seemed to me to possess the enviable quality of serious frivolousness, which is in some measure a stoic quality. He did not advertise his homosexuality, but I felt certain that he did not deny it either.

I was happy not to be a criminal in 1967. My partner and I drank champagne to celebrate our new-found legality. Yet there were those – the painter Francis Bacon was one of them – who did not welcome the cautious move towards liberalism. 'I don't want to be tolerated,' an ageing landscape gardener remarked to me. 'Tolerance is so boring.' He had enjoyed the 'thrill of the chase' for nearly half a century, and regarded the Labour government's modest bill as a 'terrible omen'. He died before the cottage clearances of the 1980s and the destruction of the Biograph, the cinema in which he had rarely looked up at the screen.

The Biograph was situated by Victoria Station. Its regular visitors could not be described as cineastes, despite the fact that it often showed films that were worth seeing. If you wanted to sit through the programme unmolested, you were advised to avoid the first six rows on the left-hand side. The movies were carefully selected by the management – war epics with deafening sound tracks covered up the myriad noises echoing in the auditorium, and darkly lit, studio-based thrillers reflected the faintest light on the clientele. The cashier on duty did his or her best to discourage women from entering, and a long-serving usherette with a club foot showed people to their seats. She, too, had been chosen with care.

The Biograph vanished, and many of London's popular cottages were sold off to private organizations. The under-ground lavatory at Shepherd's Bush Green is now a snooker club; the brick urinal in King Street, Hammersmith, has been converted into a pizzeria, and the cottage-like cottage in Battersea Park has become the offices of a firm of solicitors.

One of the minor sights of London for three decades at least was a cheerful man who wore a raincoat and a trilby hat in all weathers. He was referred to as the Unknown Cottager by those who frequented the same haunts. It was suspected that he was a deaf-mute, for nobody had ever heard him speak. Any attempt to engage him in conversation was met with a smile or a nod. What was never in doubt was his patriotism. In the centre of the handlebars of the ancient bicycle that transported him from cottage to cottage was fixed an unmistakable Union Jack. The doughty old veteran was still pedalling across the city in the late 1980s, a wizened reminder of a dying breed. I last saw his bicycle propped against a wall in a Soho back street, its flag moving limply in the autumn wind. I walked on, knowing that he was pursuing his silent occupation somewhere down below.

1. 'The Wavy-Haired, Blue-Eyed Adonis'

Fred Barnes (1885–1938)

In the spring of 1907, the young singer, dancer and accomplished light comedian Fred Barnes wrote the song that was to help make him a star of the music halls. 'The Black Sheep of the Family' came to him while he was in a despondent mood. Although he had achieved his ambition to perform as a solo artist in London, making his debut at the Empress, Brixton, in April as the second act of the evening, he was still in the unfortunate position of having to 'follow the overture'. At both the Norwich Hippodrome and the Ipswich Hippodrome, he had the unenviable task of trying to catch the interest of a restless and talkative audience, who usually ignored the first act on the bill. Fred sang 'Raise Your Hat to the Lady' as people drifted into the theatre, chatting and laughing and paying only scant attention to the immaculate newcomer on stage.

He gave an impromptu performance of 'The Black Sheep of the Family' to one of his many landladies, who declared it would be a hit. Fred was not convinced. Perhaps he was wary of the effect its lyrics might have on the public. At this early point in his career, he was impersonating smart young men-about-town, and 'The Black Sheep of the Family' needed to be sung and acted, as it were, by someone who had been ostracized from society. Six months after its composition, Fred again performed it in private, to a group of fellow artists who were appearing with him in Leeds. He remembered that it was raining steadily as he went to the piano and played it through. His friends expressed approval and also their amazement that he had written it. They urged him to try it out in London the following week.

'A disappointment awaited me in London,' Fred revealed in one of a series of articles entitled 'How Success Ruined Me' which were published in *Thompson's Weekly News* between January and April 1932. 'I found on arrival at the Hackney Empire that once again I followed the overture. But, although I didn't know it then, my first-turn days were nearly over; or, at any rate, for a time. "The Black Sheep of the Family" was going to do for me what no other song had succeeded in doing.'

He made a 'nervous entry' in a 'ragged suit' to a packed house. 'Never in my life have I been so afraid of failure as I was that night. But as I sang I gained confidence. I put everything I knew into that song. I felt that my reputation was at stake in a double sense.'

Before he had finished singing it, Fred was sure that his unusual song 'had struck home to the hearts of the people, whose faces I could see dimly in front of me. A stillness had fallen over the house. For me the quiet spelled triumph. The experience was new to me, but even as I sang I understood.'

He took several curtain calls and, at the audience's clamorous insistence, repeated the chorus:

> Yes, I'm the black, black sheep of the family.
> Everybody runs me down.
> People shake their heads at me,
> Say I'm a disgrace to society . . .

The words of 'The Black Sheep of the Family' were to prove sadly prescient seventeen years later, when Fred was arrested in Hyde Park, charged with drunken driving. A half-naked sailor, clothes in hand, was seen running away from his car.

★

Frederick Jester Barnes was born on 31 May 1885, in a 'little bedroom' above his father's butcher's shop at 219 Great Lister Street in Saltley, a poor district of Birmingham. He was not christened Jester in a spirit of mischief, but rather as a mark of respect for his mother, whose maiden name it was. Fred liked to boast that she was Lady Alice Jester, but his birth certificate simply records the names Mary Alice. She might have been called Lady as a term of endearment by her husband and relatives, though Fred probably wanted people to think there was aristocratic blood in his family.

In 'How Success Ruined Me', Fred acknowledged the debt he owed to the father with whom he had sustained an edgy, and sometimes difficult, relationship. He noted that Thomas William Barnes 'began as a workman butcher in a slaughter-house at a meagre salary of eight shillings a week and his food. He worked from early in the morning until late at night. He was thrifty, industrious, ambitious . . . My father has told me that it took him years to save his first £20.'

With this money, Tom Barnes rented the small shop in Great Lister Street. Now that he was almost a man of property, and being prudent by nature, he found the confidence to ask Mary Alice Jester to be his wife. Fred, the couple's only child, was born a year later. By the time Fred was two, Tom was in possession of a thriving business, and rich enough to buy 'larger premises higher up the street', at 214.

Fred was very attached to his mother, who seems to have encouraged his early need for play-acting. 'I remember when I was quite a little chap – not more than seven or eight – how fond I was of dressing up, making up my face, and posing before the mirror in my bedroom.' Lady Alice didn't smack him or chastise him for behaving in a manner more commonly associated with a butcher's daughter. It was her make-up he was applying to his pretty face while Tom Barnes – 'Butcher and Slaughterer' were the words beneath his name on the sign outside the shop – toiled away, unknowing.

Fred's childish fantasies were not sparked off by theatrical ambitions. He knew nothing of the famous stars of the music halls whom he would begin to meet in his teenage years. 'My first dream of the stage came when I was ten, and the great Vesta Tilley was the artiste who inspired it. The incident has always remained most vivid in my memory.'

He was in the shop with his mother one afternoon when a carriage and pair drew up on the opposite side of the street. Carriages were a rare sight in Saltley, so Lady Alice took Fred to the door of the shop to get a better view. 'As we watched, two beautifully dressed ladies alighted and walked up the mean little courtyard . . .' Fred pulled at his mother's apron and asked her who the ladies were, '"The one on the right," Mother whispered, "is Vesta Tilley, a great actress."'

Lady Alice was 'deeply impressed' to see such a distinguished person in their humble street. She told her gaping son that Vesta Tilley was playing principal boy in *Dick Whittington*, the pantomime at the Prince of Wales Theatre in Birmingham.

'I remember waiting in the street for the return of the ladies and watching with childish awe when, about half an hour later, they re-entered their smart carriage and drove away.'

Fred announced that he wanted to go to the pantomime, so his mother took him for his Christmas treat. They sat in the pit, in sixpenny seats, sharing a bag of oranges. He had never been inside a theatre before.

'My first glimpse of Vesta Tilley on the stage came when Alice Fitzwarren, the principal girl, while struggling with the villain in the market square gave the cry "Who will save me?" The lid of the pannier basket in the square then opened, and out jumped a dapper little figure clad in grey silk tights. With a cry, "I will!", she sprang to the rescue of the struggling Alice.'

Her 'wonderful dresses, beautiful voice, and charming stage

presence' captivated him. 'For weeks afterwards, I used to steal away to my bedroom and, before the mirror, try to imitate the gestures and mannerisms of Vesta Tilley in *Dick Whittington*.'

Vesta Tilley, who made her debut at the age of three as 'The Great Little Tilley', was one of a trio of celebrated male impersonators on the halls – the others being Ella Shields and Hetty King. Unlike them, she didn't look even remotely masculine as she strutted about dressed as either an officer or a civilian. She was the original 'Burlington Bertie', though the song 'Burlington Bertie from Bow' became even more popular, and much more sinister, in a version rewritten for Ella Shields, the American who came to England during the reign of Edward VII and stayed for ever. Tilley's Bertie was a pretend toff, handsomely attired, whereas Shields's was a down-at-heel tramp with pathetic and hopeless aspirations towards the good life. Tilley had her greatest success with songs intended to raise the nation's morale in times of conflict. In his book *Sweet Saturday Night*, Colin MacInnes suggests that Tilley's renditions of 'Jolly Good Luck to the Girl Who Loves a Soldier' proved her to be as persuasive a recruiting ser-geant during the Boer War as Lord Kitchener was in 1914. The petite and obviously feminine Vesta Tilley, disguised as a subaltern, would shout out over the final line of the chorus of 'Jolly Good Luck . . .': 'Girls, if you'd like to love a soldier, you can all love me!' MacInnes describes this invitation as 'equivocal'.

The 'beautiful voice' Fred heard in 1895 has not been captured on disc. She was, of course, much older when she went into the recording studio, and the noise she makes is shrill and unpleasing. In the edition of the *Era* – the precursor of the *Stage* – dated 5 August 1914, a reviewer mentions the 'obstinate success which continues to pursue the career of the well-known artiste Fred Barnes' and goes on to call him 'the male Vesta Tilley'. There is no evidence to indicate that Fred was offended by the elaborate conceit, with its implication that he was pretending to be a woman pretending to be a man. It's more likely that he was flattered by the comparison. He was not disheartened, after all, when the boys in the gallery greeted his every appearance with cries of 'Hello, Freda!'

It was Tom's wish that Fred would partner him, and succeed him, in the business. Fred's training began while he was still attending the Council School nearby. The boy often served behind the counter in the evenings or delivered meat to privileged customers in order to earn his weekly pocket money of a shilling.

From the age of eleven, Fred was a pupil at Beechfield College, a boarding school in Malvern. Tom removed him from the college when he was fourteen, and shortly after his return home Lady Alice died. If he experienced grief, as he surely must have done, he was reluctant to talk about it to the readers of *Thompson's Weekly News*. He observed instead that he was put in charge of the financial side of the business, because Tom now had two shops to run. His time as a clerk lasted until he was sixteen, when he managed to persuade his father that – given the horror he endured at seeing animals slaughtered – he could never begin to function as a butcher.

Tom greeted Fred's announcement that he wanted to go on the stage with predictable dismay. It was perfectly acceptable for him to sing in the choir at St Matthew's Church, but the idea of his doing so in front of a theatre audience was not one that Tom could accept. His attitude was not entirely puritanical, however, because he was alert to the insecurity of the average actor's life. He would have preferred his son to have chosen a more respectable and stable profession. He hoped Fred would come to his senses.

Fred was not to do so. On hearing that his fifteen-year-old friend Dorothy Ward had auditioned successfully for the pantomime at the Alexandra Theatre in Birmingham, Fred was determined to emulate her. As a consequence, he too had a successful audition, and was informed that he would be hired for the following year's pantomime at a salary of £3 a week. Since Fred was under-age, the contract had to be signed by Tom, who had been kept in ignorance of his son's scheme. He did sign it, eventually, with reluctance, warning Fred yet again of the uncertainties ahead.

Fred was twenty-one, in fact, when he made his official panto-mime debut as the Duke of Solihull in *Cinderella*, so five years of his performing life remain unaccounted for. In March 1906, he appeared as a 'character vocalist' at the Gaiety Theatre in Birmingham, where he was also engaged early in December. In 1901 he performed at the Birmingham Music Hall. Topping the bill was Charles Coburn, singing 'Two Lovely Black Eyes'. But what happened to him between that performance and the engagements in 1906 is a mystery which isn't solved in either the *Weekly News* articles or an interview he gave to a reporter from the *Performer* in May 1908. From the latter one learns that he was educated at Morecambe College and that his professional career began as a singer of 'straight' songs on the concert platform at the age of ten. He also claimed that he was 'working variety theatres with light comedy songs', but he neglected to supply corroborating evidence such as dates or place names.

'Mr Fred Barnes as the Duke of Solihull dresses immacu-lately and sings and walks the stage in the most perfect manner,' commented the reviewer for the *Era* of 29 Decem-ber 1906.

'My part in *Cinderella* was only a small one,' Fred recollected in 1932. 'I had to sing one song – "He is Never Without a

Girl" – and do a little dance. I was more successful than I had ever dreamed. The storm of applause from every part of the theatre on opening night overwhelmed me.'

Fred's performance impressed several important people, but none more important than George Lashwood, the most celebrated light comedian of his day. One, at least, of the songs Lashwood made famous still survives – 'In the Twi-Twi-Twilight'. Lashwood had been a star in London for seven years when he saw Fred as the Duke of Solihull, and had already perfected his formidable technique. He had the ability to 'change from light comedy to broad fun, and from sentiment to drama', according to M. Willson Disher, whose *Winkles and Champagne* is the classic study of the halls. As well as singing songs about capturing the love of a beautiful girl – the verb 'to spoon', meaning 'to court', appears in many of them – Lashwood also excelled at the dramatic monologue, with titles such as 'The Last Bullet', 'The Tipster' and 'My Poll'.

Lashwood, who was born and raised in Birmingham, met Fred and Tom backstage at the Alexandra. 'I was only a boy at the time. George was not speaking so much to me as to my father. "I have seen an artiste to take my place," the great George told him. "It is your son, Fred. If I can do anything for him, I will."'

Lashwood proceeded to give him expert advice.

'He taught me how to use my hands, to carry my stick, how to walk on the stage, and how to manipulate my eye-glass. What George did, in fact, was to place at my disposal, free and unasked, the lessons of his long and brilliant career,' Fred recalled. 'As a lad I made George Lashwood my hero, and I am still convinced that I couldn't have fashioned myself on a better man.'

On 16 March, 1907, the *Era* mentioned him again, on its gossip page:

Mr Barnes impersonates types of the beau-monde, which he invests with an easy, graceful deportment, and a pleasing and picturesque stage presence, plus a melodious singing voice and distinct enunciation.

These qualities, it is to be assumed, were acquired during that five-year apprenticeship the otherwise loquacious Fred preferred not to talk about in any detail. What is certain is that by 1907 he had started to gain recognition.

When the run of *Cinderella* came to an end, Fred joined a troupe called the Eight Lancashire Lads, who had also appeared in the pantomime. They made straight for London, playing the bottom half of the bill at various theatres. They were at the Cambridge in Shoreditch in May, and at the Palace, Blackpool, in early summer, where Fred was noticed as 'a comedian who is rapidly coming to the front' in a local newspaper. He was a member of Adeler and Sutton's Pierrots at Llandudno in July. But it was in Brixton, in April 1907, that Fred's solo act caught the attention of the agent George Foster, who took over his business from another agent, George Brooks, who had promised Fred more than he was able to deliver.

It must have been the Eight Lancashire Lads who were honoured with the performance of 'The Black Sheep of the Family' that rainy day in Leeds. Their surprise that he had written it was remembered by Fred in 'How Success Ruined Me', but how they reacted to the words

> It's a queer, queer world we live in
> And Dame Nature plays a funny game –
> Some get all the sunshine,
> Others get the shame

has not been recorded. The song continues:

> I don't know why but since I was born
> The scapegrace I seem to be.
> Ever since I was a little boy at school
> A name has stuck to me

Was that name, in reality, 'queer', or one of its many variations? The lyrics of 'The Black Sheep of the Family' don't seem coded today, but rather brazenly obvious. Perhaps Fred's initial reluctance to perform it in public may have had something to do with the song's very frankness and openness. In his early twenties, Fred was cautious and careful of his growing reputation. He was also anxious to prove to his father that he had the talent and strength to survive in a profession that numbered as many failures as successes. He would confess, in 1932, that he had written the song in a mood of despondency caused by his having to be the first turn on the bill, but the truth might go deeper. He did not, as yet, have the sexual confidence that comes with fame and money, and he may well have looked upon himself as the equivalent of a 'black sheep'.

The song ends on a note of optimism:

> But I'll try my luck in the colonies.
> There I'll rise or fall.
> And when I come back
> The sheep that was black
> Will perhaps be the whitest of them all.

Bankrupts and petty criminals were still trying their luck in the colonies in 1907, and disgraced – or about-to-be-disgraced – sons of wealthy families were fleeing Britain to avoid imprisonment. When Fred walked on to the stage of the Hackney

Empire in his tattered clothes that long-ago Monday evening, he was displaying extraordinary courage.

When I had finished singing, the silence continued for fully a second. Then, with a mighty roar, came the storm of applause which instinct told me was bound to come . . . The people at the back of the stage, the waiting artistes, the scene shifters, and the management were amazed. It was an unheard-of thing for a first-turn artiste to create such a furore. A few rushed forward to shake me by the hand in congratulation. Others glared at me as though I were a monstrosity.

This last remark hints at jealousy or rivalry, but the 'others' might have glared at him because they had understood what the song was really saying. A queer who admitted to being queer and actually sang about it must have struck them as a monstrous freak. Fred continues:

What made me happy was that the song with which I had scored the success was my own. I had written it, words and music. I think I know the secret now, though I failed to grasp it at the time. There is real human appeal in 'The Black Sheep of the Family'. It touches chords in the hearts of the women in an audience, and my experience is that when the fair sex respond you are sure of success.

The members of the 'fair sex' who responded affectionately to Fred were the same kind of women who adored Ivor Novello, Rudolph Valentino and – more grotesquely – the preposterous, diamond-studded Liberace, who presented himself as a simpering mother's boy. Fred was beautiful in his youth. Naomi Jacob, writing in 1957, remembered him as

one of the most handsome men I have ever seen. His features were wonderful, he carried himself with grace, and he had one of the kindest hearts in the world. Moreover he was a fine artist and no mean dancer . . . His voice, while pleasing, was not particularly outstanding, but he had that all-important attribute – charm.

But twenty years earlier, in *Our Marie*, her biography of Marie Lloyd, which was written while Fred was still alive, she offers three different impressions of him. The first is of a young, struggling entertainer, occupying a tiny room at the top of the Royal Hotel in Bristol, taking tea with Marie Lloyd and her eccentric Aunt Betsy and barely uttering a word. He knew that he had to behave respectfully in such exalted company. The second glimpse is of Fred in the 1930s, already in decline, visiting the Lloyd sisters's dressing-room and 'looking so thin, poor fellow'. The third, and most substantial, vignette shows him at the height of his fame:

Marie once stood near him at the side of the stage of the London Palladium and looked him up and down, her expression quizzical. He was wearing his immaculate, tightly waisted coat, beautifully creased trousers, snowy white shoes and hat, and his make-up – well, Fred had always affected a slightly 'pink and white' make-up, with eyelashes built out like the 'park palings'.

Marie leant towards him and whispered: 'Boy, you've forgotten your brassière – don't go on without it whatever you do!'

As a result of his triumph at the Hackney Empire, Fred won favour with the theatre's owner, Oswald Stoll, who engaged him, 'at a greatly increased salary', to perform at some of his other theatres. For the next few months, he was no longer first or second turn, but found himself climbing steadily up the bill. In May 1908, he appeared at Stoll's principal London house, the Coliseum.

At Christmas 1907, he had been in *Mother Goose* at the Opera House, Middlesbrough, as part of a double act. 'Mr

Fred Barnes and Mr Leonard Maitland are very successful as
the Dandies,' the reviewer for the *Era* noted. The following
summer he was at Llandudno again with Adeler and Sutton's
Pierrots, playing the role of the Honourable Bobbie Carruthers
in a mini-musical comedy called *The Gay River*.

Pleased though he was to be working for Oswald Stoll at
the Coliseum and the Alhambra, Fred was aware that he had
to play the other major theatres on the West End circuit before
he could be acknowledged as having reached the peak of his
profession. On his return to the capital from Llandudno, he
was summoned to the London Pavilion by its manager, Frank
Glenister – who had probably seen him as Bobbie Carruthers
– to give an audition. Fred recalled the ordeal in 'How Success
Ruined Me':

I walked on to the stage, deserted except for the pianist, and was
about to begin my first song when my eyes wandered to the
auditorium. There, seated in the front row of the stalls, was not one
figure but three. On one side of Mr Glenister was Whit Cunliffe,
the famous light comedy star. On the other side was the one and
only George Robey.

(Whit Cunliffe, who invariably wore a grey frockcoat, topper
and spats on stage, had one immensely popular song – 'Girls,
Girls, Girls' – which he went on singing until the 1930s.
George Robey, who was knighted in old age, was a medical
student in Dresden and a Cambridge undergraduate before
embarking on his music hall career. It was in the 1890s,
performing 'The Simple Pimple', that he first dressed up as an
unfrocked clergyman in a shirt minus its dog collar, a long
black coat and a very flat hat shaped like a soup dish. He made
his entrance swishing a vertebrate cane, and raised his enormous
eyebrows in dismay and disapproval when the audience
laughed. He would chastise them with the words 'Desist from

mirth' and carry on with his patter. He often began his act by saying 'Balls', pausing, and then as the laughter subsided, continuing with the words 'parties and celebrations'. He was known, fondly, as the Prime Minister of Mirth. In 1935, he played Falstaff in *Henry IV, Part One*, raising his eyebrows at every impropriety he had to utter. He is preserved on film as Sancho Panza to the Don Quixote of the Russian bass Feodor Chaliapin. A tender aspect of his rich talent is captured on the wonderful recording he made with Violet Loraine of the song 'If You Were the Only Girl in the World'.)

Is it any wonder that my performance suffered? I was fully fifty per cent below my best. All that time I was singing, my subconscious was telling me how terrible I must seem to the big men in front. My voice faltered. Sometimes it was scarcely audible. I was glad when it was all over. I went to my dressing-room convinced that I had failed dismally. My clothes were wringing wet with perspiration.

Fred had changed back into his street clothes when the three judges came to tell him he had passed the audition. He tried to apologize, but George Robey interrupted him with consoling words. 'That's all right, my lad. We have all been through it. We've a pretty good idea of what you can do.'

He was hired to perform at both the Tivoli and the Oxford at a considerable drop in salary. He was also required to be first turn again, a millstone he accepted with grace. Since the big names of the halls played regularly at these venues, the audience came with higher expectations of the acts that opened the show. Fred was grateful for the opportunity to appear alongside his heroes and seized it with enthusiasm:

The work was hard. It was no uncommon thing for me to play as many as three theatres in a single night. I would appear first at the Oxford, which was once a night; at the Tivoli, also once a night;

and the Canterbury, twice a night. This meant four performances in all.

Fred traversed London in a brougham, waiting for him at the stage door of the Oxford. He would already have changed back into the appropriate costume for his first song at the Tivoli, having quickly collected his props and band parts. From the Tivoli, the brougham took him to the Canterbury, once again dressed in the clothes for his first number and once again clutching his props and the band parts for the musicians in the pit. It was common practice when the music halls were flourishing for the artistes most in demand to work in three or four different areas of the city in a single evening.

The harder Fred worked, the more his confidence grew:

There is something about the West End of London that brings out the very best in one. I know that I myself acquired a finish and a polish that I had never had before . . . It brought me into the limelight. I got publicity, which is the very breath of life to a stage artiste.

He got money, too. His weekly salary rose from £4 to £100 in the course of three years. His pantomime roles increased in size and quality as well. He was Lord Pudsey in *Mother Goose* at the Theatre Royal, Portsmouth, singing 'Fall In and Follow Me' and 'Sunshine'. He was the Prince in *The House That Jack Built* at the Theatre Royal, Edinburgh: 'He cuts a handsome figure, and bears himself with vivacity, especially in the closing scenes, when the love affairs that run through the play are reaching their climax,' wrote the drama critic of the Edinburgh *Evening News*. As the Prince he sang 'We All Go the Same Way Home' and 'I'm Going to be Married in the Morning'. The following Christmas, he was the Prince again, in another

version of the same pantomime at the Theatre Royal in
Glasgow. He received a glowing notice in the *Era* of 21
December 1912:

. . . the management have evidently decided that this is to be a very
swagger [*sic*] boy's part, as he is provided with a change of costume
for nearly every scene in the pantomime. His first song was 'Ragtime
Violin', which made a hit, and later on in a special costume he gave
'Alexander's Ragtime Band' with striking effect. He has another
clever song, 'Mr Cupid', which is worked up with special business
and goes extremely well.

In 1909, the sheet-music publishers Francis, Day and Hunter
brought out 'The Scapegrace; or, I'm the Black Sheep of the
Family', thus confirming the song's growing popularity. Two
years later Fred recorded it for the Columbia-Rena label with
'My Boating Girl' on the reverse side. The record was on sale
for an entire decade before its deletion in the early 1920s. In
April 1911, Fred talked to the *Era* about his present fame and
his future prospects. He made an agreeable impression on his
interviewer, who observed fulsomely:

Mr Barnes is gifted with a singularly pleasing personality, but it is
his virile dramatic methods and his skill in the portrayal of character,
which have vividness and truth to nature, that place him on terms
of the greatest favour with every part of the house.

After referring to Fred's gifts as a songwriter, the interviewer
continued:

Another novelty which Mr Barnes has in hand is a *scena*, registered
and fully protected, written and composed by himself entitled 'Don't
Be One of the Boys' for which he will carry his own special scenery
and effects.

The article ended with the information that the singer, dancer, comedian, lyricist and composer had secure bookings for the next five years.

It has been said that music hall artistes came in two kinds – those who hoarded money and those who spent it extravagantly. The sublime Marie Lloyd, whose admirers included Max Beerbohm and T. S. Eliot, belonged in the forefront of the second category. A philanthropist by nature and inclination, she parted with hundreds of thousands of pounds. Her beneficiaries were the world and his wife: the needy, the greedy, and the last of her three husbands. She left a comparative pittance at her untimely death in 1922.

Fred became a dedicated spendthrift as the result of a tragic event that took place in August 1913. What caused Tom Barnes to kill himself must remain, as with so many cases of suicide, a matter for speculation. The impresario Don Ross, who was working as a theatrical agent when he first met Fred, was convinced that the reason was the shame Tom felt at his son's increasingly flamboyant behaviour. Fred had ceased being discreet and cautious. The effeminacy he had kept in check was now expressed openly, his 'virile dramatic methods' confined to his stage act alone. It was plain to everyone that Fred was a nancy. He was famous and he was moderately rich and he could do as he pleased.

In an article in the winter 1979 edition of the *Call Boy* (a magazine devoted to theatre history), Ellis Ashton revealed that Don Ross had been partly responsible for saving Fred's life. A man carrying a meat axe had turned up at the stage door of a Birmingham theatre threatening to 'put an end to Fred's cavortings', and Ross had pacified him. Ross claimed that he and Gertie Gitana, whose interpretation of the song 'Nelly Dean' survives on record, persuaded Fred to leave the building by the front entrance. When it became clear to Tom that Fred had escaped, he was 'so thwarted that, unable to take Fred's life, he went home and took his own'.

The story, which might have been imagined by Dostoevsky, sounds deranged enough to be plausible. Don Ross always insisted it was true, but there is no trace of any substantiating evidence. What seems certain is that Tom was appalled and embarrassed by the effete and dandified creature Fred had become, and by the epicene friends he had in tow. Tom was respected and admired in the tight-knit Saltley community. The idea of having his reputation tarnished by gossip about his son's peculiar way of life could have made him suicidally depressed. This is a reasonable supposition, given that he had no history of depressive illness.

Tom's death was reported in the *Birmingham Gazette* of Monday 11 August 1913:

The residents of Great Lister Street were painfully surprised to learn yesterday that Mr Thomas William Barnes, aged 52, a butcher, had been found dead in the sitting-room behind his shop, with his throat cut.

The tragic discovery was made by a domestic, the only other person in the house. When she came downstairs the lifeless body of Mr Barnes was stretched on the hearthrug, which was saturated with blood, death having taken place several hours before his discovery at 9 a.m. (on Sunday morning).

The fact that the right hand held a large butcher's knife, which Mr Barnes was accustomed to use in the shop, seemed to point to suicide.

The inquest was held two days later, in the city's Victoria Courts. Evidence was given by Edith Law, the domestic; by two neighbours, Mr and Mrs Tonkinson, and by Fred, who had travelled up from London after receiving a telegram instructing

him to come home. Fred disclosed that Tom had visited him
in the capital and had been 'very low and run down' and
'not in the best of health'. They had argued over Fred's contracts
and Tom had 'once said that if witness (Fred) did not take the
position he thought he should he would kill himself'. Fred
'did not think that anything was meant by this'. The jury
returned a verdict of 'suicide while temporarily insane'.

Fred's inheritance was valued at nearly £10,000 in money
and property. The days of lavish spending and manic drinking
were soon to begin. He bought a 'luxurious flat' in Clarence
Gardens, off Baker Street, and 'spent something like £4,000
on its elegant furnishings': 'I kept a butler, personal valet, and
two maids, as well as a chauffeur for my four cars – a Vauxhall,
a Talbot, and two run-about sports models.'

Gertie Gitana and Don Ross were walking along Charing
Cross Road one day when Gertie noticed Fred coming towards
them. He was dressed in a white cashmere jacket with matching
plus fours and knee-length pink stockings. The distracted
Fred seemed unaware that the marmoset on his shoulder was
defecating down his front. 'Cross the road, now, and don't
speak,' Gertie ordered. They managed to get to the other
side without Fred seeing them. He had become a public
embarrassment for some of his colleagues.

Twenty years before the young Denis Pratt reinvented
himself as Quentin Crisp and embarked on his long, and
ultimately triumphant, career as an exotic outsider, Fred was
alarming ordinary citizens wherever he went. He had been
rejected for military service on the grounds of his 'nervous
condition' – the phrase he used at his trial in 1924 – despite
his enthusiasm to join the ranks. Perhaps it would be accurate
to substitute 'because of' for 'despite'. It is tempting to picture
the 'male Vesta Tilley' in his pink and white make-up

reducing the board of examining officers to a state much like apoplexy with his eager insistence on becoming a soldier.

In 'How Success Ruined Me', Fred spoke of the great love he had for Tom:

I don't know whether during his lifetime my father had exercised a restraining influence over me, or whether it was that in my abject misery at this time I developed a spirit of 'don't care'. Whatever the cause I began to show tendencies in the wrong direction. I started to associate with people whose influence upon me could be baneful.

Those baneful influences are easily identified. It was impossible for him to admit to the readers of the *Weekly News* that he had revelled in their company. The guardsmen, sailors and labourers who kept Fred satisfied found him to be a very generous 'twank' – the word they used for a man who required, and bought, their sexual services. Fred was the least discreet of London's many twanks, especially in the 1920s when he did his cruising in a Rolls-Royce.

The 'wavy-haired, blue-eyed Adonis', as he was described in the *Era* in August 1914, could claim, without boasting, that 'there was not a better-dressed man in the West End of London':

My tailors in Hanover Square were in the habit of receiving orders for £200 worth of new clothes at a time. My wardrobes were stocked with suits for every conceivable occasion. Many of them I never wore. Once, I remember, I was mad enough to give an order for £100 worth of shirts at one time.

If this senseless extravagance was a desperate form of camouflage to conceal the guilt and despair induced by his father's suicide, he kept the knowledge a secret until 1932. A fortnight after Tom's death, he was on the bill at the Birmingham

Hippodrome, 'which was a place full of memories of my father. To this day, I don't know how I got through that week. I had to sing, and I had to smile with a heavy weight upon my heart.'

He went on singing and smiling, like the trouper he was, introducing new routines and numbers to please his adoring fans. Wealthy women proposed marriage, and 'lovesick flappers' wrote to him 'by the thousand'. He was featured on picture postcards, and during the First World War he sang the rousingly patriotic 'Boys in Khaki, Boys in Blue' to cheer the spirits of wives, mothers and sweethearts. He sometimes appeared in 'plantation costume' with a 'shadow chorus of hula girls in the background' singing of life back in Alabama and Mississippi. No one, apparently, ever questioned the presence of those nubile Hawaiians in the Deep South.

In the immediate years before he made the move to Clarence Gardens, Fred had lived in fashionable West End hotels, where 'peers, politicians, actresses, actors and celebrities of all descriptions accepted my all-too-lavish hospitality'. These same people were invited to his flat, which had three large reception rooms and four bedrooms. He kept open house, he recalled, throwing parties 'without the least regard to cost': 'I gave away a fortune at one time and another. I was flattered and fawned upon. I loved it. My perspective was all wrong. Success and popularity completely turned my head.' He went to Monte Carlo and lost £1,500 at the tables in a single evening.

In 1920, Fred could look back on a decade of achievement. He had performed in every important variety theatre in Britain, while his records of 'Samoa! Samoa! Some More!' and 'What's the Matter with London?' were selling steadily. The 'obstinate success' an interviewer for the *Era* had mentioned six years earlier was still asserting its obstinacy, in spite of the fact that his offstage behaviour had become more and more erratic. 'I lived in a castle of conceit,' he confessed twelve years later, when he was trying to stave off total ruin:

The Fred Barnes of those days was a fool. Other people may have realized it. I certainly didn't. I woke up when it was too late. I was going downhill then. My friends were deserting me. Scores who had been glad enough to batten upon me in Clarence Gardens looked the other way when they saw me coming.

Fred was undoubtedly foolish, but he wasn't entirely irresponsible. He gave his public what they wanted. He honoured all his engagements. Although he drank heavily, he was never so drunk that he failed to perform. Not until 1922, that is, when he surpassed himself in foolishness.

He was in Australia, where he had been hired to do a ten-week tour of the major cities, topping the bill at the Tivoli in Melbourne and earning £200 a week. His first week in Melbourne went brilliantly:

Every day I drank more than was good for me without, however, endangering the success of my performance.

Then, on the second Wednesday, I forgot myself completely. I found myself with a party of hard-bitten Colonials and kept pace with them in a hard-drinking bout which lasted throughout the afternoon and evening.

He was still keeping pace with them when the time came for him to go to the theatre. He was 'blissfully unconscious' of it. In a state of 'hilarious' intoxication, he laughed at those who reminded him of his professional duties. Some people from the Tivoli were scouring the city for him, and when they finally discovered him it was very late in the evening. 'My condition was so bad that a stage appearance was out of the question.'

The manager of the Tivoli had no alternative but to apologize to the audience for Fred's absence. He summoned Fred to his office the following morning and told him he was fired. The tour was cancelled. Fred had been set to make £2,000 but the financial loss was as nothing as the blow to his reputation and pride.

The Tivoli's manager must have been an exceptionally kind and forgiving individual. He sent for Fred a couple of days later to say that he had been in touch by cable with the African Theatres Limited and that the company was prepared to offer Fred engagements in Johannesburg and Cape Town at a weekly salary of £130. Fred accepted with surprised gratitude. He sailed to Durban on the SS Diogenes and opened at the Empire Theatre in Johannesburg in the last week of November. He sang the well-known standards 'Sally', 'Italian Skies' and 'The Sheikh of Araby', but yet again it was with 'The Black Sheep of the Family' that he made the strongest impression. 'Blessed with an attractive personality and a fine appearance, he was an instantaneous hit, and had to return after repeated encores to thank the house for the enthusiastic welcome they had given him,' wrote the reviewer for the South African Pictorial.

The experience in Australia probably chastened him, to judge by the triumph he scored in South Africa. He returned to England in a relatively sober condition and stayed that way for most of 1923. Then, one night, he staggered on to the stage of the Brighton Hippodrome and shocked the audience by his inability to sing or dance. He was instantly axed from the bill.

On the evening of Sunday 19 October 1924, Fred was arrested in Hyde Park and subsequently charged with 'being drunk in charge of a motorcar, failing to stop and give particulars after an accident, and by wilful neglect causing bodily harm to Eric

Stanley Mitchell, and driving without a licence'. The report in *The Times* made no reference to the sailor who attempted to escape and failed.

When the policeman who was making the arrest told Fred he would be taking him to a nearby station, Fred responded with the words 'Oh, don't do that. It will ruin me.' He then offered the man money, starting at £5, rising to £10, and culminating at £1,000. 'His screams and cries of distress must have chilled and alerted hundreds of people up to no good from one end of the park to another,' noted Harry Daley, the intellectual policeman who befriended both E. M. Forster and J. R. Ackerley, in his entrancing memoir *This Small Cloud*, which was published posthumously in 1986. 'This was bad luck for the sailor.'

Fred's offer of monetary compensation was accepted by Eric Mitchell and his parents. Mitchell, who was standing by his motorcycle when Fred's car hit him, received only minor injuries and was discharged from hospital the next morning. Fred's trial took place in November. The magistrate, Mr Chancellor, spoke of a 'bad case'. He found the defendant guilty of being drunk in charge of a car and sentenced him to a month's imprisonment with £5 costs. He ordered Fred to pay a fine of £15 with £5 costs for driving in a dangerous manner. The charge of failing to stop immediately after the accident was dismissed. For driving without a licence, Fred was fined a further £3.

Fred's appeal against the conviction was heard on 9 January 1925, but the sentence was upheld. He was sent to Pentonville Prison, where he was not treated harshly. He was convinced that his career was finished, his life in ruins, but such pessimism turned out to be unwarranted. Soon after his release in February, he was engaged to appear at the Camberwell Empire. His return to the stage was greeted rapturously, with packed houses every night. Then he took the starring role in a revue called *Love, Life and Laughter*, which toured Britain for almost a year. He was earning good money again – £100 a week, plus twenty per cent of the box office takings. There were no more incidents of drunkenness.

It might have been the severe Mr Chancellor who banned Fred from attending the Royal Tournament – the annual naval, military and aviation tattoo – at London's Olympia Stadium. Fred was deemed a 'menace to His Majesty's fighting forces' and warned that if he was sighted in the Kensington area while the tournament was taking place he would suffer the consequences. It seems right to assume that the sailor was either let off with a caution or fined on the spot, since his name is not mentioned in the newspaper reports of Fred's trial.

The ban upset Fred – 'This to him must have seemed like being so far in the depths as to be almost a distinction,' observed the wise Harry Daley – but it did not deter him. Year after year he found ways of evading the cordon of military police and 'getting into Olympia to watch the soldiers, sailors and airmen at their exercises'. Harry Daley's evocative account in *This Small Cloud* of Fred's persistent efforts to elude his tormentors deserves to be quoted in its entirety:

Gradually there would be a vague stirring in the distance; then shouting and the sound of running feet. What are they saying? What? 'He's in again!' 'He's in again!' Everyone starts to run – some this way, some that. But they are not all running for the same reason. The military police and their self-righteous sympathizers feel personally insulted and are running to catch Fred Barnes if they can, and throw him out neck and crop. But scores of young sailors are running to find him first, to warn him of danger and hide him until excitement dies down, when it will be written off as a false alarm. We must be realistic and admit that Fred Barnes was generous, if now not so rich, but surely the laughing young sailors also had sympathy for a hunted thing; and perhaps amused admiration for one who, confronted with this frightening restriction imposed by the combined authority of the War Office, Air Ministry and Admiralty, should remain undaunted and successfully defy it.

The reviewer who described Fred as a 'model man' was not referring to his masculine qualities and virtues, but rather to the fact that he wore his expensive clothes with style. He continued to be that kind of 'model man' throughout the 1920s, retaining his idiosyncratic dress sense even when he was otherwise insensible.

In the spring of 1927, Fred took a short holiday in America, where a 'New York audience thrilled to his unscheduled appearance', according to the *Era*. He was offered several engagements, but had to refuse them because of his commitments in Britain. He was under contract to the Gulliver Syndicate and to Moss Empires and had bookings to fulfil. He promised his new admirers that he would come back one day.

On his return to England he announced his engagement to Rose Tyson, the daughter of a millionaire. A few weeks after the surprising announcement, a photograph of the happy couple – he in top hat and tails; she in a flowing wedding dress – appeared in the newspapers. He told incredulous reporters that he was looking forward to married life and the love of a good woman. He spoke with convincing sincerity.

Fred was unrepentant when the hoax was discovered. He had enjoyed the attention and publicity his bogus marriage had generated. Rose Tyson vanished before the press could interview her, and Fred was once again the Freda who caused the War Office, the Air Ministry and the Admiralty to be vindictive each autumn.

Fred survived both the debacle in Australia and the shame of being sent to prison by reducing his intake of alcohol and dedicating himself single-mindedly to his art. It was in his power to achieve something like stability for months at a time.

Then he would become complacent and overconfident and ignore the advice given him by concerned fellow artistes and two increasingly agitated managements. He tried the often superhuman patience of his personal manager, Charles Watson, who warned him not to drink to excess. Watson had negotiated a lucrative nine-year contract with Moss Empires in 1923, which guaranteed Fred annual appearances at the London Palladium. Five years on, the 'male Vesta Tilley' was slipping down the bill. His act had lost its former polish, and there were nights when he forgot the words of songs his audience knew by heart. Watson's dismay at his client's steady decline, and his own inability to curb it, can be readily imagined.

The decline of Fred Barnes was accelerated when he missed a performance at the Holborn Empire. The Gulliver Syndicate and Moss Empires responded by relegating him to first turn on their bills. He was not allowed to sing more than two songs and in some theatres one was considered enough. A brief item in the *Era* stated that he was 'becoming a liability'.

Under the terms of his contracts, he was paid well for his humiliating work. Yet it wasn't long before the two leading managements informed Charles Watson that they were prepared to pay Fred off. Watson secured £2,500 from the Gulliver Syndicate and £3,500 from Moss Empires – generous sums in 1929 for dispensing with an artist who was still comparatively young. Fred accepted the money and proceeded to spend it, mostly on alcohol, which he consumed in massive quantities. The remorse he felt at being unemployable was heightened when he visited the halls where he had sung 'The Black Sheep of the Family' and 'On Mother Kelly's Doorstep', the last big hit he had introduced to his once-loyal fans as recently as 1926. He sat among the audience and watched the acts of other singers and comedians – many less talented than he – and went home, with or without a companion for the night, and drank.

In 1930, he decided to finance a comeback tour, leading a small company of his own choosing. He was barred from all the major venues, so he had to settle for bookings at second- or third-rate theatres in Dublin, Belfast, Cork, Glasgow, Chesterfield, Bootle and Leicester – the real fleapits on the circuit. He learned a terrible lesson as he and his troupe played to half-filled houses, and it must have hurt him deeply. He was virtually forgotten, his name no longer a draw. The tour was eventually abandoned when it became clear to him that he was making a huge loss. He paid the company's salaries and returned to London, to a life of abject dissipation.

He was now almost dispossessed, having lost his flat, his cars, his servants and, worst of all, the friends who had once enjoyed his hospitality. He was not altogether finished, however. One day, wandering in a desperately poor area of the city, he came across a number of down-and-outs, emaciated and filthy, and the sight of these piteous wrecks horrified him. It also compelled him to think seriously about the possible consequences of his drinking habits. He became, by painful degrees, teetotal; he practised singing and dancing regularly each day, and he recovered some of his pride in his physical appearance. As a result of this belated self-discipline, he was invited by the impresario Lew Lake to join a company of music-hall veterans in a show called *Stars Who Never Failed to Shine*. Stars like Vesta Victoria and Harry Champion were genuine veterans, though Champion was always strangely coy and cagey about his exact age. They were more than twenty years older than Fred, who was then forty-six.

(Even when she was in her sixties, Vesta Victoria could still endow the most innocent song with a wealth of innuendo, whilst pretending to be extremely decorous. When she sang the lines

I've got a little cat
And I'm very fond of that

in 'Daddy Wouldn't Buy Me a Bow-wow', she challenged the audience to imagine anything rude with her sweetly appealing look. One of her lesser-known songs ends with the heartfelt question 'Now what's the use of an old tin kettle to a woman if it hasn't got a spout?'

Harry Champion sang three of the great perennials of the music hall – 'Boiled Beef and Carrots', 'Any Old Iron?' and the indestructible 'I'm Henery the Eighth, I Am' – for over half a century. The enormous grin which was his trademark indicated that he found the world and its ways excessively funny, particularly when he was singing of everyday disasters and mishaps.)

Fred performed in *Stars Who Never Failed to Shine* for two years, from 1931 to January 1933, before illness prevented him from carrying on. The young Colin MacInnes saw him at the Victoria Palace interpreting the song that was his autobiography in miniature. He and the other artistes on the bill were in their 'splendid decrepitude'. Fred looked prematurely aged. He was tubercular and desperately thin, a shadow of the handsome creature who had once strutted proudly along the London streets.

He moved to Southend-on-Sea, ostensibly for the sake of his health, living in furnished rooms with John Senior, his new manager and lover. He was drinking again, and Senior was matching him glass for glass. He was offered a few first-turn engagements, but his act met with mocking laughter, and the cries of 'Freda!' were now derisive instead of affectionate. His career dwindled away.

At that time, Southend was the seaside resort most popular with working-class Londoners. They swarmed into the town in their thousands during the summer months. Fred entertained them in public houses for small change or a free drink. Some of the older holidaymakers must have been saddened or embarrassed by the spectacle of Fred, his ravaged features covered in make-up, singing to the accompaniment of a rackety pub piano. They had seen him in Hackney, in Camberwell, at the London Palladium, perhaps, and here he was, with a pet chicken perched on his shoulder, struggling to be heard above the noise of the customers.

In the summer of 1938, he sang his familiar songs, minus the chicken, in the lounge of the Cricketers Hotel, at nearby Westcliff-on-Sea. The patrons were respectful and appreciative, and neither he nor John Senior was required to beg for tips with an upturned hat. His pride was restored in some measure because the hotelier was paying him a weekly salary. This final engagement was terminated at the end of the season, in the last week of September. On the morning of Sunday 23 October, John Senior found Fred lying on a bolster in the sitting-room of their lodgings in St Ann's Road with 'his nose right in the centre of the gas ring'. The tap was turned off. There was no smell. Senior shook him and discovered he was dead.

The doctor who undertook the post-mortem told the coroner's court that Fred's body was 'very wasted', and that there was 'fatty degeneration of the heart and both lungs were diseased'. Death was due to coal-gas poisoning.

The court heard that Fred Barnes knew he had only months to live. His former manager and friend, Charles Watson, had recommended that he go to Switzerland for treatment, but doctors in London had decided against the move, taking the view that his life should run its course. Watson revealed that he had been sending money to Senior for Fred's care and that he had paid the rent for the two rooms the men occupied. A week before Fred's death, Watson had tried to persuade him to enter a nursing home, but Fred had answered, 'Let me lie here and die.'

A verdict of suicide could not be returned, since there was 'not sufficient evidence to show how the poisoning was caused'. A detective-sergeant said that inquiries showed that Mr Barnes was well-liked and that he and Mr Senior were the best of friends. Foul play was not suspected.

'He was a great man,' said Charles Watson as he stepped down from the witness box.

Fred was buried alongside his father in the churchyard of St Saviour's in Saltley. The funeral was attended by hundreds of mourners, who crowded into the neighbouring streets.

'Fred Barnes had his faults, but most of them were to his own detriment,' wrote the obituarist in the *Birmingham Mail*:

There are old schoolfellows in Birmingham, and old admirers among the public, who will remember him for his kindliness of manner and his personal charm. He had an attractive personality, and his easy grace on the stage, with a voice which had excellent qualities, made his act a popular one.

Fred Barnes was often silly to the point of recklessness. At the end of the twentieth century, a man like Freddie Mercury, of the aptly named rock group Queen, was free to be as camp and outrageous as he wished – as camp and outrageous as Fred was, in another, dismally puritanical, Britain from 1908 onwards. I picture the butcher's son in his cashmere plus fours and pink stockings and feel bound to salute him for his misguided courage. I smile at the thought of him dodging past the military police at the Royal Tournament, protected by smiling young sailors. And it pleases me that one of his most successful songs was 'Give Me the Moonlight, Give Me the Girl', which continues 'and leave the rest to me'. That girl was always safe in Fred's hands, which only wandered in the direction of uniforms. It was a 'queer, queer world' he lived in, this kind, harmless man, and he was never afraid to say so.

2. 'Like a Boiled Monkey'
Naomi Jacob (1884–1964)

Naomi Jacob liked to astonish new acquaintances by telling them the story of how she smuggled herself aboard a destroyer during the First World War. She 'masqueraded as a matelot' with absolute confidence, addressing her fellow ratings in the light baritone voice that would deepen and darken with the passing years. She took part in two naval battles, she boasted, before leaving the ship and returning to her life as an independent woman.

The exploits of Able Seaman or Midshipman Micky Jacob are not recounted in any of her numerous volumes of autobiography. The revelation that she had posed as a sailor, working and fighting alongside men who had received rigorous training, would have caused havoc at the Admiralty and beyond. Such unnatural behaviour constituted a threat to national security. What had begun as an act of personal daring, an escapade, might have ended in a trial and possible imprisonment.

Or perhaps it didn't happen. Perhaps the brief adventure was invented by Micky in order to impress the girls she met in the late 1920s and early 1930s, when she was already becoming established as a popular novelist. She was Naomi to her readers, but Micky or Jake to her friends and lovers. Her sole concession to femininity was to put on a skirt when she attended Mass. She kept her hair cropped short and wore men's tailored suits. She was seldom without a collar and tie. Her footwear was similarly masculine – brogues, boots and lace-up two-toned shoes. She smoked a cigar after dinner, and only told risqué jokes in male company, with the ladies safely out of earshot. Her claim to have gone undetected as a jack tar could not easily be discredited, given her appearance and general demeanour. Her assumption of the self-created role of Micky the sailorman might have been the outstanding triumph of her acting career, if she had had an audience to appreciate it.

Selina Sara Collinson, who was known from childhood as Nana, met Samuel Jacob at a picnic in the summer of 1883. She was struck immediately by his 'unEnglish' manners, for he bowed deeply on being introduced to her. She registered, too, that he was physically unprepossessing. He had a large, fleshy nose, and thick, very red lips. He was practically bald, his light brown hair having receded far from his forehead. She noticed his plump hands, his slight paunch, and guessed correctly that he was considerably older than her other suitors. So she told her eldest daughter, Naomi, in the last months of her life, when they were reunited in love and friendship after years of separation.

The seventeen-year-old Nana Collinson was sought after by several well-connected young men in Ripon, where her father, Robert, was elected mayor four times in succession. She was attractive and high-spirited, and naturally intelligent. She had a pleasant singing voice and was an accomplished dancer. She spoke adequate French, was persevering with Latin and Greek, and was able to recite passages from Shakespeare and entire poems by Tennyson and Robert Browning. She adored Jane Austen and the Brontës, but her favourite novels at this time were Louisa May Alcott's *Little Women, Good Wives* and *Jo's Boys*. Nana felt that she had much in common with Jo March, who cuts her hair short and writes plays and stories when she isn't otherwise occupied about the busy household. Nana's pretty sister Nellie was more like the gentle and compliant Meg.

Nana's mother, Jenny, had died of consumption at the age

of thirty-four, the disease exacerbated by the fact that she had lived in a state of almost permanent childbirth throughout her marriage. There were three surviving children – Nana, Nellie and Tom, who would emigrate to Australia. A year after Jenny's death, Robert married his new housekeeper in secret and took her for a brief honeymoon in Scarborough. The woman was kind and good-natured, and endured with equanimity being called Mrs Collinson instead of Mother or Stepmother by Nana and Nellie, who resented her close attachment to Robert. His second wife bore him three more children – Eva, Daisy and William – all of whom were cared for by their half-sisters.

Robert Ellington Collinson was a considerable figure in Ripon society. His hotel, the Unicorn, was patronized by a diverse clientele, which included racehorse owners, politicians, gentleman farmers, actors and stars of the music hall, and even members of the higher clergy who had come to preach at the beautiful cathedral. He managed to be at once respectable – he was an alderman and a justice of the peace – and happily dissolute. He was an inveterate gambler, a copious drinker of whisky, red wine and port, and a lover of the theatre in all its forms. Henry Irving, the first actor to be knighted, was a good friend. Robert was admired by everyone in the community except ardent radicals and those of a stern religious persuasion. Methodists such as the rich Mrs Hewson, whose only son was interested in marrying Nana, regarded Robert as the 'devil's spawn'. 'It will break my heart if my boy marries that girl Nana Collinson,' she announced in public. 'He's got a future. She'd be the ruin of him.'

The remark got back to Nana, as Mrs Hewson intended it should. Nana was angry at being dismissed as a 'publican's daughter'. She had been given the best education any middle-class English girl of that period could expect, while Robert was no ordinary hotelier, intent solely on running a successful business. Although he was celebrated in the West Riding of

Yorkshire, there was nothing provincial in his outlook. He thought of himself as a man of the world. He was proud of his eccentric and adventurous ancestors, among whom was a great-uncle whose desire to be a jockey had been thwarted by his outraged parents. Sam Collinson ran away from home and disappeared for several years, his family ignorant of his whereabouts. Then, one day, his father received a letter with the news that Sam was going to Persia to groom a 'string of horses' owned by the Shah. Some time later, Sam's father committed suicide because of the debts he was unable to settle, and Mrs Collinson moved to another, more remote, part of Yorkshire to avoid the scandalous gossip of neighbours.

The story of Sam's return to England to buy bloodstock for the Shah and to visit his elderly mother was one that Robert delighted in telling. Sam turned up at Maria Collinson's house on the outskirts of Beverley on a rainy winter's night with a couple of veiled women who, he explained, were two of his wives. His startled mother asked him how many wives he had, eliciting the reply 'I *think* I've six.' She ordered him to take a room at the Black Swan, a nearby hotel, because she wouldn't have him sleeping under the same roof as the 'misguided creatures' he had brought with him. Listrano and Morganita stayed with their bemused, and increasingly affectionate, mother-in-law for a week, eating strange dishes like Yorkshire pudding with their fingers. Whenever Maria attempted to persuade them to use knives and forks, they stared at the curious objects and broke into gales of manic laughter. At the end of their stay, they presented her with a carpet they had embroidered, with a design of birds, flowers and twisting vines.

Maria Collinson never saw Sam again, though he sent her money regularly, via a London bank. She knew that he was called San Colenso in Persia, but she remained unaware of the large number of grandchildren she had. Sam was too embarrassed to disclose that it probably ran to dozens.

The young Nana loved to hear about the great-great-uncle who had lost count of his wives. 'I *think* I've six' became a family joke, savoured by generations of Collinsons. It was daunting to realize that she had relatives, distant cousins, who had been raised in an alien, Muslim culture. The strict Methodists of Ripon would have been horrified to learn that there were Persian Collinsons, who worshipped Allah in mosques.

Nana spurned the attentions of Mrs Hewson's God-fearing son, as she did those of the other dependable young men who pursued her. It was the ungainly Samuel Jacob she chose to marry, for a variety of confused reasons. She was not in love with him, as she had imagined herself to be with Arthur Wells and Manny Harrison, who were of the same age and from a secure, familiar background. Nana was envious of her sister Nellie, who had married James Binns, a local businessman, and would soon be living in a fine house of her own. She was desperate to escape from the Unicorn and the hated presence of her stepmother. When Samuel Jacob proposed to her, she accepted him instantly, despite her reservations concerning his age and appearance. Although German was his first language, he spoke English fluently, if over-correctly, in a pleasing, resonant voice. He was obviously cultivated. He talked of Goethe and Schiller with a true scholar's enthusiasm, and impressed her with his knowledge of Shakespeare. He could sing many of Schubert's songs from memory. He had renounced his Jewish faith and now belonged to the Evangelical sect of the Church of England. He was, he assured her, a devout Christian.

Samuel Jacob had come from Manchester to Ripon to take charge of a private school for boys in the Claremont district. A few weeks before he married Nana, he was appointed headmaster of the Choir School at the minster – a timely confirmation, he believed, of his Christian status. He was, his wife conceded, an exceptional teacher, especially when the subject was one that involved him personally, such as literature, history or religion. That concession was almost all she had to say in his favour when she talked about him to Naomi in her daughter's suite at the Albergo Catullo in Sirmione during the last winter of her life. Nana's serious troubles with Samuel began on their wedding night, when she discovered that he was capable of physical brutality. It was not the gently romantic occasion she had anticipated. Samuel satisfied himself quickly and roughly, leaving his youthful, sexually inexperienced bride alarmed and frightened.

They were married in Ripon minster, with most of the city's dignitaries among the congregation. Only two members of the Jacob family were present – Samuel's sister Clara and his brother Benjamin, whose brash manner offended Robert. Samson Jacob, Samuel's sweet-natured, white-haired father, did not attend the ceremony. Although not strictly orthodox, he still felt uncomfortable at the thought of being associated with a Christian marriage. He sent the couple his blessings.

In the 'family chronicle' *Robert, Nana and – Me*, published in 1952, Naomi describes the moment when her parents were joined in holy matrimony:

The Canon, a man for whom Robert had a great respect, began the service. Robert thought, 'The flag's dropped, we're off!' Nana made her responses very clearly and steadily, he was pleased, the girl could keep her head. Jacob spoke in a voice charged with emotion and Robert experienced a moment of suppressed fury when he fumbled with the ring. The tall brother looked sardonic and cynically amused.

It was over, he had spoken his 'one line' – 'I do' – in a voice which was out of control and far too loud. Nana had turned and smiled at him.

They took their honeymoon in Germany, staying with Samuel's relatives and visiting the castles along the Rhine. An aunt – a 'monumental woman' – asked Nana if she had 'nothing more quiet to wear'. Her clothes were considered 'too flamboyant'. Nana, who understood little German, was soon exhausted by the interminable arguments and discussions the various Jacobs indulged in: 'Oh, how they like to talk and never use one word if they can use twenty!' She sensed their disapproval, and they probably sensed hers.

Nana was happy when they were back in Ripon, where people spoke their minds plainly and simply. She had her own household to run, with servants and a cook. She befriended her husband's pupils and the choristers at the minster, whose singing she praised. The boys adored her. Some of them wrote to Naomi when they were old men, remembering Mrs Jacob as their second mother: 'She did everything in her power to make us forget that we were away from home, and she succeeded.'

Two weeks into their marriage, Nana surprised Samuel with the parlourmaid in the corridor leading to the kitchen. She pushed open the 'green baize door which swung so noiselessly and heard a stifled exclamation, caught sight of the whisk of a quickly vanishing print skirt and met her husband face to face'. Samuel hastily explained that, as the corridor was dimly lit, he had bumped into Ada and 'frightened her to death'. It had been a good thing, he added, that 'she wasn't carrying a tray loaded with glasses'. In the early 1960s, Naomi informed James Norbury, whom she had appointed her biographer, that Samuel had actually seduced Ada. The parlourmaid was the first of several extramarital conquests. In the coming years, he would become known as the 'gay Lothario of Ripon society' – a sobriquet that would ensure his being relieved of the head-mastership of the Choir School.

'Did I ever imagine a daughter of mine marrying a dirty, undersized foreign piece of scum?' Robert Collinson is quoted as saying to the doctor who delivered Naomi. The splenetic rhetorical question appears in the Introduction to *Robert, Nana and — Me*, and the attentive reader can only wonder how it came the author's way. Perhaps Robert repeated the outburst for his daughter's benefit, and Nana duly passed it on. What is disconcerting is that Naomi seems to concur with her grandfather's view of Samuel. Robert was convinced that Nana's firstborn would be a boy, and Naomi has him observe to the same doctor in the course of the same private conversation: 'She [Nana] and I will somehow manage to snaffle this lad, we'll bring him up as decent Englishmen are brought up. Never mind Homer, Ovid and Xenophon — let him learn what will be useful to him . . .' That decent English lad was not to be, though Naomi — in her Micky persona — can be said to have resembled him. That she was indifferent to Homer, Ovid and Xenophon is evident from her voluminous writings. 'Who the hell cares for cleverness? Not me' — thus Robert, as reported by Naomi, who didn't care for cleverness either.

Samson Jacob had escaped from Poland as a child during a Russian pogrom in which his parents were killed. His mother died as the result of a brutal flogging. The Russians, learning that Samson's father was cantor in the synagogue, cut out his tongue and left him to bleed to death. Samson's uncle had taken him to Germany, where he was raised by relatives who had fled from Poland years earlier. He came to England in his twenties with his wife and young family and set up a small tailoring business in Manchester, which eventually flourished into a larger concern. He became a naturalized Englishman, speaking faltering English. Although he spoke German with his wife and children his principal language was Yiddish, which he reverted to in moments of enthusiasm or excitement. Whenever he did so in his son's presence, Samuel would snap at him, using words like 'filthy' and 'beastly' to indicate his abhorrence of Yiddish and all it suggested of a Jewish culture he had disowned. Only the poor and dispossessed conversed in Yiddish. Samuel was continually reminding his father that they were no longer in the ghetto.

Naomi was born on 1 July 1884. The event is recounted in detail in the opening pages of *Robert, Nana and – Me*. She was sixty-eight when she recreated her arrival into the world at her desk in Casa Mickie (sometimes spelt Micky; on one occasion Micki), her villa overlooking Lake Garda. The baby was a 'scarlet, squirming little creature, bald as a coot, with bandy legs and tiny, tightly clenched fists'. Mrs Pluse, the elderly cook at the Unicorn and a close family friend, was the first person to hold the infant, whom she considered the 'image of Master Robert – might 'a' bin spat out o' his mouth' – which felicitous phrase, one assumes, was heard by the exhausted Nana and bequeathed to Naomi fifty years later in Sirmione. Samuel was not in the bedroom when the baby appeared. He was downstairs, smoking cigars and drinking too much whisky, in the company of his temperate father.

When Mrs Pluse brought the newly washed child to the bedside to be inspected by her mother, Nana reacted with revulsion. The creature had an old face and no hair. 'My God, it's hideous,' she said, turning her back on the baby and ordering Mrs Pluse to take it away. 'Don't have it drowned – like kittens. Find someone to be kind to it,' she went on. 'I don't want it hurt. I don't want anything hurt. Just take it away, Plusey, take it away.'

Mrs Pluse carried the newborn Naomi down to the sitting-room, which now reeked of stale tobacco and spirits. Samuel Jacob, having been told by the doctor that his wife had presented him with a 'beautiful little girl', was in a foul mood. 'Damn it, I wanted a boy' was how he greeted the news. It was Samson, not he, who asked Mrs Pluse if he could see the child. 'He held it very tenderly and carefully, swaying backwards and forwards . . . "*Ken ain hora! Gebenscht!* No evil eye, little blessed one, no evil eye."'

Minutes passed before Samuel decided to peep at his daughter, whom Samson had returned to the arms of the cook. 'Good Lord, what a nasty-looking object! You'd have thought that my wife and I could have produced a better-looking specimen than that. It's like a boiled monkey!'

It's indicative of the abiding hatred Naomi felt for Samuel Jacob that she should have chosen, at such a late stage in her life, to set down the very first words he addressed to her. The implication is that she had reason to despise him from the day of her birth. Samuel is an anonymous shadow in her earlier autobiographies, a 'he' or 'him' who was the cause of pain and distress to Nana, Naomi and her sister Muriel. He is the father it is necessary to forget, or at least to consign to the periphery of memory. He was safely dead when she came to write *Robert, Nana and – Me*, and the relish with which she emphasizes his every failing – his unstoppable sexual appetite; his drunkenness; his inability to bestow affection on those who ought to have been dearest to him – is apparent throughout. His most grievous fault, however, is one she dwells on in other books, especially the novels concerned with the fortunes of the Gollantz family. She could not forgive him for wanting to be accepted as an upper-middle-class Englishman, the equal of her maternal grandfather and his cronies. She presents him, always, as the upstart Jew, an embarrassing misfit in the drawing-rooms of Ripon, wearing the wrong clothes, saying the wrong things, lacking the proper social graces. A true gentleman would never dream of displaying his intelligence in polite company, as Samuel Jacob had been prone to do, to everyone's annoyance. In her fiction, he is transmogrified into a variety of 'bad Jews' – men or women who think they are clever; who renounce their faith; who pretend to be more English than the English; who bring shame on their race. Her 'good Jews', by comparison, remain Jewish, make their money through hard work, manage to be at once proud and modest, and seem to be content to be awarded the enconium 'If all Jews were like him, the world would be a better place' and similar dubious expressions of respect.

It remains a mystery why she did not change her name, which proclaimed a Jewishness she tended to be guarded about. She was part-Jewish, she insisted – 'only twenty-five per cent'. Her mother became Nina Collinson after divorcing the bankrupt Samuel Jacob, and she urged Naomi to follow her example. She made the suggestion in 1899, just before her departure for America, where she would have a successful career as a journalist. She took Muriel with her, leaving the fifteen-year-old Naomi, who was estranged from her father, to fend for herself. Over thirty years later, Nina Abbott, as she then was, wondered why her stubborn daughter had retained a surname that was synonymous with so much unhappiness. She refused to call Naomi by the 'silly nickname' that had been hers from childhood. By this time, Naomi was known to everybody in Sirmione as *la signora Micky*.

She was christened Naomi Ellington Collinson Jacob in Ripon minster at the end of July 1884. Nana was at home in bed, recovering from the rheumatic fever she had contracted hours after giving birth. The baby was 'screamingly indignant' before the ceremony that made her a 'member of Christ, the child of God, and an inheritor of the kingdom of Heaven', and she continued to bawl as the Reverend Samuel Reid, the precentor at the cathedral, anointed her. 'It's good when a child yells at the font – it's the devil getting his marching orders,' remarked Naomi's Aunt Nellie to the clergyman, who seemed not to approve of the old saying.

Naomi grew into a stout child with curly hair. She was looked after by a nurse, Annie Thompson, while Samuel taught his pupils and Nana supervised the household and did voluntary work in the community. She saw her parents early in the morning and in the evening before bedtime, when Nana would read her a story.

It was Annie who gave her the nickname she was happy to keep for life. She was, on her own admission, a dirty little girl, despite the fact that she vowed every morning to stay 'very clean'. Annie was accustomed to dragging her in from the garden to wash her hands, face and knees, and one occasion she made the comment that Naomi was a 'proper Mick':

The Irish, in those days, only came to Yorkshire for the harvests and were not popular. They were considered, for no particular reason, to be wild and lawless, and very dirty. Hence a dirty child is a 'proper Mick'. The name has stuck, and I am still called Micky by everyone.

The quotation comes from *Me: A Chronicle about Other People* (published in 1933), which contains absolutely no reference to her father. The stable years of her early childhood are accounted for in the opening chapters, and then she is suddenly living in Whitby with her mother and sister. No explanation is given for the move. Samuel's school in Claremont is referred to as the Old House, an enchanted place unoccupied by boys in the evenings, where Naomi, Nana, Annie, Ann Peacock the cook and baby Muriel knew security and happiness. Apart from Lumley the gardener, the only males on Naomi's early horizon are Nana's relatives and various clerics and doctors. It's an unusual autobiographer who can discard a parent in this cavalier fashion, and some of her many readers must have been bewildered by the absence of a Mr Jacob, and by the fact that she lavishes pages on her maternal grandfather, who died when she was still very young.

In *Robert, Nana and – Me*, written two decades later, Samuel Jacob is presented as the worst husband and the nastiest father any wife or daughter could have. She remembers that Nana 'always smelt so nice, like the lavender hedge in the garden' and that 'She *felt nice* too, it was pleasant to touch her hair with the tip of your finger, very gently so as not to disarrange it, to lay your cheek against hers', whereas '"he", when he came with her [to Naomi's bedside] didn't smell nice at all, he smelt of tobacco, and something else to which I couldn't put a name – a stale, heavy smell which made you want to put your head away.' She goes on, once again placing the pronoun within quotation marks to signal her disgust:

'His' face was covered with hair, hair which felt like the coconut matting when you slipped down on it and it hurt your bare knees. You couldn't touch [the hair on his head] with your fingertips because, except for a little frill near his neck, he had none . . .

One afternoon she played with her kitten in among the rows of peas in the vegetable garden. For an entire hour she chased after the little creature, regardless of any damage she might be doing. She was having tea with Annie when her father stormed into the room. 'His voice was like the sound trains made when you stood under a railway bridge to hear them pass overhead.' She could only make out the word 'peas', and then 'Must learn to – ' and finally the order to 'come here'.

She experienced fear for the first time in her life. 'Sheer terror, someone bigger than I was, catching me, putting me over his knee, daring to unbutton my small drawers, and bring a large, heavy hand down on my bare skin.' She 'kicked and screamed' while Annie protested.

'Then the door swung open, and I was set down, my drawers flapping round my knees, and my mother stood there.' Nana was horrified that a grown man should strike a little girl, and demanded that he apologize to his daughter immediately. He did so. He asked Naomi to kiss him, but she scowled and hid her face from him in her mother's skirt. 'I never liked him again; all through my life I have remembered that indignity, and always shall.'

Naomi's first school was at Skellfield, run by the 'forbidding' Miss Ling. It was only a short walk from the Old House, and most days Annie or some other servant would accompany her. She was happiest when 'they' had too much work to do. It was then that they watched her until she reached the turning by St Agnes gate, where she waved them goodbye. She had to cross the river Skell on her way, and she often stood alone on the bridge, imagining herself as Horatius Cocles defending the bridge over the Tiber against Lars Porsena and his 'false Etruscans'. 'Hew down the bridge, Sir Consul, with all the speed ye may!' she commanded. She was dressed in a 'blue reefer and a tam-o-shanter cap' as she rallied her invisible troops – the Consul, Spurius Lartius and Herminius. She was often late for school but, being a 'proficient liar', she usually had a convincing excuse for her lateness.

At home in the attic, 'where there were curtains hanging in front of a lot of old trunks', she played the roles of Hubert and Arthur from Act IV, Scene 1 of *King John*, 'doubling the parts in a most masterly fashion'. She 'stamped her foot and bawled' at the executioners:

> Heat me those irons hot; and look thou stand
> Within the arras: when I strike my foot
> Upon the bosom of the ground, rush forth
> And bind the boy which you shall find with me
> Fast to the chair. Be heedful: hence, and watch.

Muriel was entrusted with the Executioners, though not with the two lines allotted to the First of their number. When Micky as Hubert shouted, 'Come forth!', Muriel 'came through the curtains holding – rather gingerly – a piece of old iron'. She was a shy, timid girl, not given to showing off and play-acting like her sister. Later, when Micky performed Mark Antony's oration over the body of Julius Caesar, Muriel lay on a 'deckchair extended to its full length' with her eyes closed, acting dead.

Naomi had other accomplishments. 'I played cricket, with proper rules,' she reveals in *Me – Looking Back*, published in 1950. 'I could kick footballs with my left foot too. I played whist and solo . . . I could skate and use an oar, though I was not very good at it.' She was an avid reader of books the polite ladies of Ripon considered unsuitable for a girl – Henty's *The Young Fur Traders*; Ballantyne's *Coral Island* and *Dog Crusoe and His Master*. She was entranced and frightened by *Treasure Island*, and amused by *Little Lord Fauntleroy*:

He was a nice little boy, and if the illustrations were to be relied upon, a good-looking little boy with proper sporting instincts. I blamed his mother for allowing him to be dressed as he was, and for not having his hair cut.

She loved Christmas time, but hated the parties she was forced to attend, with Annie cautioning her to 'behave like a little lady' and not to 'play only with the boys': 'Remember that you're a little girl and behave like one, not gallumphing about like some lad or other.' She recalls, in *Me – Looking Back*, handing Doris – whose birthday party it was – a 'lovely present' bought by Nana. 'I hated Doris; she hated me. I had pushed her into the fountain near the bridge which led to the station a few weeks previously, and she was so small-minded she allowed the fact to rankle. She smiled stiffly at me. I scowled at her.'

Naomi refused all the food she was offered, except bread and butter:

There were ices. 'Naomi dear, have a strawberry ice.'

'No, thank you.'

'Don't you like ices, dear?'

'Yes, but my stomach doesn't.'

Dead silence, children staring. You didn't mention stomachs openly in those days.

She was relieved when, towards evening, the fathers, uncles and grandfathers arrived. She adored the handsome Dick Wilkinson, who 'came to our house sometimes and was generous with shillings, which he found in your hair, ears or down the back of your neck'. The arrival of Robert Collinson especially pleased her, making her forget about Doris and the other goody-goody girls. He asked her if she was enjoying herself, and she told him to lean down so that she could whisper in his ear, 'No, I'm not.' He laughed, and said that he was going to play whist with his friends in the next room. 'I'll come and play with you,' she demanded.

I was taken by the hand into a smallish, darkish room, which smelt of cigar smoke. Books were put on a chair to make it sufficiently high for me. My grandfather said, 'I demand to play with my grandchild!'

. . . My hand was full of trumps. It was my lead. I played ace, king, queen and then the nine and got away with it.

When the rubber ended, one of Robert's companions remarked to Naomi 'If only you'd been a boy we'd have had you a member of the club in no time.'

Annie took her home in a cab that night, and the 'tired and excited' child told Nana about the game of whist. 'My *dear* child, what was your grandfather thinking of?' she asked, and Naomi replied, 'Whist, I think.' The following morning she received a note, which she preserved among her papers:

My dear Naomi, here are your winnings. A good five shillings. You were lucky, for you will see that the stakes were deplorably high.

Your affectionate grandfather, Robert Ellington Collinson.

She went with Annie to Ripon market, and bought her mother 'two pairs of scissors in a leather case lined with plum-coloured velvet'.

The idyllic life in the Old House came to an end when Naomi was eight. The family moved to a 'horrible tall modern place with disgusting gardens covered with "rockery"'. She had made the acquaintance of a retired Scots guardsman named Black, who bet on the horses for her – 'threepence to win and threepence for a place' – and sometimes she made as much as half a crown (two old shillings and sixpence). With the money, she treated herself to Woodbines, which cost a penny a packet, or the more expensive Ogden's Guinea Gold. When funds were low, she would steal the odd cigarette from the box in her father's study and smoke it in the lavatory, whilst reading Marie Corelli's *The Sorrows of Satan*, or some other daring novel Nana had added to her collection. Samuel surprised Naomi once and scolded her, but Nana came to her defence, as she invariably did. Naomi stopped stealing his cigarettes, but when the horses let her down she took to smoking brown paper, strips of cane taken from the seats of chairs or dried herbs. 'They were all uniformly nasty and burnt the tongue.'

Educating Naomi was problematic. She was imaginative and intelligent, but inclined to laziness. She had a furious temper, which often went out of control. 'By the time I was ten I had been to three different schools, to say nothing of governesses who came and went – some charming, some dragons in more or less human shape.' From Skellfield she was sent to a private school run by a Miss Meade and a Miss Brown. The ladies

improved her handwriting and taught her to use the Greek
'e', but they didn't care for this truculent and unladylike pupil
and politely asked Nana to remove her. She fared better with
the Misses Dixon, two elderly sisters who tried to teach her
good manners. They didn't teach much else, and Naomi
sometimes experienced 'acute boredom'. She began playing
truant – 'to play the nick' was the popular term then – on
Wednesday afternoons in order to sit behind the horses on Mr
Wells's cart when he delivered beer to the public house in
Sharrow, the village outside Ripon where the Dixons had their
school. The kind old women were always sympathetic when
she told them she'd had a bilious attack or a blinding headache.
She befriended the local blacksmith, who let her blow up the
fire in his forge. She was a 'strange girl' – the phrase she heard
most frequently on the lips of the matrons of Ripon – who
enjoyed running wild whenever she could. Her sister, who
inherited Nana's good looks, conformed to the accepted
notion of what a little girl should be like: quiet, demure and
feminine.

It gradually became apparent to Naomi that her parents
were not happy together. They were edgy in each other's
company, forever arguing over trivial matters. There were
fewer boys for Samuel to teach in the new, ugly house, where
the atmosphere was usually tense. Naomi was bewildered and
upset when her mother came up to the nursery one evening
and fell weeping into Annie's arms. She caught snatches of
what Nana was saying, and guessed correctly that it had to do
with her father. She was not to know that the move from the
Old House in the shadow of the cathedral was necessitated by
the fact that Samuel's womanizing and drinking had lost
him the headmastership of the Choir School. His income had
fallen as a result. Nana felt humiliated, not least because her
beloved 'Da' had warned her against marrying a man he
considered 'exceeding dull' and 'completely unattractive'.

Nana had threatened to leave Samuel as soon as the gossip about his involvements with girls of a lower class had started. She took her daughters on holiday to Whitby or sent them to stay with their Aunt Nellie and her husband James at Kirkstall, near Leeds. It was during these absences from Ripon that Nana was making plans to extricate herself from a relationship that was in every way disastrous. It was only when life with the feckless Samuel became completely unendurable that Nana decided to file for divorce – a truly desperate, even shocking, measure in the 1890s. Naomi was certain that changes were soon to take place when her great-aunt Mrs John Stonehouse 'descended upon the household' to have a long and serious talk with Nana. Now that Robert was dead, Mrs John – as she was always called – was the senior figure in the Collinson family, a fount of common sense and practicality. James Binns was there, too. Annie and Naomi had joined them when Samuel entered, staring with 'those cold blue eyes' and said, 'Do you always entertain your servants in the drawing-room?', to which Nana replied, 'I entertain my friends wherever I wish to entertain them.'

The meeting with Mrs John and Nana's brother-in-law had been, in effect, a final conference. Nana wanted their support for her decision, and they gave it to her, after listening to details of her married life she had hitherto suppressed. She had no future with Samuel Jacob. The children weren't safe with him, either.

Then it came. The hall was filled with boxes and bags, we had on our hats and coats and carried our little cases; it was obvious that we were going away. There didn't seem to be any boys anywhere, or servants – yet surely they must have been there? 'He' was there, talking a great deal. My mother scarcely spoke, except to say, 'I gave you every chance! I ought never to have come back! But – it's over!' . . . 'He' bent down to kiss me, 'He' only stared at Muriel. We went down those nasty steps, past the ugly garden and got into a cab and drove to the station.

Nana, Naomi and Muriel were bound for Whitby, where Nana was to be manageress of the newly decorated Crown Hotel. The decorating was still in progress when they arrived, so Nana arranged for the girls to stay on a farm near Malton until there was accommodation for them at the hotel. 'It was a lovely farm and Muriel and I had a big bedroom and our own sitting-room, which made us feel terribly grand.' The farmer's wife spoilt the 'two little misses' with beautiful food. 'She let us help ourselves, which was additionally attractive.'

It was an enchanting time, and our mother used to come over for the day sometimes, and she seemed younger and laughed a great deal and made us laugh too. It was as if that cloud which had hung over us for so long had been dispelled, and the sun had broken through.

The day school in Whitby was very different from the ones Naomi had previously attended. Latin wasn't on the syllabus, and History was confined to England alone. Nana was of the conviction that children should be taught that other European nations had histories too, and her daughter was frustrated by the parochial manner with which the subject was treated. The stress was on 'fancy work and needlework' – appropriate concerns for budding wives and mothers.

(In *Me*, Naomi mentions the parish church where they worshipped on Sundays. 'It stands on a hill and one hundred and ninety-nine steps lead up to it. I used to count them both going up and going down, and always found that there were two hundred.' But in *Robert, Nana and – Me*, she writes, 'We knew the pier, and the church perched high up with ninety-nine steps leading up to it – I had counted them, and decided that there were a hundred and that someone had made a mistake.' At some point between 1933 and 1952, one assumes, a hundred steps went missing.)

At the age of eleven, Naomi believed that all arguments could be resolved by fighting. She must have been the terror of the playground. She was bored again, particularly in winter, when there were few diversions other than reading. There were donkey rides on the beach at Whitby Bay in summer, and evening visits to the Spa with Nana to hear the band and to gaze in wonder at the beautiful women – the wives and widows of millionaire industrialists – strolling along the promenade.

They were still living in Whitby when Naomi was sent off by herself to stay with Samson Jacob and her aunt Clara at his home in Towcester, near Manchester. Although she missed Muriel dreadfully, she enjoyed the old man's company. From him she learned the Yiddish expressions she uses in her Gollantz novels, and his simple goodness and modesty were in striking contrast to her father's brashness and pomposity. Samson took her for gentle walks in the countryside. 'I always pretended that he walked too quickly for me, which used to make him laugh.'

On the return journey to Whitby, she stopped off at Bradford, where it had been arranged that she should spend an evening with her father. During dinner at the hotel 'he grew sentimental over me' and promised to buy her a pair of boots in the morning. She told him she didn't want boots, but he insisted:

I cannot remember the shop, but I can remember the boots. They were of glacé kid, and had a design of flowers embroidered on the toe-caps. They were hateful boots, they didn't look, somehow, like English boots at all. Then I was put on the train, and finally arrived at Whitby – still wearing the boots.

I tried to tuck my feet under the chair, but my mother saw them and said: 'My dear child, where did you get those boots?' It was less a question than an exclamation.

I told her.

She said, 'Let me see them!'

I showed them; she looked at them gravely, then said: 'No doubt a kind and thoughtful present, but not suitable for you to wear at school. Let me have them and I'll give them to you when you are older.'

'Then I'll have grown out of them,' I said hopefully, 'and then they'll do for Muriel, won't they?'

'Perhaps – I don't know.'

I never saw those boots again; through all the years that followed they were the only thing my father ever gave me, except a very inferior dinner at the Grand Hotel, Middlesbrough, when he ordered kidneys which were so underdone that I couldn't eat them.

Naomi records in *Me* that Nana took her out of the inadequate school in Whitby and placed her in the Higher Grade School in Leeds. While she was there, she lived in nearby Kirkstall with Aunt Nellie and Uncle James and their already expanding family. James Binns was 'my idea of how a man ought to look. I always believed that he had been a soldier, and to this day I still think he ought to have been.' He particularly impressed her when he was wearing his tweed suit, and she confesses in *Me* that her own fondness for tweeds stemmed from the sight of her uncle in them.

She was given money to pay for her meals at the school, but managed to save two shillings to spend each Saturday. She told her aunt that she was detained for extra work on Saturday mornings, but her cousins knew she was going to matinées at the Grand Theatre, which she had first visited years before when Nana took her to see the pantomime *The Forty Thieves* with Bessie Wentworth as Ali Baba. (Bessie was the last of three sisters who all died at the age of twenty-six.) Naomi would rush to the gallery entrance as soon as she arrived in Leeds and wait there patiently – with a book to read, and an apple or a bar of chocolate to stave off hunger – until the doors opened. 'I was the first person to make that mad rush up the endless stairs.' At the Grand she saw Henry Irving in *The Lyons Mail* and Ellen Terry in *Madame Sans Gêne*. Although she couldn't understand French, she managed to follow the plot of *La Dame aux Camélias* and appreciate the intensity of Sarah Bernhardt's acting. She remembered a performance of *The Three Musketeers* starring Edmund Tearle because of an intervention from someone in the gallery: 'When the beautiful queen, standing well down to the footlights, declared her love for Buckingham, taking us – the gallery – into her confidence, Richelieu walked down the wide stairs, listening.' It was at this point that a boy was moved to shout: 'Shut up, missus. The old bastard's behind you!'

Naomi was removed from the school in Leeds when Nana discovered that the playground was on the roof. There were no more matinées for the 'fat, very chubby-faced small girl' who startled the ticket collectors (and, occasionally, the passengers) on the train back to Kirkstall with her impersonations of Henry Irving and Sarah Bernhardt. Those luminaries never appeared in Whitby. A production of *Lady Windermere's Fan* at the Spa Theatre seemed tame stuff after the excitements of *The Lyons Mail* and *The Three Musketeers*.

Her time at the Higher Grade School is not mentioned in the later autobiographies, for reasons known to Naomi alone. In *Me – Looking Back*, she goes from Whitby to Middlesbrough, where she and Muriel were pupils at a prestigious boarding school. Muriel, who could never bear being parted from her mother, left after a single term, but Naomi stayed on. 'I was invariably in trouble; the same old story, I never meant to do wrong, but things *went* wrong.' She earned more bad conduct marks than any other girl in Form Five.

The teaching was of a high standard. Naomi liked all the teachers except the deputy headmistress, Miss Davenport, who 'never attempted to hide the fact' that she disapproved of the badly behaved girl. 'She was tall and very thin and the end of her nose always looked cold.' The Misses Wilkins, Hawley and Jennings were dedicated women who inspired the restless Naomi to concentrate on her studies. She was at the boarding school for 'about a year' (this most industrious of autobiographers scorns anything as mundane as a date; she often seems to be functioning outside time) before moving on to Wantage (*Me*), Taunton, or 'it might have been Wantage' (*Me – Looking Back*), or Manchester (*Robert, Nana and – Me*). 'The next thing was that we left Whitby. For some reason my mother went to manage some hotel in Manchester. Where it was, and what it was called, I have not the faintest idea.'

Nana, Naomi and Muriel were unhappy in the grimy city. They missed the sea and the moors, and the friendly people who came to the Crown Hotel with chickens and eggs and other produce to sell. The wind in Manchester sent dirt rising and paper scattering. Nana soon handed in her notice. She hired a cottage in Loudwater, near High Wycombe in Buckinghamshire (Micky moves the town to Surrey). It was owned by two sisters named Raleigh. Muriel asked one of them if Sir Walter Raleigh was her father or uncle. 'It appeared that he was neither.'

Naomi and Muriel were sent to a 'small and select' school in either Wantage or Taunton. It was 'generally utterly unsuited for a child of my regrettable proclivities'. She detested having to learn to play silly songs on the piano, and she argued with the teacher during the Scripture lesson. Muriel was miserable without Nana. There was no alternative but to escape, which they did. (In *Me*, Naomi acts alone, tying up her box with a length of clothes-line, but in later volumes Muriel is her willing accomplice.) They drove in a milk cart to the nearest station and took the train to Chichester (*Me*) or Bedford (*Me – Looking Back*) or wherever it was the nomadic Nana was now living.

The sisters spent several happy months with Nana in either Chichester or Bedford. The stolen clothes-line was posted back to the school in either Wantage or Taunton, and the 'unmanageable' Naomi settled down to read 'anything and everything' that was available. She believed her schooldays were over, but Nana's sudden decision to go to America ensured that this belief was to be unfounded. Nana, through the help of distant relatives, had been invited to take a job in journalism and had to accept or decline the offer quickly. Would the girls like to join her? Muriel, not surprisingly, said yes; Naomi, no. 'I still don't know what prompted me, I still wonder sometimes what would have happened had I gone with them, if I should have made good or just been swamped by Nana's brilliance and – have done nothing.'

There are three versions, at least, of what happened when Naomi announced firmly that she would remain in England and become a teacher. In *Me*, Nana is reported as saying, 'I never heard such nonsense. Teach where – teach who? It's ridiculous.' In *Me – Looking Back*, Nana's immediate response is 'I must do something about it, if you really mean it', and in *Robert, Nana and – Me*, she says, 'But, my dear child, you'd need to go to college, to get a degree, I don't think that I could afford it.' According to the third, and final, version, Nana remembers that her father had been friends with an influential clergyman in Middlesbrough who ran a church school in which teachers were trained.

Nana duly wrote to the Reverend John Kay Bealey, who

responded in an 'astonishingly short time' with the offer of a place for Naomi in St Hilda's School as a pupil teacher, with an annual salary of £12 10s, to be paid in quarterly instalments. 'The name of the school delighted Nana . . . She seemed quite convinced that, as I had lived for a time in Whitby, I should without doubt be under the powerful protection of this saint, and she would undoubtedly occupy herself on my behalf.' (In her latter years, St Hilda governed a double monastery in Whitby, with men and women in adjoining quarters. Among her subjects were the future St John of Beverley and the herdsman Caedmon, the first English religious poet. 'All who knew her called her Mother, such were her wonderful godliness and grace' is how the Venerable Bede describes her in his *Ecclesiastical History of the English People.*)

Naomi did not feel she was 'under the powerful protection' of St Hilda when she arrived in Middlesbrough after a brief holiday 'somewhere in Norfolk, I think'. Nana and Muriel were already in New York, and Samuel was preoccupied with his own self-inflicted problems. She was alone, in a northern city totally unlike the Ripon of her childhood. The Reverend Bealey had arranged for her to lodge with Ted, the Scripture reader, and his wife Ada in their modest terraced house 'in a small street, the sort of street which is beloved by provincial builders. On each side were thirty small houses, all exactly alike, even to the pots of aspidistras in the front windows.' The view from her bedroom window was of backyards with outside toilets. There was no bathroom. In common with Ada and Ted, Naomi took a bath once a week, in a tin tub placed before the ever-burning kitchen fire.

Naomi was never quite sure what the duties of a Scripture reader actually were, though she did ascertain that her landlord provided the bread for Holy Communion. On Sunday mornings, Ted would cut a large chunk from the breakfast loaf and then slice it into sections about half an inch square. These he would place in a box which 'might have held cigarettes', and then he would go off to church. Naomi found this process 'somehow and somewhere – all wrong'.

Her first weekend with Ada and Ted passed awkwardly. The usually voluble Naomi was tongue-tied in their presence. They had no interest in the world beyond Middlesbrough, so conversation was limited to small talk. Ada and Ted were kind to her, but she sensed that the childless couple would have been happier without the responsibility of having to look after a teenage girl. This state of awkwardness was to continue while she lived with them. There were no scenes or arguments, yet the atmosphere was always slightly strained.

The Reverend Bealey called for Naomi on the Monday morning and took her to the school to meet the headmistress. Louisa Butterfield hated Naomi on sight. The new pupil teacher responded in kind. Louisa was powerfully built and accustomed to having her own way. She cast a cold eye over Naomi, asking her questions to test her general knowledge. The girl had been foisted on Louisa, who welcomed every opportunity to criticize her and put her in her place. Naomi fought back.

Naomi, along with the other pupil teachers, was addressed as Miss Naomi by the staff and children. 'The school was in the lowest part of the town, and if you have ever been in Middlesbrough, you will agree that nothing could be much lower.' In the mornings she went through her training in the pupil teachers' class; in the afternoons she taught; and in the evenings she studied. Nana had promised to send her money at regular intervals, but the intervals increased in length: 'My clothes wore out and I had no money to get new ones. My shoes wore through and I had to put in cardboard soles, I remember. A good thick bit of cardboard lasted two days if the weather was fine. I always cleaned my own boots, so that Ada couldn't see how worn they were.'

She was 'utterly and entirely miserable'. The only bright spot in her day was a visit to the Free Library, where she borrowed books which took her out of Middlesbrough in imagination and dispelled some of the ugliness about her. She would later find consolation by singing in the church choir ('growling' alongside the busty Louisa, the lead soprano) and by going to concerts organized by Felix Corbett, the choir master. It was Corbett who brought the violinist Fritz Kreisler, then at the beginning of his illustrious career, to Middlesbrough. 'He was a young fellow then, with heavy brown hair and a thick moustache. He stood there looking very shy and delightfully young, and played like an angel. The whole hall rose to this young Austrian, and cheered and applauded as if they had gone mad.'

From the outset, she was at odds with Louisa Butterfield and the teaching methods the headmistress had inherited without qualms or reservations:

I didn't understand that rigid discipline was the primary necessity in order to teach children that two and two make four; I didn't realize the enormous importance of making small children sit with their arms folded behind their backs, in what seemed to me an unnatural and rather ugly attitude; I didn't understand why a child should be caned because it was late, when the whole of the blame lay with its mother.

These same children were 'barefooted, most of them were underfed, and badly clothed, and a great number were dirty'. What Naomi did understand, almost as soon as she began teaching, was that the boys and girls were not just frightened but bored. 'They came from ugly, dirty homes and they ached for brightness, light, sunshine, and a little laughter.'

It was this last that Naomi provided. She told them stories. She introduced them, from memory, to the Brothers Grimm and Hans Christian Andersen, whose books she had read in the nursery of the Old House. To 'hear fifty-five small children suddenly shout with laughter is one of the very nicest things in the world,' she writes in *Me*. (Her godson, Carlo Pagiaro, who ran the elegant Caffè Grande Italia in Sirmione, remembered that she told him and his brother funny stories in simple Italian. He was christened Carlo Augusto, but his parents added Michele, by way of tribute to his affectionate *padrona*, Signora Micky.)

Naomi's hatred of the system, which she did not conceal from Louisa Butterfield, inspired her to work hard. Her efforts led to her passing an examination known as the King's Scholarship, which entitled her to a salary of £40 a year and the right to use her surname, if she so desired. She did. The headmistress 'came round to my class, to collect the daily registers, and I took the opportunity of pointing out that I was now a qualified teacher, and as such refused to be called "Miss Naarmy" any longer'. She added that she expected to be addressed as Miss Jacob in future. She also added 'a few remarks to the effect that I would not be corrected before my class, and that if such correction was needed it must be made in private'. She was sixteen.

Her teaching methods were unconventional in 1900, and would have been criticized as such in 1950. Her principal concern was to keep the children interested – and that meant all the children, not just the ones who were naturally clever. The other teachers – Miss Mabel, Miss Ethel, Miss Annie and Mrs Johnson – resented her popularity, especially when the secretary of the local Education Board, Mr Calvert, wrote a report in which he commended her 'well-taught class'. It says much for her independent spirit that she continued with her pioneering work in the face of open hostility from her peers. 'When the inspectors came, I refused to become white and shaking before some elderly gentleman who in all probability knew less about the job than I did.' One particular inspector asked 'with icy disapproval' if her children could recite the names of the rivers of England. She answered that they were unable to repeat anything in lists. She didn't approve of lists. They were 'a lazy way of teaching'. The old man stared at her. She stared back. 'Good gracious, I believe you're right' was his response.

Naomi went on fighting her lonely battle against discipline for discipline's sake and for stirring the children's imaginations. At that time, Middlesbrough was virtually ruled by the iron-masters, who owned grand mansions overlooking the countryside, while the men who worked for them were forced to live in hastily and shoddily built houses that soon constituted the city's first slums. 'I have known a yard where there were ten houses, none of them with running water. The only tap was in the yard itself. The water trickled out as if it was too tired to run. At the end of the yard were two privies.' These ten houses were occupied by almost a hundred people, some of whom were the boys and girls in her charge. They came to school with lice in their hair, and their arms and legs were marked with flea and bug bites. No wonder they responded to her storytelling. They had little else to laugh about.

Then Jane Brentnall arrived at St Hilda's, to look after the infants' school. Naomi had a supporter at last. Jane shared her reforming ideas and ideals, and the two became conspirators and friends. She 'burst like a meteor into my world', Naomi writes in *Me – Looking Back*. Jane brought in games and toys, coloured chalks and wools, as well as paint and modelling clay. She taught the children the basics of mathematics without having them recite their multiplication tables, sing-song fashion. Naomi, who was hopeless at arithmetic, followed her example. With the confidence she had gained from Jane's support, Naomi 'agitated' for lead pencils and exercise books to replace the slates and slate pencils her pupils had been using and never cleaned properly. Then she 'agitated' for pens and ink, and was again successful. She also contrived to introduce botany lessons on to the school's curriculum. These were an excuse for an outing to the park every fortnight. 'I can't say that it was much of a park,' she writes in *Me – Yesterday and Today (1957)*,

but it was a change from the narrow streets, with their smells and dirt . . . My children used to come home with wilting wild flowers in their hot hands, having had a glorious time, rolling on the grass, racing about and getting their lungs filled with air which was – if not completely pure – at least a good deal cleaner than that which they inhaled in school or in their narrow streets.

Having attained the King's Scholarship, Naomi went on to collect the Elementary School Teachers' Certificate, which increased her salary to £70 a year, with an annual rise of £5. She said goodbye to Ted and Ada and moved in with a family who were 'very good' to her and introduced her to many influential people in the community. She started going to dances, and her dancing was of such a high standard that she received invitations to the Charity Ball and the County Ball. She was now a fixture of Middlesbrough society. 'So life, apart from school which I grew to hate more fiercely every day, assumed a slightly brighter aspect.'

Because it was considered expedient to amass as many certificates as possible, Naomi decided to take private lessons in drawing. She enrolled for a course taught by nuns at a convent in Newlands Road. She eventually gained her drawing certificate, but it was the benign Mother Superior, Mary Brigid, and her devoted sisters who were to have a lasting influence on her. None of them attempted to convert her; there was no proselytizing. It was the atmosphere in the convent that she found most appealing:

Whoever and whatever made me change my religion and become a – very unworthy – member of the Church of Rome, it was emphatically not the dear nuns at Middlesbrough. And yet, sometimes I wonder. I was teaching in a school where everything was ugly. I was listening to lessons which were made dull. I saw children caned for small misdeeds, shouted at and so forth. At the convent there was beauty – the exquisite beauty of complete cleanliness . . .

She remembered the beauty of the convent fourteen years later, when she converted to Roman Catholicism after her relationship with Marguerite Broadfoote was brought to an abrupt and cruel end.

Nana returned to England for a brief holiday while Naomi was still teaching in Middlesbrough. They stayed together in a rented cottage at Thames Ditton. Nana loved rowing, so they spent a lot of time on the river. They made frequent trips to Hampton Court, where Nana talked about the pictures with such enthusiasm that other visitors often stopped to listen. In *Robert, Nana and – Me*, Naomi recalls an afternoon when two small boys and a girl joined them. One of the boys read out 'very slowly and carefully' the notice 'The Public Must Not Touch The Exhibits' and, turning to the girl, said, 'But *we* may touch them if we like.' The girl replied, 'We may *not* touch them', and then asked Nana, 'We may not touch them, may we?' Nana smiled and said, 'Perhaps, Your Highness, it would be wiser not to.' The girl was the future Princess Royal, and the boy was Prince David, who would become the uncrowned Edward VIII and then the Duke of Windsor.

They were on the river one evening when Naomi suddenly experienced stomach pains of an alarming kind. Nana took her to a doctor on the way back to the cottage, and he diagnosed a burst appendix and recommended its instant removal. Naomi decided to return to Middlesbrough. 'If anyone was going to carve me up it should be Mr Driffield Levick, with his brilliant wife acting as his assistant.' Mrs Levick was Naomi's doctor.

In those days women in the medical profession were regarded as something very nearly approaching freaks; they were certainly felt to be slightly dangerous, and perilously near that dreadful, but slightly vague – thing – unsexed. I never discovered what 'unsexed' meant, but it was a term frequently applied to women who dared to think or act for themselves.

Dr Levick was noted for her kindness and ability, and for the good humour with which she countered prejudice and opposition. Her happy marriage was proof enough that she hadn't been unsexed.

The operation was a success. Mr Levick, visiting her in the nursing home where she was convalescing, told Naomi that she had used 'some shocking language' to Dr Howell, the anaesthetist, when she was coming round. Nana came to see her every day, and Louisa Butterfield, accompanied by a Mrs Medcraft, also honoured her with a visit. Nana, who was at the bedside, was appalled to hear Miss Butterfield remark that she and her friend had 'never been in a nursing home before and wanted to discover what it was like'.

Among Naomi's new-found friends in Middlesbrough was a young man called Wilkinson, with whom she 'indulged in a small sentimental interlude'. He wrote a poem for her on violet notepaper with the intriguing title 'The Mistaken Jewess'. He was so besotted with the music halls that he threw up his job and went on to the variety stage with an act that Naomi found 'very highbrow and harmless' and 'slightly depressing' in *Me*, but 'pleasantly musical and nicely dressed' in *Robert, Nana and – Me*. He gave himself the name Wilkie Warren, and as such was first on the bill at the Middlesbrough

Empire on the night Naomi met Marguerite Broadfoote. She had gone backstage to congratulate Wilkie, and perhaps get a glimpse of Nellie Wallace, the gangly, buck-toothed, bespectacled, would-be *femme fatale* whose catchline was 'If you're looking for something tasty, what price *me*?' She didn't see Nellie Wallace that evening because Wilkie Warren introduced her to the beautiful singer who was topping the bill. As Marguerite Broadfoote was leaving, she said to Naomi, 'I shall be back here for pantomime. I hope that we shall meet again.'

For the rest of that year – 1905, by my calculations – Naomi toiled at St Hilda's:

So there I was, a member of the Socialist Party, a suffragist, hating the dirt and squalor; doing what I could, with the aid of a diluted solution of carbolic, to keep the children's heads as free from vermin as was possible; mixing boric acid and hot water for their 'sore eyes', providing ointment for chilblains, washing cuts and abrasions, and growing more unpopular every day with my superiors.

She had been seen walking in the street arm in arm with a young man (Wilkie Warren?) who wasn't her fiancé, and Louisa Butterfield had chastised her for such unseemly behaviour in public. Her fellow teachers, with the exception of Jane Brentnall, were horrified that she went to theatres unaccompanied by a responsible adult. She was often accused of setting her pupils a bad example. If the poor were to be taught anything, it was morality. Naomi, who was more concerned with the children's health and well-being than with patronizing moral values, felt continuously trapped and frustrated.

Marguerite Broadfoote returned to Middlesbrough to play Principal Boy in the pantomime. The twenty-year-old Naomi, who still had long hair, which, in the fashion of the time, she tied up in a bun, fell in love with the older woman. Marguerite was married to a theatrical agent, Ernest Edelsten, who was too much like Samuel Jacob for Naomi's comfort. She 'disliked him at their first meeting', according to James Norbury, who describes him as 'a Jew who could be extremely generous at one moment and the most close-fisted of men at the next'. Everyone, including his wife, knew of his philandering.

Marguerite called Naomi Micky, and Naomi called her Meg. Micky invited Meg to St Hilda's to meet the children. She brought with her 'huge bags of sweets, more sweets than the majority of the children had seen in their lives. She stared at the poor little souls in their rags and their dirt. She smiled at them, talked to them, made them laugh.' When Louisa Butterfield observed frostily, 'I didn't know that actresses liked children,' Marguerite Broadfoote replied, with a smile, 'Even actresses are human beings, surely.'

Naomi was called into the head mistress's office, where she was reminded, yet again, that St Hilda's was a church school. The Reverend John Kay Bealey had recently died, and in his place was a young clergyman with severely puritanical views regarding the theatre, which he associated with vice in all its manifestations. Was Miss Jacob aware that the woman she had brought to the school 'appeared on the stage wearing tights'? Naomi answered that she *was* aware, and that a 'very celebrated actress' had played Rosalind, in tights, in *As You Like It*, only a few weeks before. This remark elicited the response, 'There are tights – and tights' from Louisa Butterfield. 'Admitted,' Naomi parried, 'but all worn in the same way, on the legs.'

Naomi listened as the head mistress and the vicar ran through her failings. They said nothing of her achievements. They overlooked the obvious fact that she and Jane Brentnall were the only teachers the pupils both liked and respected. The vicar spoke sternly when he pointed out that she had been sighted leaving the *stage door* of the Opera House. He put particular emphasis on the words *stage door*, thereby implying that she was consorting with music-hall artistes, who were even more immoral than actors. It was then that Naomi lost her temper, banged her fist on a desk, and said that she was sick and tired of it all and was going. 'They didn't want to lose me. I was a good teacher and they knew it. They recovered their breath to tell me how foolish I was, how I was abandoning a very grand and noble profession.' But Naomi was adamant. In her anger, she had made a decision she would never regret. The clergyman remonstrated with her. What would she do? She told him that she was 'going on the music halls', which was a near-truth because Meg had asked Micky to be her secretary and travelling companion. 'He expressed consternation as to my moral welfare,' she writes in *Me – Looking Back*. 'Then followed seven of the happiest years I have ever known – or shall ever know. I entered a new world, a world where people were kindly and open-hearted.'

The children were very upset when Miss Jacob said goodbye to them. She was upset as well, and wondered fleetingly if she was acting wisely. She reminded herself that she was young and had no fear of the future. She was also in love with Meg, and Meg with her, although she doesn't say so directly in any of her autobiographies. She joined Meg in London, and met Ernest Edelsten and their son Bobbie, a weak child who needed plenty of cossetting. The hated Edelsten is rarely mentioned in the various *Me* books, and always in a non-committal manner – as a successful agent who owned a grand house in Brixton. 'He was a difficult man to live with and an impossible partner in the marriage,' observes James Norbury in his biography *The Seven Ages of 'Me'*. Edelsten was indifferent to Micky at first, and probably grateful that Meg had acquired such a devoted companion. He could spend more time, now, with his many mistresses.

From 1905 to 1912, Marguerite Broadfoote was much in demand as a singer of tasteful ballads. With Micky to answer her letters, to arrange her billing, to seek out suitable boarding houses to stay in, she performed in music halls and theatres throughout the British Isles. Micky was always with her, and eyebrows weren't raised when they shared a room, because women could sleep together in all innocence then. It was generally known that Meg was married, and even after Micky had her hair cropped short no one assumed they were lovers. Fellow artistes may have had their suspicions about Meg's masculine-looking secretary, but since many of them were having adulterous affairs or casual encounters with members of their own sex, they didn't give voice to those suspicions in public. Meg, with her soft Edinburgh accent and pleasant demeanour, was treated respectfully wherever she went. Micky, in her triple capacity as friend, secretary and adviser, 'was accepted and given a good time'.

'She wasn't clever; in fact, I have rarely met any woman who possessed so much intelligence but not intellect,' Micky writes in *Me*.

In other words, she was a fool – but one of God's Fools. I have her favourite books still. They are *Captain Desmond V. C.*, *Candles in the Wind* (both by Maud Diver) and *The Way of an Eagle* (by Ethel M. Dell). There is also a little book of poems bound in dark violet suede, called *Poems of Passion*, several of which are marked in pencil as demanding special notice.

Poems of Passion by Ella Wheeler Wilcox was published by Gay and Hancock in 1908. It's possible that 'Artist's Life' was one of the poems marked by Meg:

> Of all the waltzes the great Strauss wrote,
>   Mad with melody, rhythm-rife
> From the very first to the final note,
>   Give me his 'Artist's Life'!

It stirs my blood to my finger-ends,
　　Thrills me and fills me with vague unrest,
And all that is sweetest and saddest blends
　　Together within my breast.

It brings back that night in the dim arcade,
　　In love's sweet morning and life's best prime,
When the great brass orchestra played and played,
　　And set our thoughts to rhyme.

It brings back that Winter of mad delights,
　　Of leaping pulses and tripping feet
And those languid moon-washed Summer nights
　　When we heard the band in the street.

It brings back rapture and glee and glow,
　　It brings back passion and pain and strife,
And so of all the waltzes I know
　　Give me the 'Artist's Life'.

For it is so full of the dear old time –
　　So full of the dear old friends I knew.
And under its rhythm, and lilt, and rhyme,
　　I am always finding – *you*.

Yet in *Me – Looking Back*, Meg is described as 'well read, a very fine musician, possessing a real appreciation of art', and in *Robert, Nana and – Me* Micky notes that 'she was a woman of considerable education [who] loved to prowl round old churches, to visit beautiful cathedrals'. Perhaps James Norbury is right when he suggests that Meg was a 'mother substitute' for Micky, who was hearing less and less from Nana. What is certain is that Micky's relationship with Meg was both more stable and more loving than any she sustained in later life. There were no scenes, for none was necessary. Micky was happy to be the attentive companion Ernest Edelsten wasn't, and Edelsten was pleased to be entirely free of a marital responsibility he never honoured.

The stars of the music hall – even the greatest, like Marie Lloyd – preferred to stay in lodgings rather than hotels. They appreciated the home-from-home atmosphere of digs, where breakfast in bed could be served as late as ten or eleven in the morning. They enjoyed, too, the often alarming company of landladies, who ranged in character from the angelic to the diabolic. Landladies provided excellent copy for Dan Leno, the tortured comic genius who made use of their tics, mannerisms and eccentric turns of speech when he was playing Dame in pantomime. The angelic ones supplied fresh food, clean linen and hot and cold water, and were cheerful and friendly. The diabolic served jaw-breaking chump chops at every meal, considered baths an extravagance, and let it be known that they only catered for theatrical lodgers out of the kindness of their hearts or under duress. When Micky pointed to a grease mark on the wall at a particularly grubby boarding house, the landlady looked at it and nodded before observing, 'I'll tell you what that is. That was where Mrs de Vere chucked a leg of mutton at Mr de Vere, when they were playing here in that drama *What is Life Without Love?*'

Among the music-hall artistes Micky met during her involvement with Meg were a strange couple called John and Cissie Lawson. He was the son of a Jewish mother, but was raised as a Christian in Lancashire. He achieved fame in both America and Britain with a dramatic sketch he adapted to perform on the halls. It was entitled *Humanity,* and such was its success that the title became his nickname. 'Humanity' Lawson appeared as Jacob Silveni, a Jew whose wife is betraying him with a Gentile. Lawson walked on to the stage, 'a smallish dark fellow, looking like an undertaker in a poor way of business', and bowed to the audience. 'What have we here? Flowers for my wife and a note. I'll open it and read it, just for fun' were the lines that precipitated the action. He opened the letter, read it to himself with increasing anger, and spoke the last sentence out loud: 'And leave for ever your husband, who is only a Jew.' As soon as he said the words 'only a Jew', the orchestra played the opening bars of the song 'Humanity' Lawson had made his own:

> Only a Jew, the insult I'll remember.
> Only a Jew, then why not Christians too?
> For the same sunshine is o'er us,
> And the same road lies before us,
> Then why should *he* refer to *me* as only a Jew?'

Lawson sang, with a Yiddish accent.

There then followed what the public had really come to see – the spectacle of Jacob Silveni, with the assistance of an actor playing his wife's lover, breaking twenty pounds' worth of crockery on stage. 'The set was magnificent, it was Lawson's idea of what a "swell house" was like.' The two men ran up and down a big double staircase, flinging pottery at each other:

There was enough crockery standing about to have stocked a small shop, and – every bit was broken! Everything that was flingable was flung, everything that was smashable was smashed. Tea cups, decanters, 'art pots', chandeliers, plates, huge vases on even larger pedestals – all went crashing to the floor!

Micky was impersonating 'Humanity' singing 'Only a Jew' at a party one evening when a 'very slim young woman, with a mop of ash-blonde hair' entered the room. As soon as Micky finished, the woman came over and introduced herself as Lawson's wife. Cissie Lawson congratulated Micky on her impersonation, and from that moment they became friends.

Cissie Lawson was described by a drama critic as 'the Gutter

Lady Macbeth' because of her fondness for 'low-life-high-tragedy'. She played a succession of fallen women in sketches with titles such as *A Bride for a Living, Devil's Sunday* and *Again the Woman*. According to Micky, Cissie herself wrote the pieces in collaboration with members of the Lawsons' company. *Again the Woman* was inspired by a couple of lines of doggerel she found in a book:

> She was a harlot, and he was a thief,
> But they loved each other beyond belief.

Micky attended the first performance: 'For all its crudities, its lack of polish, and its starkness, I have never been more moved in my life.' Cissie, who had received little education and no training, was an instinctive performer; a 'natural' whose simplicity and patent sincerity compensated for her rather inadequate technique. She was, Micky hints, more in love with her husband than he was with her, and the authenticity of her acting may have been rooted in unhappiness. Nothing John Lawson did could make Cissie fall out of love with him. In *Me*, Micky pays tribute to the dead Cissie as one of the tragic wives of the music hall, but in *Me – Looking Back*, written seventeen years later, she salutes an artiste who is obviously alive: 'Dear, gallant Cissie Lawson. Life hasn't treated her too well, but her courage remains unimpaired. What a trouper she was – and still is!' Micky's more attentive readers may have wondered if Cissie, who had been a widow for fifteen years when *Me* was published, read her premature obituary, with its suggestion that Lawson's inconsiderate behaviour had led her to an early grave.

Micky was also briefly acquainted with an acrobat named Muzuz, who followed her everywhere for an entire week, to Meg's annoyance, for he was scarcely able to speak English and looked distinctly smitten. Micky was bewildered whenever she caught his admiring gaze. Then, on the Friday evening, while Meg was singing, Muzuz asked her to marry him. She 'thanked him and declined'. He persisted in his attentions, stumbling to make it clear that his was no ordinary, romantic proposal. It was her sturdy physique that commanded his admiration, Micky learned, especially her shoulders. She could be part of a double act, he assured her. 'I'll soon teach you to carry me on your head,' he promised. But Micky still declined. She didn't feel that her mission in life was to carry Signor Muzuz about on her head.

She saw the conjuror and juggler Paul Cinquevalli frequently, since he was usually topping the bill. He was Polish by birth, and began his career as a trick cyclist on the trapeze. He was known as the Little Flying Devil. It was while he was convalescing after a near-fatal accident, lying on his back in a hospital bed, that he taught himself to juggle. 'He could juggle with cigarette ends, visiting cards, bits of paper, as well as cannon balls, billiard cues, and lighted lamps.' Cinquevalli was much respected in the profession for his courtesy and quiet dignity, but his life ended in tragic circumstances. During the First World War, a rumour was started that Cinquevalli was not a Pole but a German, and as such was working as an enemy spy, using his brilliant juggling act as a cover-up. Despite the absurdity of the allegation, 'people who ought to have known better believed the stories, people cold-shouldered him, and whispered about "German spies". Always a man of intense nervous temperament, always sensitive in the extreme, he noticed it, and suffered.' He suffered, in fact, a massive breakdown, from which he never recovered. He died in 1918.

Every summer during their years together, Meg and Micky spent a couple of months at Meg's bungalow in Selsey, on the Sussex coast. The bungalow was made out of two railway coaches, 'joined by a corridor, and faced with a wide veranda overlooking the sea'. It is safe to assume that the sickly Bobbie was sometimes with them, playing on the beach and enjoying the fresh air.

Meg's immediate neighbour was the Liberal member of parliament and crusading journalist Charles Masterman, who wrote many articles about the appalling working conditions in British factories. It was through Masterman that Micky was introduced to G. K. Chesterton, one of the very few writers of distinction she met in the course of her long life. She was disconcerted by the fact that 'such a large and robust-looking man had such a tiny and squeaky voice'. Chesterton's reaction to Micky's forceful baritone has not been recorded.

Masterman was initially amused and intrigued by the 'odd-looking, rather masculine woman he had seen next door' – the description is James Norbury's in *The Seven Ages of 'Me'*, where Charles Masterman is transformed into C. W. Massingham. (The real C. W. Massingham was not a politician, but an explorer and anthropologist who ventured into the Australian bush in the mid-nineteenth century.) Masterman called on Meg and Micky one day to tell them that a very important person, the leader of his party no less, would be staying at his bungalow the following weekend. He asked Micky, 'very earnestly', to refrain from any suffrage work while Lloyd George was in Selsey. Micky promised to behave herself, but then, as she says, she 'fell from grace':

I couldn't resist the temptation. I got a large biscuit tin, and cycled into Chichester to buy a cheap alarm clock. This I placed inside the biscuit tin, and sealed the box up with lots of adhesive tape and large lumps of sealing-wax. The whole contraption I placed under the Masterman bungalow. The noise was terrific. Try putting an alarm clock in a biscuit tin!

I placed it there about 6 a.m. Now, having come to years of

discretion, I would not go out at 6 a.m. even to play a joke on Mr Lloyd George. At eight, Masterman and his illustrious visitor came down the steps of the bungalow to bathe. They heard the noise and stopped, located it, and Masterman waved his guest away from the danger zone. He then, with commendable pluck, advanced to the tin, lifted it and carried it down to the sea, flinging it far out into the waters of the English Channel. The politician wrung his hand, and congratulated him on his courage. I don't dispute the courage, but it was amusing to witness.

That is how she accounts for her little jape in *Me*. In *Me – Looking Back*, Meg is involved in the practical joke:

When Lloyd George came down to spend a weekend at Selsey the Suffrage movement was at its height, and Marguerite and I went into Chichester – nine miles away – and bought an alarm clock, one of the kind that existed in those days, costing about three shillings and possessing a tick which would have wakened the dead without the alarm being used at all. We brought it home, wound it up and placed it carefully in a biscuit tin, adding a couple of large stones and sealing it with adhesive tape. This, late at night, we placed under the Masterman bungalow. The next morning we watched – assuming an air of complete nonchalance – as we ate breakfast on the veranda.

Lloyd George and his host issued forth, attired for bathing. They stopped, and they looked, and they listened – the clock was ticking away bravely and noisily in its tin box. They 'registered' that this was obviously one of the diabolical plots of the Suffragists. They had hidden a time bomb under the bungalow. Then followed a kind of 'Sir Philip Sidney' act. [Should Micky have written 'Sir Walter Raleigh'?]

It was obvious that one of them was determined to outdo the other in bravery and self-sacrifice. In the end Masterman went and dived under the bungalow. He emerged bearing the box in triumph and, running down to the water's edge, plunged in and finally hurled the biscuit tin out to sea. Then they both decided against a bathe and returned to their bungalow congratulating one another.

When, some days later, Micky told Masterman the truth, 'he didn't think it in the least funny'. Masterman's response to Micky's confession seems unusually moderate and dignified, given the fact that the Suffragists had recently burnt down Lloyd George's favourite golf-club house.

Micky's behaviour offended other residents of Selsey in the last summer before the outbreak of the First World War. One afternoon she was seen riding a horse along the east beach, dressed only in a bathing suit. Meg's outraged neighbours sent indignant letters to the land agent, who in turn wrote to Micky saying that it must never happen again or he would be 'forced to take steps'.

The carefree Micky continued to offend the respectable old ladies who lived nearby. They sighted her returning to the bungalow one morning without her beach wrap:

That afternoon, one of the old ladies called on Marguerite in person to complain. It appeared that she had a nephew staying with her, who was going to take Orders, and she felt that the sight of me – in a bathing suit – might shake his faith, or generally upset him in some way.

Meg listened to the woman's recital before remarking that she and her friends 'had minds that would be better for a good spring cleaning'. She further commented that if the nephew's future depended on his not seeing a woman in a bathing suit, then the sooner he was away from the Church the better it would be for the Church. Meg spoke in measured tones, in the soft Edinburgh accent that so beguiled her admirers.

As a result of the woman's visit, Meg decided to give a midnight bathing party. Most of the guests that weekend forgot to bring bathing suits, but Meg always kept a supply on the premises. She handed out a dozen of them, including Micky's. Meg decided that Micky would have to swim in her pyjamas. 'You'll be well enough clad, this time, even for old Mrs C's precious nephew.' Micky was only in the sea for a few minutes when she realized that she and her pyjamas were quickly parting company, and soon she was swimming in the nude. Meg swam out to her with a wrap, thus denying the old ladies – watching this Dionysian orgy from behind their curtains – the spectacle of a naked Micky scrambling up the beach.

It was in that year, 1914, that Meg and Micky's relationship was brought to an unwanted close. The painful episode is not mentioned in any of her autobiographies. Ernest Edelsten, who treated his wife's liaison with Micky with indifference, had grown jealous of Micky's influence on their son Bobbie. The boy regarded her as mother and father combined, and made his affection for her evident. Edelsten was furious, accusing Micky of perverting his son's mind and turning Bobbie against him. He told her that the ailing Marguerite (who had retired from the stage two years earlier) no longer required her services and ordered her out of the house. She went. Meg died on 10 July 1915, 'of a broken heart', according to James Norbury, whom Micky entrusted with the story of Ernest Edelsten's insane jealousy.

Micky moved into a very small flat in a street off Edgware Road. The rent was cheap and her fellow residents friendly. Among them was an impoverished journalist and poet, T. W. H. Crossland, whose sonnets she considered 'one of the glories of English literature'. Two days before his death, he told Micky, with a chuckle, that he had just written his last sonnet in order to pay his funeral expenses.

Shortly after war broke out, Micky applied for a post with

the Women's Emergency Corps. This organization, which was founded by three women – Eva and Decima Moore, and either Lena Ashwell or Gertrude Kingston, depending on which of the *Me* books you are inclined to believe – aimed to give employment to people who had been dismissed from their peacetime jobs as well as to those who wished to contribute to the war effort. Its offices were in Miss Kingston's Little Theatre. 'Every class of woman who could be organized was provided for there.'

Micky 'was not received with any great delight'. She was instructed to present herself to Mrs Charlesworth, known as Charlie, who asked her what skills she possessed. Micky answered that she could ride and box. The startled Charlie told her the Corps needed a messenger. 'For days I hung about behind the bar in the Little Theatre, giving out stationery, stamping letters, and when I was doing neither of these things, hammering nails into the walls, to support the thousand and one notices that appeared everywhere, about everything.'

It was Micky's task to write those notices in bold lettering – WALK IN, KEEP OUT, BY APPOINTMENT ONLY, DO NOT MAKE A NOISE, and, a farcical touch, DO NOT DRIVE NAILS INTO THE WALLS. She had no idea what the many typists were typing, though she assumed it was something 'important and necessary'. At that early stage of the war, the Emergency Corps was providing food and clothing to Belgian refugees, who – to Micky's knowledge – never expressed an iota of gratitude.

Micky discovered that the women who swarmed to join the Corps were from every level of society:

Hearty women who obviously hated London and belonged to the shires; delicate creatures who looked as if they were ordained to spend their lives doing exquisite needlework; efficient women; women who – you realized on sight – would make a complete muddle of anything they were given to do; masterful women;

women who exerted 'charm'; women with ideas; others without an idea in their heads.

In which category would Micky have placed herself? Among the masterful, I think. It is a tiresome characteristic of certain Yorkshire people to boast that they always speak their minds because they alone are in possession of a common sense denied to the rest of the human race, especially those unfortunate enough to be born in the south of England. J. B. Priestley, in particular, seldom wasted an opportunity to remind his readers and listeners of the commonsensical qualities that were his by right as a Yorkshireman. Micky did likewise, as she is at pains to record in her many volumes of autobiography. It is Micky who always has the last word; Micky who deflates pomposity; Micky who comes out with the plain, unvarnished truth, simply by virtue of being a Yorkshirewoman.

Micky became secretary of the Toy-making Department, after being interviewed by Lady Aberconway (James Norbury calls her Lady Abercrombie) and the Corps secretary, Mrs Falk, 'a beautiful young woman with fair hair and a slightly vague manner':

'And what,' said Lady Aberconway to me, rather in the tone you might use to a new housemaid, 'what were you before the war?'

'Me?' I said. 'Oh, I was manager and secretary to a bill topper.'

Her eyes grew larger and larger.

'Mrs Falk,' she said, 'what is a bill topper?'

Mrs Falk, who has always regarded me as a harmless and rather amusing lunatic, said, 'What's a bill topper, Jacob?'

Lady Aberconway tapped her on the arm, and said in a hurried and slightly agitated whisper, 'It doesn't matter, it doesn't matter.' I fancy she thought it was some rather obscure form of white slavery.

Some eighty women were employed to make toys. Micky

'slogged away trying to learn something about the toy trade which we were trying to capture from Germany'. She taught herself 'something about paint and varnish, about deal, and three-ply, about fret-saws and hand-saws, about lathes and nails and screws'. Although hopeless at arithmetic, she also managed to keep accurate accounts.

The Women's Emergency Corps was eventually disbanded, its various departments incorporated into schemes organized and funded by the government. Micky's toy-makers moved to Lord Roberts's Memorial Workshops, and she was politely told that her services were no longer required. She worked briefly for a man called Gooch, who owned a factory in Watford, but she didn't care for him and said so to his face. 'I left in a blaze of glory and truculent conversation,' she observes, bewilderingly, in *Me*, the first of her autobiographies.

It was while she was employed in the toy business that she received a second proposal of marriage. Her unlikely inamorato was a stout, elderly German Jew who invited her to dine with him in a smart London hotel. She was under the impression that he was about to offer her a contract for Mr Gooch's toys when he leant forward over the fish, pressed her hand, and said 'Naomi – how would you like one day to be my widow?'

Micky's refusal must have been tempered with amusement or disbelief, because the old man persisted in his efforts to marry her. He sent her bouquets from Gerard's, the exclusive florists; numerous boxes of Turkish cigarettes, which went unsmoked, as they were not to her taste; and Belgian chocolates, which she resisted eating. She does not reveal if she returned his expensive presents, but after some weeks 'he retired from the chase'.

Following a short spell in an agency in the West End of London, where she was required to find cooks and servants for titled people, the next job Micky undertook initially appealed to her socialist principles. She was appointed by the secretary of an unseen committee to organize flag days throughout the country on behalf of the Russian poor. She travelled from city to city, talking to mayors and councillors, some of whom welcomed the idea, though others were more sceptical.

In *Me* she recounts that she was sent to Clapham – 'I think that it was Clapham or Brook Green or some such place,' she notes, with her customary disrespect for accuracy – where she was met by 'a sinister-looking gentleman at the Town Hall' who advised her to apply to the Jews, who were always charitable and kind-hearted. As a consequence, she visited the wife of the local rabbi: 'I felt instinctively that, when I mentioned Russian Flag Day, a chill fell on the air. I felt, too, that for some reason I was emphatically not the "blue-eyed boy" of the moment. In fact, I realized that I wasn't all popular.'

After asking Micky various questions about the flag day, the rabbi's wife suggested that she should address a group of Jewish ladies the following Sunday afternoon. Micky agreed to the suggestion, but 'left with that queer feeling you get when there is a row blowing up somewhere'.

Sunday arrived. I went to Clapham, Brook Green, or wherever it was, and in a few – but not too few – chosen words, drew a pathetic and touching picture of the starving Russians and their infant children. I still had this feeling that a storm was going to burst. It did – a Jewish woman rose and told me a good deal about the flag day that I didn't know. It was, she stated, organized, at the base as you might say, by a gentleman who lived in the North, and was much interested in the conversion of Jews to Christianity. This flag day certainly provided money for food, stores, medicine and so forth which were sent to Russia but – but – it was only distributed to Jews who became Christians.

Micky was suddenly aware that she had been duped – not

'He cuts a handsome figure and bears himself with vivacity.'
Period photographs of Fred Barnes

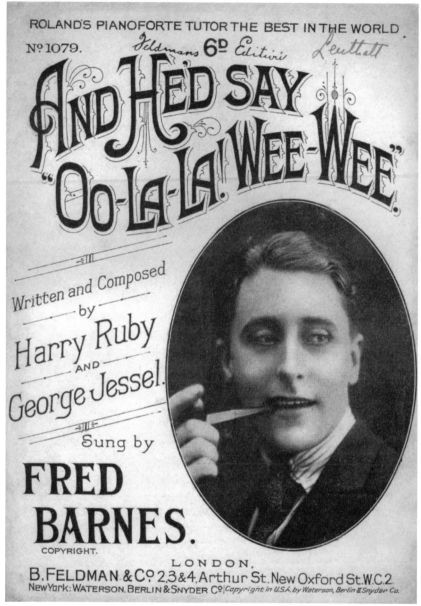

(*Above*) Cover of the sheet music for one of Fred's more humorous songs
FACING PAGE: (*Above left*) Naomi, aged 4
(*Above right*) At 20 with Marguerite Broadfoote
(*Below left*) With Percy Plate Esq.
(*Below right*) At Casa Mickie with Joan Gabbetis

Feeding the pigeons in
St Mark's Square, Venice,
with Jean Webster Brough

With Gina Cigna, who
died in June 2001 at the
age of 101

Signora Micky in Sirmione, with godsons Carlo and Sergio Pagiaro

Stuffing the Christmas turkey in the kitchen at Casa Mickie

Arthur recovering from whooping
cough at Frinton

Ballet preparations at Oundle School.
An amused fellow ballerina looks on

Oundle School staff.
Arthur holds centre stage

(*Above*) A leading member of the ADC, Arthur played Elizabeth in Somerset Maugham's *The Circle*

(*Left*) Arthur as Elizabeth, perched on the leading man's knee

Second-Lieutenant C. A. B. Marshall in a posed photograph requested by his parents

Call My Bluff with
Frank Muir and
Robert Robinson

With Peter Kelland
in Jamaica

In the garden

by the secretary, who was probably as innocent as she, but by the invisible committee and its mysterious chairman. She was forced to remark, feebly, that she needed more evidence and conclusive proof that the woman's statement was true. Even as she spoke, she knew that she was 'fighting a losing game'.

I felt rather like Paul Kruger when he was asked to open the Millionaires' Synagogue, and promised to do so on condition that he need not make a speech, only declare the building open. He arrived, mounted on to a rostrum, and removing his top hat, said firmly, 'I declare this synagogue open in the name of Our Lord and Saviour Jesus Christ.'

Micky said goodbye to the irate ladies in Clapham, Brook Green, or wherever it was they were gathered, and returned to her flat near Edgware Road, where she wrote a letter of resignation to the secretary of the committee.

'I joined the Women's Legion and went to France. I got trench feet and came home,' Micky declares, rather tersely, in *Me – Looking Back*. 'I saw men going up to the trenches,' she elaborates in *Robert, Nana and – Me*. 'They mostly seemed in good spirits, fine healthy-looking lads, smiling and holding their heads high. They were "boys being sent to do a man's job" – but they did it all right – at a price.'

Back in London, Micky went into hospital to have an operation, for her trench feet presumably. From the winter of 1916 until September 1919, she worked as either the welfare supervisor (*Robert, Nana and – Me*) or assistant supervisor of the canteen (*The Seven Ages of 'Me'*) at a munitions factory in Willesden. She was now one of 'Kitchener's Lizzies', as women seriously involved in the war effort were generically labelled.

The 500 men and women who made the signalling and arc lamps which were the factory's speciality addressed Micky as Jake. A new canteen was added to the building shortly after her arrival, with a small stage at one end, on which was placed an old grand piano. Each Friday afternoon, during their dinner hour, Jake's 'boys and girls' were entertained by some of the stars of the music hall Micky had met when she was Meg's companion. 'Marie Lloyd herself came once and was a riot', and George Robey was 'funnier than I have ever heard him'. There were improving talks as well, given by visiting dignitaries at the request of the management. Someone called Vera Holme lectured on the Serbian retreat, and Major Corbett-Smith gave a rousing speech that consisted mainly of lines from Henry V's address to his troops before the battle of Agincourt. When he finished, Jake's 'ultra-red Socialist boys and girls' were in such a state of 'patriotic fury' that she feared they might fling up their jobs and follow the major to Flanders.

In *Robert, Nana and − Me*, she provides a detailed account of a typical working day at Lyons and Wrenchs' factory:

Lathes, milling machines, drillers; benches where the signalling lamps were assembled; the tool shop where the instruments for making assembling, and the like, possible; the coil-winding shop where those complicated generators were made − fine, close work that; the paint shop which was always, of necessity, overheated with its baking ovens; the inspection shop where every article turned out had to be proved to be worthy of acceptance . . . the great belts moving smoothly with their slight purring noise, the regular pushing back of levers, the whirr of the electric drills, the nerve-racking sound of filing, the banging of hammers, the tinkle of metal. All these things went to make up the factory. At first you felt that you would never get the din of it all out of your brain, then slowly − when you were conscious that the machinery had stopped running, for dinnertime or because the day's work was over − you missed it, and felt a kind of blankness. It was curious that there were several deaf people working there and when the machines stopped running you had to bawl at them to make them hear what you said; but the moment it [sic] was running full pelt they heard every word you spoke.

In both *Me* and *Me – Looking Back*, Micky's 'boys and girls' are honest, hard-working Cockneys, the 'salt of the earth', who possess a native intelligence denied to their superiors in the War Office, but in *Robert, Nana and – Me* they are depicted as time-wasting and unpatriotic, their 'ultra-red' Socialism no longer to be admired. She praises a few, quietly productive workers, and dismisses the rest for being either scheming or slow-witted. She chastises them for refusing to eat macaroni cheese or savoury rice when meat was scarce – 'They resented anything unfamiliar' – and for wanting what they were accustomed to. This is the writer who taught her Italian cook to prepare roast sirloin of beef and a multitude of stodgy dishes containing suet and lard – the food of her ancestors she considered preferable to the oily concoctions of her adopted country.

The one break with tradition the 'boys and girls' (*Me* and *Me – Looking Back*) and the workers (*Robert, Nana and – Me*) approved of was Jake's appointing a woman, Grainger Evans, to the post of medical officer. The considerate Dr Evans broke down the men and women's initial resistance to her by dint of the effective medicines she prescribed. A cleaner with hitherto incurable wind found herself with a calm stomach instead of the 'proper roaring tempest' that disturbed her after every meal, while Big Liz Mitchell – who remained Jake's favourite 'girl' over a period of forty years – swore by the doctor's powerful cough mixture. Dr Evans lanced whitlows and extracted metal splinters from under fingernails and won the confidence of the entire staff.

It was Dr Grainger Evans who diagnosed Micky with tuberculosis and arranged for her to go to King Edward VII's Sanatorium at Midhurst in Sussex. The works gave her a 'very handsome present', and the boss made a speech, saying that as long as the factory stood, there would always be a place waiting for her. Two weeks after she entered the sanatorium, she received a letter from him in which he expressed regret at having to dispense with her services.

Micky was ordered to exercise, which meant weeding the garden and 'planting rock plants'. From this she progressed to carting dead leaves to the rubbish tip. She filled the cart, pushed it in the direction of the tip, sat down, opened a book, read it, smoked a 'forbidden cigarette' and returned 'with the empty barrow just before knocking-off time'. Since she was paying for her treatment, she considered it her right to do as little exercise, however gentle, as possible.

There were 'several dukes' – Micky does not reveal how many, nor does she bother with their titles – among the trustees of the sanatorium. Accompanied by Sir Ernest Cassel, 'King Edward's great friend', the ducal committee inspected the hospital one day. They 'were marched through my room to see how they liked the shade it had been painted':

I was lying on my bed, reading.

The M.O. asked Sir Ernest Cassel how he liked the shade of the paint.

He glanced at it, then at me, and said, 'It's more in your line than mine – what do you think of it?'

'Of what?' I asked. 'Your hat, or your manners for wearing it in my bedroom?'

The M.O. went pale grey, but Sir Ernest stared, took off his hat and said, 'Sorry – sorry – I entirely forgot.' As a matter of fact he said 'Thorry'. He was very nice about it, sat down and began to talk, told the M.O. that he could go on and see where the others had got to, and in five minutes I had unloaded three of my best stories – two were Jew stories – and he laughed immoderately. He asked if I had all I wanted. I said my only difficulty was to get enough cigarettes. He said, 'I'd give you some, but I only have cigars with me. You couldn't smoke a cigar, could you?'

'Try me,' I said, with that brevity that is the soul of wit.

He handed me his case, and the next day sent me a box of fifty half-Coronas.

Micky stayed at the sanatorium for eight months. 'No patient could have been more tiresome, no patient could have given more trouble to the authorities, and I doubt if anyone enjoyed being in a sanatorium less than I did.'

A few weeks before Christmas 1919, the medical officer invited Micky to choose some short plays for the patients to perform. He warned her that they must be 'cheerful and bright'. She found three: *The Great Look*, *A Sister to Assist 'Er* and *The Monkey's Paw*. She refused to let the staff attend rehearsals and ordered the cast of *The Monkey's Paw* not to divulge the plot. The evening was a 'great success' and the difficult Miss Jacob, who referred to the patients as 'inmates' just to annoy the M.O. was suddenly – and briefly – popular with the nursing staff.

There was a little public house about half-a-mile away from the sanatorium, kept by a retired prize-fighter. A group of 'poor consumptives', which included Micky, took an afternoon stroll each day to breathe in the fresh air. They were instructed to walk slowly, but their pace quickened as soon as they reached a 'convenient row of trees' that hid them from view. They were practically running as they approached the pub, which they entered by the back door by prior arrangement with the boxer. There they drank and smoked in a 'quite remarkably stuffy' bar, from which the hated fresh air was permanently excluded.

She was discharged in the spring of 1920, and told that her
illness had been 'arrested'. She returned to London, to a new
and larger flat in Baker Street, which she shared with Henrietta
Carlotta Francesca Maria Simione, known to her friends as
Simmy. When Micky first met her, Simmy was acting
as housekeeper to a man living above Vaughan's, the gunsmith's
in the Strand, as well as managing the Green Man in Bedford
Street. When an American soldier complained that his beer
was flat, Simmy replied, 'Well, what do you expect, it's been
waiting for you for three years.'

Micky had secured a job for Simmy (to whom *Me* is
dedicated) at the Willesden factory, where she worked on a
drilling machine. Simmy, who was as forceful as Micky but in
a more noticeably feminine way, had moved into the Edgware
Road flat, which commanded a view of the slums in the nearby
Harrow Road:

I have watched fights going on from my bedroom window, people
milling up and down a narrow staircase wrestling together, blas-
pheming, cursing, while the children cowered in a corner watching,
listening, shivering. It is a pleasant memory that after I had lived in
that district for a time I could lean from my window and yell: 'Lay
off it, or I'll come round to you. Me and Simmy!'

In *Me*, Micky tells with approval the story of how a Jew
had followed Simmy home to Baker Street from the tube
station:

He made several tentative offers to take her to Lyons and give her a
cup of tea, to take her to the movies, all of which she rejected. At
the door of the flat he enquired, 'Live 'ere, miss? Vatabout [*sic*]
asking me in for a chat, eh?'

Simmy turned. 'Now look here,' she said, 'we've been to a bit of
trouble to get Palestine for you – go and live in it!'

It is difficult to ascertain if Micky was married before or after her relationship with Simmy. Her husband's identity remains unknown, partly because in old age Micky liked to pretend that she had forgotten his name. She once asked her sister Muriel if she could remember who he was and was not at all displeased when the answer was negative. In *The Seven Ages of 'Me'*, James Norbury recounts that 'the marriage had taken place when she was sad and lonely and desperate', which could mean either the period in which she was barred from seeing Marguerite or the months after her beloved friend's death. In 1914, she read *Confessions of a Convert* by Monsignor R. H. Benson, the younger brother of the diarist A. C. Benson and E. F. Benson, the author of the Mapp and Lucia novels. All three men were gay, but Robert Hugh was the only one to experience lasting guilt and shame. E. F. Benson, whose nickname was Dodo, told his neighbours in Rye – the novelist Radclyffe Hall and her companion Una Troubridge – that after Hugh's death a box containing a 'discipline' – a scourge with small spikes clotted with blood – had been found among his effects.

Monsignor Benson's book convinced Micky, after years of doubt and anguish, that she should become a Roman Catholic. She took instruction from an elderly nun, who irritated her by being excessively pedantic:

I was perfectly well acquainted with the Catechism and, conceited little fool that I was, I longed to ask her to 'Get on!' I even went so far as to ask the parish priest if I might be given an instruction which was slightly more profound, and I don't doubt that I hinted 'and more in keeping with my own intellectual attainments' . . . He told me to go back to the old nun and learn humility!

The marriage 'as most of her friends realized' was 'doomed to failure from the start', Norbury observes. The unlikely couple 'lived together for a few weeks and were both sensible enough to realize that even after such a short time they had reached a permanent parting of the ways'. Despite this unpleasant experience, Micky contemplated a second marriage to Henry Dale Johnson, a Middlesbrough man she met some years later in Dr Harry Wadd's sanatorium in Richmond, Surrey. Johnson shared her enthusiasm for the theatre and was an amusing companion. Micky startled him one evening when he arrived at her flat to take her out for a meal at a London hotel. She was wearing a ball gown instead of her customary dinner jacket and black trousers. 'Don't stare at me like that, Henry, you make me feel like a female impersonator,' she joked.

Micky had £10 in the bank and no immediate prospects of employment. Simmy, her 'lion-hearted' partner, was now working as a barmaid at Madame Tussaud's, the waxworks museum.

In *Me*, Micky remembers – with characteristic vagueness – that 'some misguided person' said to her, 'I wonder you don't go on the stage,' to which she replied, 'I *am* going on the stage.' And that is precisely what she did.

By sheer chance, an actress called Gladys Gray, who would later marry the more famous Leslie Faber, told Micky there was a part that suited her in the play *Scandal* by Cosmo Hamilton, which the director and manager Arthur Hardy was soon to send out on tour. Micky had never met him, but that didn't deter her from going along to the Strand Theatre, where *Scandal* was ending its run, with a plan to convince Arthur Hardy that he not only knew her personally but was also aware of her, as yet untried, acting ability.

At the stage door, she asked to see Mr Hardy. The stage-door keeper wanted to know if she had an appointment. She said she hadn't:

'Better let me have your card then,' he said.

I knew that my card would convey nothing to Arthur, so I said, as lightly as I could, 'Just tell him that Naomi Jacob wants to see him.'

He said 'Better let me have a card.'

I produced the card and said, 'He'll be terribly amused at the idea of *my* sending up a card – but there you are!'

He returned, and said that Mr Hardy would see me. Up I went.

Fortunately Arthur was alone, if he'd had anyone else in the room I shouldn't have known which of them was Arthur Hardy. I went in brightly and said:

'How are you? Nice to see you again, Mr Hardy.' I didn't dare to say 'Arthur' even to make it sound real!

Her mischievous plan paid off. Arthur Hardy was too polite in the face of Micky's breeziness to insist that she was a complete stranger to him. Instead – according to her account in *Me* – he responded to her greeting with, 'Hello! This is jolly. How are you? Anything I can do for you?'

What he could do for her, she replied, was to offer her the part of Brownie in *Scandal*.

He screwed in his eyeglass, looked at her closely, and remarked, 'You'd be awfully good, too!' Then, speaking slowly, he observed that it was silly of him, but he'd forgotten where he had seen her last.

That was what I'd been waiting for. 'How like you,' I said.

'You come round after the show, tell me that you like my work, and you want me to come and see you in London – and then forget all about me.'

'No, no!' Arthur protested. 'Oh, dear me, no!'

'Nottingham,' I said. '*Now* do you remember?'

'Of course, of course.'

He offered her a weekly salary. He held up four fingers to

indicate how much he intended to pay. She, in turn, raised four fingers and a thumb, and Arthur Hardy said, 'Well, five then, as you know your business inside out.'

The rehearsals went badly for Micky, who assured the increasingly anxious director that she would surprise him by giving her all on the first night. Hardy, still convinced that she was a seasoned performer despite the evidence to the contrary, believed her and was pleased when her prediction turned out to be correct. Brownie was required to have a fit of hysterics and Micky supplied it forcefully throughout the thirteen weeks of the tour.

Arthur Hardy invited Micky and Gladys Gray to sign on for another tour with an increase in salary, but they both declined the offer. They hadn't been happy in the company. 'I think he was very hurt, and I remember him telling me, gravely and very nicely, that when my money was spent it would be too late to come and ask him to take me back.'

Micky returned to London on a Sunday, and the following morning she received a telegram from Eva Moore (for whom she worked occasionally as a secretary) advising her to go to the Comedy Theatre to audition for the part of the tipsy cook in *The Ruined Lady*. She was hired immediately. (Micky was to specialize in drunken cooks and comic maidservants during her acting career.) The leading, ruined lady was Rosa Lynd and the leading man C. Aubrey Smith, who would later go to Hollywood and appear in several films in the role of the archetypal monocled English gentleman. He was more interested in cricket than in acting and introduced the game to his American colleagues. His peculiar style of bowling earned him the nickname 'Round-the-Corner Smith'.

Micky made friends with a young actor – 'We were as bad as each other; together we must have contributed very little to the success of the play' – called Nigel Bruce. He, too, would become a Hollywood star, playing the bumbling Dr Watson to Basil Rathbone's sardonic Sherlock Holmes. He and Micky acted in a curtain-raiser to *The Ruined Lady* entitled *A Nice Thing*. Micky played an old woman, 'paralysed and half-crazy', and 'Willie' Bruce a young sergeant 'in a very badly fitting uniform'. He had to spill a cup of milk on stage, and invariably the milk landed on Micky's head – 'being paralysed I couldn't wipe it up, and had to stay with the milk slopped all over me until the end of the play'.

Micky's next appearance was as a costerwoman in an adaptation of *Liliom* by the Hungarian dramatist and novelist Ferenc Molnar. For reasons Micky does not disclose, it was given the title *The Daisy*. It was directed by Edith Craig, the daughter of Ellen Terry, whose lover Christabel Marshall had renamed herself Christopher St John. Christopher, like Micky, was a Catholic convert, and it is said that the St John surname was appropriated because of the affinity she felt to St John the Baptist. Edy would inherit her mother's sixteenth-century farmhouse at Smallhythe, near Tenterden in Kent, in 1928, and inaugurate an annual performance in its Barn Theatre in memory of the great actress. Vita Sackville-West, for whom Christopher nursed an unrequited passion, read her poem *The Land* there. In old age, William Plomer revealed to me that he had attended the reading with Stephen Spender, and that both of them had been reduced to helpless giggling at the spectacle of Vita, wearing riding boots, striding about the stage declaiming her determinedly earthy verses. She did not speak to them for many years as a consequence.

One of the first actors to perform in the Barn was John Gielgud, Ellen Terry's great-nephew. He and Peggy Ashcroft went there to act in scenes from *Twelfth Night* in the early 1930s. Gielgud recalled that the audience seemed to be entirely composed of women in tweeds and bow-ties. The sight of them terrified Peggy Ashcroft. When she walked on to the stage as Viola, dressed in breeches and boots, 'there was an

intake of breath from the audience like a kettle whistling',
to quote Gielgud. 'You must protect me, Johnny,' pleaded
Ashcroft, and Gielgud arranged for a car to meet them as soon
as the performance finished. They made a hasty exit.

   The Daisy ran for 'five or six nights' at the Kingsway Theatre.
Micky was returning to her dressing-room one evening when
she saw Ellen Terry coming along the passage.

I flattened myself against the wall, and almost held my breath as she
passed – she didn't pass, she stopped and said: 'My dear, I wish I
could speak Cockney as you do.' I ought to have said something
pretty, or at least reasonably sensible. I didn't. I just made a gurgling
noise and hoped that she might think I was overcome – which
indeed I was.

   After the failure of *The Daisy*, Micky was engaged to play
Lady Pennybroke in a tour of *Eliza Comes to Stay* by
H. V. Esmond, the husband of Eva Moore. When this came
to an end, she applied for the part of a Scotswoman in *The
Safety Match* by the young playwright Ian Hay. Hay himself
was present when Micky auditioned for Robert Courtneidge,
the most demanding and forbidding producer of the period.
He took her on, despite the fact that he found her accent too
Glaswegian and coarse. He drove her to fury in the rehearsals,
stopping her at the end of every line with suggestions for
improvement. He brooked no nonsense from Micky about
her giving everything on the first night. He wanted everything
perfect straight away. Micky rebelled, asserting that she wasn't
accustomed to being treated like a halfwit. Courtneidge
reminded her of her professional duties, and insisted that she
impersonate his inflections and gestures. She reluctantly did as
she was told. She came to love and admire Robert Courtneidge,
and befriended his talented daughter Cicely, the star of Ivor
Novello's last musical *Gay's the Word*.

The tour of *The Safety Match* was long and extensive, encompassing not only the familiar provincial cities but also Hull, Dublin and Belfast. In Hull, she and two other actors watched in horror as a newly launched battleship broke in two. 'The ends dipped earthwards, and a great rent appeared in her sides . . . The figures of the men could be seen falling out, down, down into the waters of the Humber.'

In Dublin, she had tea with the Irish republican revolutionary leader Michael Collins, who the following year – 1921 – would be a member of the delegation that negotiated the treaty with Great Britain which led to the establishment of the Irish Free State. Michael and Micky did not discuss politics. He was a 'nice boy, with very thick brown hair, and one lock which would fall over his forehead. He was very shy, laughed a great deal, and was tremendously interested in my greasepaints, and how I used them and put on a make-up.'

Micky enjoyed her stay in Dublin, which 'was still a very pleasant city', even though many shops were boarded up and there were buildings scarred with bullet holes. The week in Belfast, however, was a week too long. She 'saw a man's body torn out of his coffin, the coffin kicked to pieces, while the poor body was rolled into the gutter'. The rattle of machine-guns could be heard day and night. Once, a 'woman rushed out of a side street . . . Her arm was hanging in scarlet strips where a bullet had hit and smashed it.' The woman 'waved this terrible mangled limb' at Micky and cursed her for being one of the 'damned, bloody English'. On another occasion, when Micky was returning to her lodgings, she stopped at the corner of Donegal Pass to watch a funeral go by. She stood still, murmured a prayer and crossed herself. A huge Ulsterman rounded on her and shouted, 'Get to hell out of this, you blasted Papist!', and Micky answered, 'Now what's the good of sending me to hell? There isn't standing room there, it's chock-a-block with you Ulstermen', before running off.

★

'I forget what I did after *The Young Idea* – probably nothing. I think that it must have been about this time that I wrote my first book,' Micky observes in *Me*. In *The Young Idea*, Noël Coward's second play, she impersonated a 'hunting type' well enough to please the author. Her first book was an adaptation of H. V. Esmond's *Birds of a Feather*, in which Esmond played an 'old Jew, grand, petty, noble and inglorious, generous and impossibly mean – but really a great character'. Micky turned this dramatic piece into the novel *Jacob Ussher*. She showed the manuscript to Esmond's widow, Eva Moore, who 'didn't think much of it' but tried to be encouraging. Micky then took it to the literary agent Curtis Brown, where it was seen by Raymond Savage, who would represent her for most of her writing life. He sold *Jacob Ussher* to the firm of Thornton Butterworth, and after the moderate success of her next few novels he secured a contract with the more prestigious publishing house Hutchinson. She and Savage would remain friends for three decades, but would fall out when her books stopped selling well and Hutchinson ceased to publish her.

'I think it must have been about this time . . .': this phrase, with variations, recurs in each of the autobiographies. *The Young Idea* was staged in 1920; *Jacob Ussher* was published in 1926, and *Me: A Chronicle about Other People* was written in 1933. It seems extraordinary that she could not remember exactly when she became a novelist, since her literary career was only seven years old. She continued acting and understudying throughout the 1920s, appearing in the once-famous *Outward Bound*, a modern-day version of the sixteenth-century German allegory *The Ship of Fools*. Its author, Sutton Vane, behaved in a snooty fashion towards Micky, who expresses her dislike of him in *Me*. She had already written her second and third novels when she played a drunkard in Edgar Wallace's *The Ringer*. Wallace's first words to her at a rehearsal were 'I hear that you are one of us' – 'us' being 'novelists' – which Micky took to mean Jewish. She answered, 'Really? I didn't know that you were a Jew, Mr Wallace.' He wasn't, and he didn't take offence, as many other well-known writers of the period might have.

Micky was happy acting in *The Ringer*. She had to make her entrance singing her head off, struggling to escape from the clutches of two burly policemen. She sang – or rather, howled – a different song each night. Hearing that the music-hall star Kate Carney was in the audience, Micky honoured her with a mangled rendering of 'Three Pots a Shilling'. On another occasion, she serenaded Gus Elen with his 'Nature's Made a Big Mistake'. She had to leave the cast, to her considerable dismay, when the tuberculosis that had been arrested reasserted itself. She feared that she would have to return to the sanatorium in Midhurst, but, on the recommendation of Lady Harris (whose husband, Sir Percy, was the Liberal MP for Bethnal Green), she found a place that was nearer to London and much more congenial.

It was called Metcalfe's London Hydro, and was situated on Richmond Hill in Richmond, Surrey, next door to the house in which J. R. Ackerley's father, Roger, lived with the first – and legal – of his two families. This establishment – part clinic, part convalescent home – was run by Dr Harry Wadd, described by Ackerley's biographer, Peter Parker, as a 'dirty-minded old fraud who spent as much of the time he could spare from fleecing his patients exchanging smoking-room stories with Roger'. Joe, who regarded Wadd with contempt, records the following conversation between him and Roger in *My Father and Myself*:

WADD: Rog, old bean, if you gave up that rotten old claret of yours I could promise you another ten years of life.
MY FATHER: Thanks. I'd sooner have the claret.

Roger's riposte 'sent Wadd into one of his squealing, leg-slapping bouts of laughter'. Although Wadd occasionally attempted to dissuade him from eating and drinking to excess, he always accepted a glass or two of Roger's 'rotten old claret'.

Micky found Dr Harry, who 'looked like a cross between a barrister and a racing man', greatly to her liking. On her first visit to Richmond, he told her she would have to cure herself. She recalls the advice he gave her in *Me*: '"Make up your mind to enjoy yourself. Sleep with your bedroom window open wide, eat as much as you can, and if you don't like the food that's given you – ask for something else and see that you get it."'

She stayed at the Hydro for four months. She had no treatment except 'sunlight'. (She does not reveal the cost of her sunlit medication, but it must have been steep.) She was allowed to smoke and drink wine and spirits. Harry's wife Mollie supervised the meals and acted as hostess every evening at the cocktail hour, which started at six. Micky remembers in *Me* that there were 'two brothers – named Wood – who were always ready to talk about anything under the sun, and indulge in long and quite good-tempered arguments on any subject whatever'. Henry Dale Johnson, who would become one of her closest friends, lightened the conversation whenever it got too serious, and Olivia Etherington Smith was present as well.

'Olivia detested Micky on sight,' observes James Norbury in *The Seven Ages of 'Me'*. 'She [Olivia] was very beautiful and very county, [and] had the arrogance and lithesome loveliness of a well-bred tigress,' he continues, in the manner of Elinor Glyn or Ouida. Despite Olivia's initial detestation, which Micky reciprocated, the two women – the 'well-bred tigress' and the plump Yorkshire terrier – were soon lovers. Micky and the 'strong-minded' Olivia became, in Norbury's words, 'ideal companions'.

From Harry Wadd's Hydro, which accommodated six dogs

(including Wadd's favourite Bedlington called Zitty Nanny) along with the patients, Micky set off for the Lake District with her new companion. 'There is something in the Lakes which gets you. Nowhere are the larches so green in spring, nowhere are the hills so full of colour, and nowhere are there kinder and more amusing people.' If her account in *Me* is to be trusted, Micky and Olivia spent a great deal of their five-month convalescence in a variety of public houses, where they listened with keen appreciation to the local – usually ancient – storytellers. The stories they told are set down in the novel *The Man Who Found Himself* and in *Me*. '"Ah wear on the 'ill-side one mornin' doin' me best, wi' 'elp of t'dog, ter get sheep in"' is how one of them begins. The rest of this interminable anecdote is transcribed, with a generous sprinkling of apostrophes and deliberate misspellings, to indicate something of the disarming naturalness of the speaker. Micky was splenetic when a critic, reviewing *The Man Who Found Himself*, alluded to her 'musical-comedy yokels':

I don't mind critics saying that I write poor English – I am sure that I frequently do . . . but when I reproduce conversations word for word, when I repeat what John William Wilson, or James Henry Turner actually said, then it is just a little hard.

Or, perhaps, 'ard. Throughout her long writing career, Micky liked to 'reproduce' the accents or dialect of her characters by having them drop aitches, elongate their vowels, substitute 'v's for 'w's, and vice versa. There are nightmarish pages in the novel *Barren Metal* when a Yiddish-speaking Jew, a Cockney and a Yorkshireman are conversing in what Micky believes to be idiomatic English. The apostrophes come at the hapless reader like shrapnel.

★

In the years before she made her home in Italy, Micky involved herself in politics. She joined the suffrage movement during her time in Middlesbrough, but the evidence suggests that she was never a wholehearted suffragette. (An old lady I interviewed in Sirmione in 1998 told me how shocked she was to learn that Signora Micky had been *una suffragetta*. This terrible revelation had come to her after Micky's death in 1964.) She records in *Robert, Nana and – Me* that she heard Christabel Pankhurst speak at a meeting, 'I think in Middlesbrough':

The audience was distinctly hostile, they hurled the usual arguments about woman's place being the home, and begged her to 'go 'ome and mind the baby'. Finally one weedy-looking individual rose and put his question.

'Now, Miss Pank'urst, I want you to answer me one straight question. In your 'eart of 'earts don't you wish you were a man?'

She looked at him with grave attention, then said, 'I don't think so, but – don't you wish *you* were?'

Micky wrote to Miss Pankhurst, asking if she 'might go to prison for the Suffrage Cause'. She was granted an interview, as she relates in *Me*:

Christabel Pankhurst wore a red tam-o'-shanter, and her hair was inclined to be wispy. She listened, and tapped on the desk with a pencil all the time I was talking.

When I finished she said, 'No, you can't go!'

I said, 'Why can't I?'

'Because you'd make a joke of it all, and play the fool.'

Later she talked to me seriously, and said, and said very nicely, too, 'You might be quite a useful person, if you could overcome your idiotic love of popularity, Jacob.'

Micky joined a few marches, held a banner or two, but she didn't smash any windows or frighten any racehorses.

I remember one exceedingly pretty and clever Suffragist walking along the Strand breaking windows. She was a painter by profession, and a very good one, too, even though she did paint a portrait of me which made me look like an actor made up as a Labour leader.

Which actor? Which Labour leader? She wrote about the portrait painter in 1951, long after her involvement with socialism was over. The actor the adult Micky most resembles is the chubby, bespectacled Edward Chapman, who played bank managers, sadistic schoolmasters and blunt-speaking northern businessmen on stage and screen. (It was Chapman who, in 1953, attempted and failed to have John Gielgud ousted from the theatrical profession.) The Labour leader she refers to might be Philip Snowden or a clean-shaven Ramsay MacDonald, but certainly not Clement Attlee, with his bald head and distinctive moustache. Perhaps, with her usual inattention to detail, she meant 'leading figure' rather than 'leader'. Perhaps the Labour politician she has in mind is the great Ernest Bevin, who was Foreign Secretary from 1945 to 1951, the year of his death.

The suffragettes were known as the 'wild women' and the 'shrieking sisterhood'. It's impossible to imagine Micky shrieking, but she must have been wild with rage on the day she was ducked in a village pond 'somewhere in Cleveland'. In *Me*, she blames her failure both as suffragette and Labour Party candidate on her sense of humour. The British electorate are famously suspicious of politicians who tell jokes, and Micky's convoluted stories of gnarled Yorkshire rustics outwitting effete southerners must surely have perplexed the people in London and Birmingham who attended the meetings she

addressed. She remembers, in *Me*, how she fared at an adoption
meeting in Sevenoaks:

Almost the first question they asked me was regarding my attitude
to birth control. That was a facer, because I am a Catholic, and
anyway, I have never felt that birth control was a political issue at all.
Housing was, and still is, my strong suit, and I played it then for all I
was worth. I don't think that I was very good. I don't even think
that I was very sound, but in some way I managed to satisfy them
and I was adopted.

Returning to London that evening in an open car, she
caught a cold and the following morning was confined to bed.
She was visited by Dr Ethel Bentham, the 'socialist member
for East Islington', who arrived at the same time as the telegram
confirming Micky's adoption. Dr Bentham, telegram in hand,
sat on Micky's bed and reminded her that electioneering was
no occupation for the unhealthy. She would have to make
speeches in the open air, in all kinds of weather, and her body
was not strong enough to take the strain. It was more than
likely that she would be 'letting her constituents down pretty
badly':

Was it fair to let them take such a risk to gratify – here she spoke
very slowly and patted my hand to show that she didn't really mean
to be hurtful – a very natural vanity?
     I said, 'No, it's not fair – I'd better call it off.'
     'I'm sure you're right,' she said, 'and I'm sure that the people –
who matter – will think that you are right, too.'
     I left for Italy the next week, and that was the end of my political
career.

Micky and Olivia took two or three holidays in Italy before
deciding to settle there. They chose Sirmione on the shores of

Lake Garda as their new home. They hired a suite of rooms on the first floor of the Albergo Catullo.

In the years preceding their departure from England, Micky worked as a journalist and continued with her acting career. She also found time to write more fiction:

Once, when novels of a particularly outspoken character were having a great vogue, I said to Raymond Savage, 'I ought to write a real sex novel, I suppose, if I could.'

He said, 'Don't, Micky, leave them alone. If you have anything new to say about sex, anything enlightening – say it. If not – leave it alone.'

She heeded his advice, alas.

She says little of interest on the subject of her journalism in her many memoirs, though she does mention the occasion when a newspaper editor sent her to Whitechapel (forever associated in the public imagination with Jack the Ripper) to investigate a murder. She told him she didn't care for the idea, and he told her that since she was demanding a man's wages she could do a man's job.

In Whitechapel she asked a suspicious policeman to direct her to the scene of the crime. He was hesitant to tell her, but after a few bluff exchanges – in which Micky got the better of him, of course – he confirmed that the house was in Pennyfields Street. 'An' a nastier, stinkinger 'ole I never wish ter see,' he added in Micky Cockney.

The terraced house was indeed nasty and stinking. The door was ajar and Micky ventured inside. The place seemed to be deserted. The room on the left of the dirty passage was in a 'horrible state of dirt, disorder, and with some unpleasant looking splashes on the wall, which might have been red ink, but were nothing of the kind'. She began to feel sick. She walked further along the passage, and became conscious of a

smell. She had been told by Thomas Burke, the author of the
bestselling novel of low life *Broken Blossoms*, that opium smelt
like baked beans. It suddenly occurred to her that she was in
an opium den. She sniffed, and slowly drew to one side a filthy
curtain that was hanging from the ceiling. She saw an old
man 'cooking something over a brazier'. She noticed several
Chinese seated on the floor and a few Europeans on benches
and in bunks. Some of the men were asleep, while others lay
moaning. But one man was wide awake. He shouted at her.
Micky muttered, 'Sorry, very sorry, good afternoon,' and
turned to leave. She knew it would be a mistake to run, so she
walked as quickly as she could along the dirty hallway, even as
she heard the man hurl himself down from the bunk. She
reached the front door, opened it, stepped into the street and
slammed it behind her. She hid in a nearby passageway
and wiped the sweat from her eyes. She set off as soon as she
realized that the man was no longer following her. She met
the policeman again. He was now speaking received English.
He asked her if she would 'be down this way again' and Micky
replied fervently, 'I think not.'

'It must have been about this time that I played in an
American play called *The Barker*,' Micky – blithely ignoring
days, months and years – recounts in *Me*. She appeared as a
working-class woman, dressed in rags, and was required to say,
'Oh, that's all baloney.' She was unfamiliar with the word
'baloney' and, for reasons never presented to the curious reader,
substituted 'polony'. It wasn't until the producer, Ben Weldon,
explained that she was ruining a good line that she reverted to
the original.

Noël Coward came to see the show, and paid a visit to
her dressing-room at the Playhouse Theatre. Seeing her in her
tattered dress, he quipped, 'Chanel, my dear. It's obvious. You
don't have to tell me.'

Micky did not enjoy playing a foul-mouthed New Yorker

with a heart of gold. She had a speech at the end of *The Barker*
which she transcribes in *Me* in Micky American: 'W'attever
she done, Nifty, tell me w'at right hev you ter sit in judgement
upon her. Ef she sinned, Nifty, she sinned for LOVE, and –
well, goodbye, take care o' yourself, Nifty.' Micky would turn
and take a last look at Nifty's bowed head before disappearing
into the wings. The distinguished actor Leslie Faber, who
greatly influenced the young John Gielgud, was embarrassed
by her shameless overacting: 'You don't want me to say anything about your performance, Micky, do you?' Micky replied
hastily, 'No, thank you. I know all you could say.' He extricated
himself with the words, 'I thought so.'

In the cast of *The Barker*, which starred the then unknown
Claudette Colbert, was another budding popular writer,
Godfrey Winn. Winn's obvious effeminacy, humourlessness,
indestructible vanity and soppy prose style did not prevent him
from being worshipped by thousands of middle-class women.
Known variously as Godfrey Winsome and Winifred God, he
dispensed advice to housewives throughout the British Isles on
such necessary subjects as interior decoration, simple cooking,
and – God be mocked – child-raising. This berouged repository
of instant wisdom loved his mother, his dogs and a succession of
royals, both major and minor. In *Me – Likes and Dislikes*, which
was published in 1954, Micky counts Godfrey Winn, who had
visited her at Casa Mickie, and his rival Beverley Nichols,
among those she considers insupportable:

There is a fairly modern type of journalist, I know one or two, who
have definitely 'cashed in' on God and mother love. How sincere
their religious beliefs or their love for their mothers may be I have
no means of knowing, but they fill columns about both. They are
sufficiently clever to remain strictly undenominational, so that no
particular sect can be offended and so lose the paper any readers. It
is all very 'sweetly' done, with suitable references to birds, flowers,

toil-worn hands, home comings and so forth, you feel that the
articles are written in a lavender-scented room – not real lavender,
of course, but essence out of a bottle – probably inscribed on
lavender paper while 'the scent of the honeysuckle rushes in through
my open window'.

Winn's weekly column appeared in *Woman*; Nichols's in
Woman's Own. In the last years of her life, Micky preferred to
offer her own commonsensical advice to Britain's housewives
over the airwaves. Her fruity baritone could be heard regularly
on the BBC programme *Woman's Hour*. The talks were
recorded in Casa Mickie, and were later collected in *Me –
Thinking Things Over*, which appeared in the autumn of 1964,
some months after her death.

It was while she was playing the unruly drunk in *The Ringer*
that Micky befriended Val Gielgud, who acted one of the
policemen who arrested her. Gielgud, who was later to become
head of drama for BBC radio, told Micky that her novels were
badly written. In his autobiography *The Years of the Locust*,
published in 1947, he writes:

Although I care as little for her novels as she does for my political
views, I think we have always been friends. Certainly during the
run of *The Ringer* she was extremely kind to me. I was given the run
of the dressing-room which she shared with Betty Hicks, and
which came to be known as 'St Chad's' from the girlish gossip that
continually echoed round its walls. Until it vanished as the result of
enemy action, I cherished on one of my office walls a drawing made
of me by Leslie Banks: sitting cross-legged in 'St Chad's', laying
down the law too loudly, and closuring every argument with an
emphatic, 'No, Micky – you're wrong!' Micky Jacob used to get
very cross with me when I insisted on making use of a certain
amount of specialized academic historical reading in our arguments.
She would go so far as to say that I was a snob, and showing off the

fact that I had been to Oxford. This, being about a third true, annoyed me extremely. But Micky Jacob on the Crippen Case – she had known and liked Belle Elmore and believed her a much-wronged woman – or on her memories of Marie Lloyd, was well worth listening to. Just as her performance in *The Ringer* was not only true but good.

Val Gielgud tried, and failed, to teach Micky when and how to use the semi-colon. He made his critical comments on her work in such a humorous manner that Micky was not offended. He introduced her to his younger brother John, and the two men attended Micky's weekend parties at Baker Street. In *Early Stages*, John Gielgud recalls meeting several stars of the music hall there. He, too, praises her acting ability.

Micky's mother and sister had returned to England in 1918. Muriel married Reginald Godsell, whom she had met on a visit to London some years earlier. Godsell was invalided out of the Royal Navy in the last months of the war and never really recovered from the injuries he had sustained in battle. He died after the house next door to the one in which he lived with his wife and young daughters was bombed in 1940. 'When the bomb fell, he said to my sister, "I say, that was close!"' He suffered a heart attack two days later.

Nana, now Mrs Abbott, took a flat in Kew which she didn't like, then moved to Brighton to be close to the Godsells, and finally rented a cottage in Bramber, where she seemed to be happy. She often came up to London to see Naomi, as she alone insisted on calling Micky, act. She continued with her journalistic career by writing articles on English life 'for the New York papers'. She visited the flat in Baker Street when Simmy was in residence, and what she thought of her eldest daughter's relationships with Marguerite, Simmy and Olivia

Etherington Smith has not been recorded. It must have occurred to her that Naomi, to use an expression of the period, was 'not as other women'. There are no surviving photographs of Samuel Jacob, whose looks Micky probably inherited.

Due, perhaps, to Harry Wadd's 'sunlight' treatment, Micky's problems with her tubercular condition kept recurring. She had no alternative, she realized, but to leave England and move abroad.

Micky and Olivia booked the suite in the Catullo for an indefinite length of time. Micky and the hotel's owner, Gianina Signori – 'a woman I have always admired for her business acumen but disliked for every other trait she possessed' – came to an arrangement in regard of the cost of the long-term booking. Micky and Olivia were later joined by Robert Broadfoote Edelsten – Bobbie, or Roberto – who acted for a couple of years as the increasingly popular popular novelist's secretary until he either said or did something she couldn't countenance.

Micky had been living in Sirmione for about a year when Nana decided to come and stay with her. A room was reserved at the Catullo, where Nana worked on a novel that Micky would finish, and to which she would give the title *Look at the Clock*. (It was published posthumously under the name Nina Abbott. Two others followed, written by Micky from her mother's notes – *Shadow Drama* and *Balance Suspended*.) Nana arrived in the late summer and remained with Micky, Olivia and Bobbie for seven months. It became clear to Micky that although Nana was as quick-witted, as warm-hearted and as acid-tongued as ever, she was getting increasingly frail. She went for walks by the lake with Micky and her Pekinese, Sammy, and made the wigs for the pantomime in the Children's Convalescent Home, which was run by Maria Guazzini, one of Signora Micky's best friends. Each evening at the Caffè Grande Italia, Mario, the owner, would prepare for Nana a glass of *grappa* with hot water, a slice of lemon, sugar and a pinch of cinnamon. He brought this concoction to the table with the words '*Per la Principessa*' and she would respond with the only Italian she knew: '*Grazie, Signor Mario.*'

Throughout the winter months, Nana told Naomi many of the family stories her daughter would use in her volumes of memoirs and in her fiction. The true nastiness of Samuel Jacob was finally, and exhaustively, revealed. She read Dickens, Carlyle, H. G. Wells's *An Outline of History*, Chambers's *Encyclopaedia* in its entirety, and dismissed Catullus, who was born and lived in Sirmione, as a 'dull dog'. It takes an eccentric reader to accuse Catullus of dullness. There have not been many poets, before his time or since, who have written lyrically, and indeed comically, about the act of fellatio. Did Nana's Latin encompass the word *fellat*?

Micky watched as Nana's health deteriorated. 'I often wish that you took more after *my* family,' Nana would scold her in moments of irritation. She also rebuked her for 'sticking to that common name', meaning Jacob, and for wearing slacks that weren't fashionably tailored to look feminine. Since Micky prided herself on her masculine appearance, the criticism was shrugged off. She simply stated that she preferred the slacks the local tailor made for her. They felt comfortable. Nana must know that she valued comfort above elegance.

Nana lost her appetite and began to sleep badly. 'I begged her to see a doctor but she refused unconditionally. She hated doctors, she refused to have "some Italian doctor saying things about me that I don't understand".' Then, as Nana became more and more irritable, Micky asked her 'point blank' if she wanted to go back to England. After a moment's thought, Nana smiled and said, 'That is what I want to do.' She added, 'I have no particular wish that "some corner of a foreign field should be for ever England" through me. Yes, I should like to go home.'

Micky drove Nana and Bobbie to Milan. At the railway

station, Nana had to be persuaded to use the lift and sit in a bath chair, because the platforms could only otherwise be reached by mounting a steep flight of steps. She agreed to enter the lift, but balked at the idea of the chair. When Micky remarked that the bath chair would add to her prestige, Nana responded, 'My lass, I'm not concerned about my prestige. That can take care of itself without the aid of bath chairs.'

Bobbie wheeled her into the station restaurant, where she commented on her daughter's dark slacks for the last time. 'I wish that you'd not wear those dingy-looking things. You look for all the world like an undertaker in a poor way of business.' (This phrase was much employed by both mother and daughter.)

Several station officials bowed to and saluted the imperious Nana as Bobbie manoeuvred the chair along the platform. She acknowledged their deference with the one word '*Grazie*'.

Bobbie had secured corner seats for himself and Nana, who said her goodbyes to Micky from the open window. On an impulse, and to ensure that their leave-taking wasn't tearful, Micky told her mother a risqué story. Nana tut-tutted during its telling, but howled with laughter when Micky delivered the punchline. As the train slowly withdrew from the station, she asked Micky to repeat it. Micky bawled the line above the noise of the engine. 'The last thing I saw of my mother was her laughing immoderately at my improper story.'

Micky was admitted to hospital shortly after Nana's departure in order to have an operation, from which she 'nearly died'. Perhaps it was a hysterectomy, or perhaps not. She simply records that she remained in the hospital at Desenzano for eight weeks, with Olivia Etherington Smith and Leslie Faber's wife, Gladys, taking turns to sit by her bedside.

On returning to Sirmione, she learnt from Muriel's letters

that Nana had been examined by a doctor and was now in the care of a nurse. Then, one night at dinner with Olivia and Henry Dale Johnson, a telegram was brought in to Micky. It read: 'Our mother left us this morning. Muriel.'

Nana was buried in Brighton, but had left instructions that no memorial was to be put up for her. 'After all, we don't belong to this part of England. We're only off-corners here.'

Micky's agent, Raymond Savage, had negotiated a lucrative, long-standing contract with her publisher, Hutchinson, and as a result she visited him in London. She also spent a few days in a sanatorium – probably Harry Wadd's expensive Hydro – where she met the shy and placid Sadie Robinson, with whom she immediately began an affair. So enchanted was she with Sadie that she invited her to live in Italy. Thus began a *ménage à trois* that would endure, despite several vicissitudes, until the outbreak of the Second World War.

Bobbie Broadfoote Edelsten was 'not a success as a secretary', according to James Norbury. In spite of the kindness and solicitude he had displayed towards Nana – 'He was more than a son to me,' Nana wrote to her daughter on arriving in England – Micky was compelled to sack him. The doting Sadie took his place, to Micky's evident satisfaction.

Olivia, the 'well-bred tigress', was not pleased at the prospect of sharing Micky's favours with Sadie. But Micky was absolutely content with the arrangement. If she was in the mood for a spate of fiery love-making, she would take Olivia to bed; when she required docility, she would order Sadie to comply with her wishes. The atmosphere in the small villa in Sirmione, the precursor of the grander Casa Mickie in Gardone, was often electric:

At times she got irritated with Olivia, whom she thought tried to be a little too domineering on occasions; and at others she got annoyed with Sadie, who did not seem to assert herself enough in some of their triangular quarrels.

Thus James Norbury, writing of this lively threesome in 1965, when Micky – who never discussed or admitted to her Sapphic activities in public – was safely dead. Although lesbians weren't officially criminals, as male homosexuals were, few of them bothered to declare their sexuality beyond the confines of the bedroom. The publication, in 1928, of Radclyffe Hall's *The Well of Loneliness* brought female homosexuality to the world's attention. Stephen Gordon, the book's protagonist, is a man trapped inside a woman's body. She is one of nature's mistakes, doomed to a life of frustration and unhappiness. The tone of the novel is highly moral, with Stephen constantly addressing the Almighty with unanswered, and unanswerable, questions.

Cyril Connolly reviewed it in the *New Statesman* soon after it was published, and his judgement is still apt:

The Well of Loneliness may be a brave book to have written, but let us hope it will pave the way for someone to write a better. Homosexuality is, after all, as rich in comedy as in tragedy, and it is time it was emancipated from the aura of distinguished damnation and religious martyrdom which surrounds its so fiercely aggressive apologists.

The long-forgotten James Douglas, whose campaign in the *Daily Express* to have the book banned in Great Britain succeeded after a ludicrously unfair trial at Bow Street Magistrates Court, coined one memorable sentence in the first of his many diatribes: 'I would rather give a healthy boy or a healthy girl a phial of prussic acid than this novel.' He added, by way of explanation: 'Poison kills the body, but moral poison kills the soul.'

Micky wrote to Radclyffe Hall expressing admiration for her writing and support for her courage. She knew that John, as the author was known to the chosen, was the lover of Una Troubridge, and it was through Lady Troubridge that she met and became friends with the couple. In January 1929, Micky was staying at a hotel in Southend when she noticed a poster in the foyer advertising a lecture by Miss Radclyffe Hall on the theme of *The Well of Loneliness*:

I saw Lady Troubridge passing through the hall and, introducing myself, asked if it would be possible to get seats. She told me that she believed that the hall was completely sold out, but she would do her best, and leave tickets, if two were procurable, at the desk. She was successful and we [Micky and Olivia] went to the lecture.

Micky was not especially impressed with John's performance that evening, as she records in *Me – and the Swans* (1963). Although John had a 'clear, pleasing voice' she 'seemed to me to lack fire' and bored the audience with 'more facts . . . than the subject could carry'. Micky had the tact not to make these slight strictures to either John or Una. John, at this period in her life, was peculiarly sensitive to criticism. Una wrote in her diary on 25 January 1929: 'John spoke on Sexual Inversion most eloquently and with immense success.'

John and Una visited Sirmione in the summer of 1934, staying in the suite in the Albergo Catullo previously occupied by Micky and Olivia. In *Una Troubridge: The Friend of Radclyffe Hall*, Richard Ormrod writes:

Known to them only by correspondence since their meeting in 1929, Micki [*sic*] Jacob soon became a close personal friend. She shared with them not only inversion, but Roman Catholicism, a great love of animals (she kept eleven cats and various dogs), and writing. Her appearance was even more mannish than John's since she was darker, more heavily set, and wore full male suits and never skirts as John did.

They returned the following August with a third woman, Evguenia Souline, whom they had met in Bagnolles, in France. Una had been ill with gastroenteritis in the Hôtel des Thermes, and John had telephoned the American Hospital in Paris for a nurse to be sent out. Evguenia arrived, in a white uniform, and within days John was besotted with her.

Once again, they stayed at the Catullo. And once again, they went to see Mike, as John and Una called her, at the villa in Gardone. Micky was instantly repelled by the pale, oriental-looking survivor of the Russian revolution (Evguenia was John's 'Royal Chinkie Pig'; her 'Darling Most Chink Faced Little Tartar'), not least because of the virulent anti-Semitism she voiced in Micky's presence. John had purchased black shirts for the three of them as well as the Fascist ribbon to wear in their lapels. At every opportunity, she praised the achievements of Mussolini. Micky had supported him earlier in the decade, when he appeared to be uniting Italy, but by 1935 she saw him for the potential tyrant he was. 'She is openly and indiscreet to fascism [*sic*] and is contemptuous of the Italians,' Una noted in her diary. She also commented that 'Mike is fatter than ever.'

The Hall–Troubridge–Souline *ménage* was fraught with drama. John was determined to seduce Evguenia, and Una was frequently tearful and unable to hide her jealousy. Micky, sensing that Evguenia was resonsible for the highly charged atmosphere, raised the subject with Una in the restaurant at the Catullo. From Una's diary entry of August 11:

Mike said, 'May I be very rude?'
    I said, 'Of course, Mike, what is it?'
    'Well, I simply loathe your young friend.'
    'You have made that obvious.'

'Souline is a complete bitch.'

I said, 'Either you will have to leave Sirmione, or we shall.'

I got up and left the table to the sound of her apologies.

Micky waited in the restaurant for Una to return with John and Evguenia, to join her for dinner as arranged. Eventually the maid, Anita, appeared with a letter from Una, to the effect that they would not dine with her. Micky told Anita to tell them that Souline had ignored and insulted her the previous day. She set off for Gardone feeling angry and hurt.

There was a further complication. Despite the attentions of Olivia and Sadie, Micky had conceived an instant passion for Una. At the age of fifty-one, she was suddenly behaving like a love-sick schoolgirl. She spent an entire night under Una's window 'pining with love', as Una recorded with distaste. One of Mike's more passionate entreaties was written down by Una: 'Oh Una, why are you so beautiful? I don't think I'll be able to stay here long. I don't think I'll be able to bear it.'

Micky had not understood that John was Una's idol, and that nothing she did – not even her fierce courtship of Evguenia – could impair Una's devotion. The black-shirted trio left for France, to the relief no doubt of the staff at the Catullo, and the resident Merano *ménage* continued as before.

In that same year, 1935, Micky's novel *Honour Come Back* was published in America. Sometime in the autumn, she received a telegram informing her that the book had been awarded the Eichelberger Prize for 'services to humanity'. Although she had never heard of the prize, she was delighted to be given it. That evening she, Olivia and Sadie had a celebratory meal, with plenty to drink, in Sirmione, returning to the villa happily inebriated. But her joy was to be short-lived. A few days later, opening her press cuttings from England, she came upon one headed 'HITLER AND NAOMI JACOB'. 'Her novel had won the prize,' writes James Norbury, 'but she had to share it with the man who had become the scourge of Europe – Adolf Hitler, whose book *Mein Kampf* had also been nominated and coupled with hers.'

Micky's response to this alarming news has been preserved in James Norbury's biography:

You see, it didn't matter much to me what Adolf Hitler thought about Naomi Jacob, but it mattered exceedingly to me what I thought about Adolf Hitler. For years I had written novels about Jews, for years Jews had been my kind, good and generous friends. I had expressed my sympathy with those who had suffered and were still suffering and it didn't strike me that I would emerge too well from such statements as 'Eichelberger Prize for the Year – to Adolf Hitler and Naomi Jacob'.

She wrote to the Eichelberger organization in New York explaining 'with humility and regret' that she could not accept the prize.

On their first visit to Sirmione, John and Una had dined with the poet, dramatist, aviator and nationalist politician Gabriele D'Annunzio at his huge villa in Gardone. In *Me – Looking Back*, Micky quotes approvingly Max Beerbohm's observation that D'Annunzio was 'almost as great a bounder as he was a writer' and goes on to recall the occasion when he turned up in Sirmione in the company of the Prince and Princess of Piedmont. The prince was Italy's last king. The princess, Micky notes, 'had been a fine piece of work when young, but her youth was long past'. And of D'Annunzio himself she remarks:

I remember his clothes on that particular day; they struck me as slightly eccentric. He wore a yachting cap with a huge gold badge, a double-breasted blue coat with gold buttons, a white shirt with a very narrow black bow-tie, white flannel trousers and white buckskin shoes with tan strappings . . . He walked with a 'strut' which gave the impression that he was full of his own importance.

In that same book, Micky recalls going to a dentist in Salò:

I was told that he was the dentist of D'Annunzio, and his waiting-room was plastered with enormous signed photographs of the poet. I have never seen a signed photograph of D'Annunzio yet on which he merely wrote his name, he always launched out into eulogies and elaborate phrases with too many words. The dentist arrived. I spoke of the many photographs. He replied modestly, 'Signora, you speak now with the personal dentist of D'Annunzio!'

I said, 'But he's only got two teeth left!'

'Admitted, signora, but I keep them in perfect condition.'

Signora Micky loved the Italians, especially the peasants and the aristocracy, but she always regarded them as flighty and temperamental, not made of the honest, sober and practical mettle of Yorkshire folk. A succession of servants washed, cleaned, cooked and did the gardening for her at Casa Mickie. None of them was as trustworthy as her treasured Mrs Wicks, the cheerful Cockney who worked for her at Baker Street.

In *Me – in the Kitchen*, published in 1935, Micky inadvertently suggests why the cooks she employed in Gardone did not entirely satisfy her. She exhorts her readers to boil pasta well beyond the *al dente* stage – spaghetti for half an hour; tagliatelle for forty-five minutes. Several of the recipes contain lard as an essential ingredient. The Italians are justifiably proud of their cuisine, and any cook with even an iota of self-respect would have been horrified at having to obey to the letter this opinionated Englishwoman's instructions. Each new cook was required to learn how to prepare Yorkshire pudding and plum duff, and many other quintessentially English dishes.

Me – in the Kitchen is addressed to an imaginary unnamed young housewife with a husband called George. They suddenly become the parents of a boy and a girl, Tommy and Ann, in the final chapters. The tone throughout is breezily bossy and deeply patronizing:

When your cooking knowledge is in its initial stages, always keep a certain amount of imagination. For example, your first omelette. It appears, and George says – because things have been a little trying at the office, 'Is this supposed to be an omelette?' Be ready, don't burst into tears and say that you're going round to see mother directly dinner is over. Smile, and say, 'Omelette, darling? No! Scrambled eggs.' That takes the wind out of his sails. Again, if you have tried a new dish and it has turned out looking like a cross between the dog's dinner and a bad haircut, let me advise you to 'get in first'. As you serve it, say, 'Now I don't know if you'll like this, George. They *say* it's delicious, but I don't feel so certain about it myself.' If it eats better than it looks, he will say so, and – you're saved. If he says it's perfectly frightful, and can he have the cold meat that was left yesterday – you smile and say with charming brightness, 'I was a little afraid of it. I am *so* sorry.' That's an example of the old saying: 'Heads you win, tails I lose.'

Later in the book, Micky has the gall to tell George's little woman how to ensure that Tommy and Ann will eat up everything at mealtimes. The secret is not to ask them if they did well at school today. If you do, they will talk themselves out of eating. Micky advises silence.

Me – in the Kitchen certainly reflects the attitudes of its time. The housewife's duty is to keep her husband happy and her children under control. George, the breadwinner, is banned from the kitchen in which she is boiling the pasta until it's a soggy wreck and fighting back the tears when hubby's promised soufflé collapses. Micky instructs her to soldier on, to surprise George with something different and delicious every day and to be inventive with stale bread and tinned pineapple.

In her entry for *Who's Who*, Micky gave her hobby as 'writing novels'. It was a hobby of which she never tired. The fiction factory's closing siren only sounded with her death. Her industry, if nothing else, is daunting to contemplate. At the peak of her activity, in the 1930s, she was churning out at least six books a year. Apart from the sequence concerned with the fortunes (in every sense) of the Gollantz family, she was also writing sagas of Yorkshire life in the nineteenth century, often featuring the token wicked squire, virginal heroine and hard-hearted mill or mine owner; love stories set in London, Paris, Venice and Milan; and the odd historical novel with a famous cast list, such as *Mary of Delight*, about Mary, Queen of Scots, which she adapted from her own one-act play. Twenty years later, in 1954, she produced *The Irish Boy*, which she described as a 'romantic biography'. Its hero is Michael Kelly, the Dublin-born tenor whose singing enchanted both Haydn and Mozart. The two great composers appear in the novel, alongside Casanova and Prince Charles Edward Stuart, the Young Pretender. On the opening page, Michael is warbling in a 'very clear, very strong – though childish – soprano voice'. An unnamed stage Irishman, overhearing him, remarks to a neighbour in Micky's own brand of Dublin English: 'Be Jezus, it's that young Mike. Did ye iver hear such a voice, and him only t'ree years old?' Worse is to come. Casanova has a 'strange, twisted smile' and a laugh 'like dried peas rattling in a leather mug'. Mozart is simply a 'little, white-faced genius' with no interest whatsoever in the scatological. The diminutive Michael Kelly, who is frequently called Mickie, merits a serious book, but *The Irish Boy*, be Jezus, isn't it.

In *The Seven Ages of 'Me'*, James Norbury refers to Micky as an 'erratic and wayward child of genius who squandered many of her talents'. He also laments a 'slipshod quality that prevented her giving of her best to the many readers of her books and novels'. He goes on to describe the Gollantz series as 'minor masterpieces' and predicts their likely survival. When they were written, in the 1920s and 30s, casual, unthinking anti-Semitism was commonplace throughout Britain. The name Shylock was applied to landlords and shopkeepers. The fiction of the time both reflected and bolstered this prejudice. There are Jewish conspiracies galore in the Richard Hannay novels of John Buchan, which survive by virtue of being well-written, and in the thrillers featuring Bulldog Drummond, the ex-soldier who continues to battle against the Hun and other evil foreigners in peacetime. The insanely patriotic Drummond, who sometimes calls the tough, hearty men in his gang 'my dears', was the creation of Herman Cyril McNiele, an individual of limitless bigotry who gave himself the pen-name Sapper. Buchan, whose prose often invites favourable comparison with that of Robert Louis Stevenson, shares with Sapper a fondness for the adjective 'swarthy'. Whenever someone swarthy enters the narrative, dirty work is certain to ensue.

Micky means well in her Gollantz books. Unfortunately, her good intentions are more obvious than any gift for characterization or skill at unfolding a complicated story. Although she wrote about Jewish life in England and western Europe when anti-Semitism was becoming ever more prevalent, she did not do so with subtlety and wit. In *That Wild Lie*, the *Bildungsroman* that tells how young Emmanuel Gollantz leaves Vienna and becomes a rich English gentleman art dealer, Emmanuel is given some sound advice before departure by the Austrian banker Marcus Breal, an old friend of the Gollantz clan and a chuckling fount of wisdom:

'The Englishman is a strange creature. In his heart he always keeps a dislike and fear of the Jew. Jews remember, English forget. They forget that their God was a Jew, and when the unpleasant thought comes into their minds, they pray that next time he will have the good taste to come as an Englishman. But,' he held up a pale hand, 'even though they dislike Jews, they dislike still more the Jew who is ashamed of being a Jew. An English lord came to do business with me the other day. He said, "Be Gad" – they all say "Be Gad!" – he said, "You're a Jew, Breal, but, damn me, if I wouldn't rather do business with you than with half a dozen Englishmen I could name." He went on, "I always say that when a Jew deals straight, when he's honest, be Gad, damn me, if he isn't the straightest and honestest man alive!" Now that, Gollantz, is rubbish. An honest man is an honest man, no more and no less whatever his race. But once get an Englishman to believe in a Jew – and they aren't fools, oh dear me, no – and he'll trust you with every penny in the Bank of England. They may fear you, they may dislike you – but once they trust you, you're a made man.'

Breal's lecture to the grateful Emmanuel, complete with a message from Micky Jacob to her large number of Gentile readers, is typical of a particular kind of popular writing which prevails to this day. Micky's modern counterparts, such as Barbara Taylor Bradford, have dispensed with 'be Gad' and, possibly, 'damn me', but the Advice Scene – like the omnipresent Mirror Scene, in which a character looks at himself or herself and is pleased or startled or amused, depending on the situation – continues to be a convenient method of shoving ersatz wisdom and necessary information at the reader. Micky is an adept hand at the 'half-and-half trick', whereby someone has a smile that is 'half sad, half gay' or an expression that is 'half kindly, half sardonic'. These smiles and expressions, which are still in vogue, always come in halves. A smile that is nine-tenths sad, or perhaps three-quarters, is a rarity. Micky parts company with today's perpetrators of fictional schlock in one respect, in that when she has a character hiss she provides a sibilant by way of evidence.

My own favourite of her novels is the thumpingly terrible *Barren Metal*, if only because it contains the sentence 'They ate a very admirable cauliflower'. Micky must be the first novelist to apply the word 'admirable' to a vegetable. But the cauliflower that Meyer Pardo and Rachel eat is more than that – it is '*very* admirable'. It's Micky, not the characters, who makes this judgement. She reverts to 'admirable' whenever her adjectival flow looks like coming to a stop, when even she realizes that 'lovely', 'beautiful' and 'charming' have been employed to excess.

Barren Metal is a rags-to-riches saga in which a poor Jewish boy from the East End of London makes his fortune in the clothing business. Meyer Pardo, whose tailoring skills are exceptional, marries the swarthy Rachel and they have two sons – the intellectual David, whose ambition is to become a film director, and Isaac, known as Ike, who wants to be even richer than his father. But Meyer, at the height of his success, is embroiled with some crooked businessmen (not Jewish, Micky is at pains to tell the reader), and he and his companions in crime are put on trial for fraud. Meyer is given a prison sentence and all his assets are seized to cover his court costs and the money embezzled. The resilient Rachel moves to humble dwellings and starts again from scratch. The orders for blouses, skirts and dresses trickle in at first, but it isn't too long before she is a successful businesswoman in her own right, strengthened by her love for Sholto, a good Christian whom she marries after Meyer's death.

There is a scene in the middle of the novel that gives unintentionally hilarious expression to Micky's firmly held view that Jews who deny their origins cannot be trusted or admired. Ike is visiting his mother at the Pardos' home in Maida Vale:

He was pompous, inclined to strut a little. He explained at great length that he was not an ordinary tailor.

'The place has been going for two hundred years, probably longer. The old books are tremendously interesting. The Regent was a client, so were Sheridan and Charles James Fox.' He laughed tolerantly. 'I can find no evidence that the Regent ever paid his bills! You must come down one day and look round. Nothing really suggests a – shop. More like a club.'

Rachel looked up from polishing her nails. 'It sounds lovely.'

'I just wanted to make it clear that when Helen marries me, there will be no question of her marrying beneath her. Her father realized that. In fact, he has this morning offered me a junior partnership in his own firm. Very decent of him, I must say.'

'Very decent, Ike.'

He was suddenly rather more nervous, drumming with his finger-tips on the glass-topped dressing-table.

'I hope you'll get on with Helen, Mother. By the way, she always calls me – George. Likes the name, thinks it suits me. And – I don't think – I mean I have never felt it necessary to say – in so many words – where we – I mean the family – started. So many people have a prejudice against' – he shrugged his shoulders – 'the Ghetto.'

With a coldness for which she hated herself and yet which she could not conceal, Rachel said, 'I'll try to remember.'

Ike, alias George, thanks her, and says that he will go and change and fetch Helen to dinner. This conversation has been overheard by Rachel's faithful maid, Sarah, one of those working-class cautions who litter the English novel, good and bad. She speaks her mind in Micky Cockney: '"My word, young Ike isn't satisfied with 'is young lidy chaingin' 'er naime, 'e's got ter chainge 'is! Did you ever! I'll 'ave ter 'ave a squint at 'er over the banisters, that I will. Wot a life, eh?"' She adds, comically, after making a reference to the 'chimbly' (chimney)

I find impossible to decipher: "'I'd better slip a length o' red carpet down, 'ad I? It's not arf a gime, ain't it?'"

Rachel is now properly groomed and dressed, and ready to receive her prospective daughter-in-law:

Helen came, tall, with fair hair glorious in its artificiality, a long, horse face, and a nose which, Rachel decided, was 'pure Ghetto', and the Neubauer family called 'aristocratic'. She was very sure of herself, and adopted a manner of kindly patronage to her future mother-in-law.

'So sorry not to have met David. I heah he is so handsome. I almost wondah at your allowing him to go to Germany at the moment. Not afraid, no?'

Rachel said, 'Afraid of what?'

Miss Neubauer laughed, a high, snickering laugh. Ike scowled.

'This new movement against the Jews. Dreadful of course, but one must remembah that many of the Eastern Jews have brought it on themselves. Such a pity that these people can't be content with their own work, and must mix themselves up in political matters.'

Ike said, 'I don't believe that my mother takes much interest in politics – do you, Mother?'

'I don't know. Tell me, what are these Eastern Jews? What have they done, Ike?'

Again Miss Neubauer sniggered. 'So quaint to heah you call him by that name. At home, we – the family – all call him George, y'know. We like it so much better than – Ike. But then, of course, we have almost forgotten that we evah had Jewish blood in the family. You see, I'm so fair, and so are my sisters.'

Over dinner, Ike/George and Helen chatter about the latest plays and films while Rachel worries about the plight of the Eastern Jews and David's safety in Berlin. The meal is hardly finished when Helen, 'glancing at a diamond wrist-watch', screams at her fiancé: "'My dear George, unless we make a move we shall miss that divine Clark Gable! Mrs Pardo, do forgive me snatching George away. I dare not miss an inch of this glorious film."'

As these passages indicate, Micky was not a disinterested writer. The snickering, sniggering Helen, with hair that is 'glorious in its artificiality', speaking Micky Posh, is clearly set up for the reader's disapproval. It was ever thus in popular fiction. *Barren Metal* was published in 1936, when its references to the Jews of Eastern Europe were nothing if not topical. The book is now forgotten. Micky was probably unaware that she was trivializing what would soon be the tragic fate of millions of innocents. Helen is intended to be silly and vain and shallow, and that shallowness forms part of Micky's earnest message.

The 'very admirable cauliflower' apart, the book contains one other memorable sentence. It comes when Rachel, a poor woman again, bumps into Ike in a smart London street. He is embarrassed by her presence. How does Micky register Ike's embarrassment? 'He lit a cigarette with elaborate unconcern.' That takes some doing. It is too late, alas, to ask Micky for a demonstration.

Micky decided to leave Italy some months before the outbreak of the Second World War. The country's new racial laws, which barred Jews from any number of jobs in education, commerce and the legal system, were anathema to her. She called Mussolini 'that buffoon' because of his close links with Hitler. She entrusted her friend, the operatic soprano Gina Cigna, with the maintenance of Casa Mickie. Her latest secretary, Elsa Manley, was appointed to take care of Micky's library, pictures and ornaments, and the general running of the villa was left in the reliable hands of her servants, Pietro, Piera and an Italian Elsa, who were familiar with the different needs of the cats and dogs.

Olivia and Sadie returned to England, while Micky went
to live briefly in St Raphaël, in the south of France. It was to
be a permanent separation. Of the break-up, James Norbury
observes, lyrically: 'The dream of fair women, of Marguerite,
of Olivia, of Sadie, seemed now to be as fragile as the violets
that nestled in the mossy banks of the country lanes of her
beloved and threatened England.'

Micky was in London in August 1939, taking part in a
charity gala at the Victoria Palace Theatre to raise money for
the various organizations that would have to spring into action
in the event of war. Micky was the master of ceremonies. At
that time, and for the following two decades, a plump Canadian
with white hair named Carrol Levis had his own radio show
– *Carrol Levis and His Discoveries* – in which he gave unknown
singers and comedians the chance to display their talents. The
audience would decide by the volume of their applause who
was the most talented of the contestants. In the 1950s, the
ever-expanding Levis became familiar to television viewers,
but he now had a rival compère in a similar programme, in the
form of the ghoulishly smiling Hughie Green, the presenter
of *Opportunity Knocks*. On that night in 1939, Micky surprised
everyone by impersonating Carrol Levis. She wore a garish
evening suit with a floppy bow-tie and a white wig to hide
her dark hair. Forgetting her disastrous performance years
earlier in *The Barker*, she contrived to speak with a convincing
North American accent. So complete was her assumption of
the vulgar Levis personal – like Hughie Green, he had a smile
he could switch on automatically – that the dapper Hollywood
star Adolphe Menjou, who was on the bill, addressed her
as 'sir' for the whole evening. She would regard the Levis
impersonation as her finest acting triumph.

It would be accurate to state that Micky barged her way
through the Second World War. 'She had the energy of five
women rolled into one,' observed the journalist Collie Knox.

Meeting her one day in a corridor in the Theatre Royal, Drury Lane, he said, 'You look younger than ever, Micky,' to which she gave the 'happy riposte': 'Young enough to still land a decent punch on that bastard Hitler's nose and strong enough to give that buffoon Mussolini a sound kick up the rump.'

Her war began in England. She enrolled with the Ministry of Information and was sent to lecture in working men's clubs, women's organizations and youth groups. She gave broadcast talks on the music hall, among other subjects. Then, at the invitation of the actor Sir Seymour Hicks, she joined ENSA, the acronym for Entertainments National Service Association, but known to the actors and musicians who worked for it as Every Night Something Awful. Her first posting was to Algiers, as a welfare officer in the Hospital Section of the Overseas Service. In his autobiography *Mind's Eye 1927–1972*, the theatre director Basil Dean remembers giving Micky a briefing prior to her departure:

When 'Mickie' Jacob came to see me before taking up her new job in North Africa as welfare supervisor, she was wearing a khaki tunic of slightly antique cut, with claret-coloured facings and brightly polished captain's pips on the shoulder-straps. Striding about the room, telling me what was wrong with ENSA – so far as I can recall, its major defect sprang from my own appalling lack of humour – and emphasizing her points by tapping the furniture authoritatively with her cane as though to command its attention, she filled my mind with recollections of Vesta Tilley at the Palace and those smoking-room cartoons by Spy. Apparently it was the uniform of a women's organization of the First World War, but it was an error of tact on my part to ask whether she had permission to wear it.

Shortly after her arrival in Algiers a succession of signals in cipher arrived at the War Office, angrily demanding who was the woman parading about Algiers in unauthorized uniform and purporting to belong to ENSA? Finally, there came one from our senior officer: the military authorities were threatening her immediate arrest if she was not recalled. In all fairness I must add that Naomi Jacob won her point and continued to wear the uniform of the defunct organization for the remainder of the war, the only instance known to me of a 'one-man band' among all the millions of men and women in uniform on either side.

The 'defunct organization' Basil Dean refers to is probably Queen Alexandra's Nursing Corps, in which Micky had served for a short time before being sent home from Flanders with trench feet. The captain's pips were added to the uniform later.

It seems that Micky gleaned little information from that first interview with Basil Dean at Drury Lane. 'Now it was typical of ENSA that no one ever told you anything, no one ever attempted to teach you anything, and I went out to Algiers with not the faintest idea as to what I had to do or how I was going to do it,' she writes in *Robert, Nana and – Me*. En route to Algiers, she was stationed in Rabat, where 'an arrogant Caliph told her he hated the English, detested the Germans but thought she might make a worthy addition to his harem'. She declined the offer.

Micky spoke at various hospitals in Algiers, but after a visit to the kasbah she longed to be posted elsewhere. 'I shall never forget the smell of it as long as I live! I detested the Arabs, for a nastier, more cruel set of ruffians it has never been my ill-luck to meet.' The Arabs' indifference to the suffering of animals upset her deeply. What with the heat, the prevailing stench, the constant demands on her time by the hospitals, Micky soon reached breaking-point. She was relieved when she was ordered to go on to Sicily. So, perhaps, were the military personnel, who were enraged at the sight of Micky in her preposterous uniform.

The hospitals in Sicily were lacking in medicines, bandages

and, most distressing of all, soap. The doctors and nurses were having to tend, as best they could, hundreds of severely injured children. The Germans had dropped 'little packets of what looked like chocolate' into the woods and on to the mountain-sides. They were, in fact, small bombs. The boys and girls had lost hands, arms and legs. 'It would have been sufficiently dreadful for any child, but these were the children of the very poorest peasants, who would have to work in order to live and so were doomed to a miserable existence for the rest of their lives.'

The British soldiers in Sicily spent many happy evenings with 'Auntie Micky' in a four-ale bar. Despite her avowed hatred of smut, she always liked having a drink and a joke with the Tommies, as she still called them. It's possible to see her as a latterday Falstaff, surrounded by the Bardolphs, Nyms and even, perhaps, the Pistols of the fighting forces. She had the Falstaffian girth by now, and a voice made deeper by cigarettes and a generous consumption of whisky, as well as a natural talent for telling tall stories. She was never quite so relaxed in female company.

She caught malaria, which was rife on the island. 'It took my mind back to a slightly macabre joke of my father's – one of the few he ever made – when I contracted measles. "That child would take anything! Lock up the silver!"'

On recovering, she was moved to a convalescent home in Taormina. She was meant to stay there for ten days, but left after four, having signalled Catania to return a signal with the message that her services were required 'at once – if not sooner'. The home was filled with senior officers and the 'atmosphere was like that of a well-aired tomb'. One officer told Micky that he'd heard the matron say, 'Steward, take away that colonel, he's been dead for three days.' When Micky said goodbye to the matron, thanking her for her kindness, the latter replied that she was sorry Miss Jacob's convalescent leave had been cut short. The expression the matron wore as she spoke was more indicative of delight than sorrow.

Micky's next assignment was to supervise the delivery of extremely costly cinema equipment in two five-ton trucks to the ENSA office in Brindisi. There was one driver for each truck, and a sergeant was appointed to assist her. They crossed the straits of Messina easily enough, but at Messina itself she lost the trucks in the huge mass of army vehicles, 'occupying every available space'. She spent the night in an officers' mess. Locating her missing drivers and the sergeant the following morning, she tore them off several strips before they boarded the ferry to the mainland. The consequent trek through southern Italy was an upsetting experience for all of them. They were forced to take long diversions because roads had been bombed and bridges blown up. They entered villages where the shops had absolutely nothing to sell. The children who crowded round the trucks simply held out their hands in silence. They were starving. In one particular village the sergeant said to Micky, 'I can't eat anything. Look at those poor little kids.' Micky couldn't eat either, nor could the drivers. They distributed that day's rations to the boys and girls, keeping only sugar and tea for themselves.

We washed when we could, slept where we could. I have used my portable typewriter for a pillow and my British warm [an army overcoat] for my only blanket, and the roadside is not the softest bed in the world – but we got through and finally arrived at Brindisi.

To Micky's justified chagrin, she was censured by the commanding officer after she had delivered the equipment safely. She was told that no woman should have attempted such a dangerous expedition. It seems odd that the officer at ENSA did not realize that Micky was hardly some helpless female in a man's world.

She resumed her duties as a welfare officer in Bari, but her efforts failed to satisfy her boss, Virginia Vernon. Micky was supposed to fill in a weekly progress sheet, but she never did because she had no idea which or what progress had to be reported. She contracted malaria again and was sent back to Sicily, where two doctors examined her and advised treatment in an English hospital. She travelled home by ship, landing in Scotland in February 1944. James Norbury is in lyrical vein again as he recreates Micky's train journey from Glasgow to London: 'Were the soft-voiced men of Cumberland still tending the flocks and waiting patiently for the woodland daffodils that would herald the lambing season?'

In Middlesex Hospital, Micky 'had a nasty, stupid operation to the accompaniment of flying bombs', and she then went to Bradford to recuperate among friends. She resumed her acting career, playing the mother of a troupe of performing acrobats in a stage adaptation of Margery Sharp's novel *The Nutmeg Tree* and the bawdy nurse in William Congreve's *Love for Love*, starring John Gielgud as Valentine. (On the radio programme *Desert Island Discs*, she told the presenter, Roy Plomley, that she did not enjoy acting in Restoration comedy, expressing once more her disapproval of smut.) She visited the dying Radclyffe Hall at the Ritz since Una had written Mike a letter of sympathy on hearing of the death of Sammy, the favourite Pekinese (the three women were friends again), but when John was moved to the London Clinic, Una insisted that she alone would sit with her beloved. Micky called at the clinic many times, leaving messages for John and Una at the reception desk.

In January 1945, Micky donned her uniform and went to Naples for ENSA, this time as public relations officer. On boarding the ship at Liverpool, she was horrified to discover that she would have to share a cabin with five other women, one of whom was in the habit of singing 'Mares eat oats, and does eat oats, but little lambs eat ivy' very early in the morning.

After enduring a restless night, she complained to the purser, who sympathized with her predicament and invited her for a drink before lunch. Later that day, the commanding officer sent for her. He had heard that she carried a portable typewriter and asked if she would make a précis of the BBC daily news bulletins so that he could have them posted all over the ship. Micky replied that if she accepted the job she would need to have complete privacy and quiet. An empty cabin was immediately found for her.

In the adjacent cabin, which he shared with another artist, was the young actor Harold Lang, who had recently completed his training at the Royal Academy of Dramatic Art. Lang had noticed the diminutive, broad-beamed martinet when the company had assembled outside the Theatre Royal, Drury Lane, and had been amused by the spectacle of two grieving women who were saying goodbye to her. The peaked cap, the uniform and the cane had all made an impression on him. And then, on the second morning at sea, his slight interest in her suddenly developed into what would be a lasting obsession. On hearing Micky bawl out, 'Steward, where's my shaving water?', he realized in an instant that he was a lost man. His fascination with her was enhanced in Naples when he saw how casually she always entered the gentlemen's lavatory, and how no one had the courage or effrontery to challenge her.

The commanding officer in Naples was the actor Lieutenant-Colonel Nigel Patrick, who liked to fling open the door of Micky's office with the words 'Madam, a letter from the King, written in his own hand!' and peppered every conversation with remembered lines from plays as diverse as *Henry V* and *George and Margaret*. His second-in-command was a Captain Neville-Willing, a pompous individual who was the source of much harmless fun. One of his duties was to meet the artistes on the incoming ships, as Basil Dean recalls in his autobiography:

Sent to warn the Polish Ballet that their lurid behaviour elsewhere must not be repeated in Italy, he obtained the cabin number of the principal dancers, went below and tapped smartly on the door.

'Come in!' said a girlish voice.

He found three or four young men in various stages of undress, apparently in no hurry to land.

'Well, what is it, sweetie?' asked one of them impudently.

Drawing himself up to his not very considerable height, Captain Neville-Willing pointed to his shoulder badges.

'Look, boys, doesn't this mean anything to you?'

There was a chorus of laughter as one of them cried, 'Oh, my goodness, she's a captain!'

On another occasion, Micky had cause to tease him. A show called *Behold the Man* was playing at the Bellini, which had been chosen as the ENSA garrison theatre during the war:

Just before one of the evening performances Naomi Jacob stood at the corner of the street, watching the crowds, and talking to Neville-Willing. Both were in uniform and both wore slacks, Naomi Jacob with hair cut short and sporting the usual monocle. A young Cockney soldier approached, saluted smartly and said:

'Excuse me, sir or madam, is this the way to the ENSA theatre?'

As he walked away in the indicated direction Naomi Jacob murmured, 'Charming boy.'

'I thought the remark rather insolent,' said Neville-Willing.

'Oh, but he wasn't addressing me,' said 'Mickie'; 'he was talking to you.'

Micky was very busy in Naples – giving talks, writing articles for the English press, welcoming the various actors, singers and musicians who came to entertain the troops, and providing programme notes in simple language for the operas performed at Teatro San Carlo. She was also, it need hardly be said, supplying Raymond Savage with new novels to sell to her publisher.

As the year progressed and the Allies' victory seemed a certainty, Micky grew discontented with her work in Naples. She wanted to see Rome again, and Milan, and Sirmione. Nigel Patrick, who complained that she was never in the building when he needed to talk to her, agreed to let her go. In *Me – Over There* (1947), she describes how she managed to quell the mocking laughter of a group of undesirables:

One very hot afternoon I was driving along a long dusty road on the way to Rimini, it was grilling, and I was feeling sticky, thirsty and bad-tempered. I was going to lecture and give a broadcast . . .

In front of us was a huge camion filled with German POWs. They were many of them smoking, and passing round a bottle from which they drank with evident pleasure. Through the windscreen of my car they caught sight of me. The figure of an elderly woman in uniform wearing large horn-rimmed glasses was too much for that sense of humour for which they, as a nation, are so justly famous. They dug each other in the ribs, they pointed, they roared with laughter, and were regarding me as a first-class turn.

Micky goes on to relate that she told her driver to shoot ahead of the lorry and stop in front of it. He did as he was commanded. The camion was being driven by a German, and seated next to him was a young English sergeant holding a rifle. It was impossible for them to see what was going on in the rear of the truck, and the sergeant was somewhat astonished to be ordered to stop by a woman who said, 'I just want a word with the bodies at the back. I shan't keep you a moment.' Micky, facing the 'bodies at the back' inquired if any of them spoke English. A silence ensued. She repeated the question 'in a slightly louder tone'. She then received two answers in Micky German. The first, given by a 'sheepish-looking fellow', was

'I a little Eengleesh spik' and the second, by an unidentified man, 'Und I allzo.'

I said, 'Then listen to me and then repeat what I said to all your little friends. No one laughs at me – get that? And –' I stopped and bawled, 'Put out those damned cigarettes when I'm speaking to you!' They put them out and I continued: 'But still less does anyone laugh at the uniform of the King of England which I have the honour to wear. It has been worn by better men than you, or you'd not be going to the POW camp. Now, one crack, one smile, grin or what not, and I shall be right behind you with a revolver on my knee, and it's loaded, and I'll shoot. I don't shoot well, so I've no idea if the right fellow will stop it, but someone will get hurt. That's all.'

Micky and her driver followed the camion for several miles. She watched the prisoners as closely as they watched her: 'I have never seen men so impressed. Not only did none of them dare to move, but when they spoke to each other they talked out of the corner of their mouths.' Micky had lied about having a revolver to hand. She did possess one, but it was packed away among her belongings. She only ever carried it when she was alone.

On the way to Milan, she stopped off at Sirmione and spent the night at her villa in Gardone. Her devoted servant, the Italian Elsa, greeted her warmly. She had upsetting stories to tell about the retreating German army. The Signora's cars had been stolen. An arrogant officer had ordered one of his men to erase the 'Samuelo' on Sammy's grave in the garden. 'What is that?' the officer demanded of Elsa, who was born and raised near the Swiss border and therefore spoke some German. 'The grave of a little Pekinese dog,' she answered. 'The name is Jewish. Tomorrow it will be painted out!' The following day a soldier appeared with a pot of red paint and covered up the offending Samuelo: 'You're behaving dangerously, Signora, trying to protect a dirty Jewess, and an English one at that! Be careful, I have the power to shoot you, if I wish.'

Elsa calmly instructed the officer to go ahead – her mother had died; her brother had been killed in action; for all she knew the Signora she worked for might never come back; she had few reasons to live. She asked the officer to shoot her. He glared at her for a moment and then shouted at his men to leave. They did so, in Signora Micky's cars.

Casa Mickie was occupied at that time by a number of men and women, mostly elderly, the kindly Elsa had taken in. They had been driven from their homes by the Germans. While Micky sat in the kitchen, drinking tea and listening to Elsa, the captain of the local partisans arrived bearing a bouquet for the Signora, whom he invited to inspect his soldiers the next morning.

Elsa brushed and pressed the uniform that had so incensed the military top brass, and Micky put it on. The day was fine and the air bracing. Wine was set out on a marble table in the garden. The twenty or so brave partisans, who included a Jew, marched into the driveway of Casa Mickie and drew to attention in front of its chatelaine. 'They stood there straight and stiff, with their arms bright and shining, while I asked questions and listened to their answers.' When the inspection was over, and the wine consumed, they formed an orderly line behind Micky who, cane in hand, led the march down to the *piazza* in Sirmione, where they posed for a photograph. Micky was made an honorary partisan, and was photographed wearing the red-topped cap – the cap of the German infantryman turned inside out – the partisans assumed in mockery of the enemy.

There is something about the scene that is irresistibly comic and yet oddly touching. Here were men who had risked their lives in resistance to Italian Fascists and German invaders taking the salute from a figure out of the music hall – a male impersonator with the unearned pips of an army captain. They were honouring the Signora who dressed *sempre da uomo* because she was English and also because she had made it clear she wanted to settle in her adoptive country again. Their evident decency, their firm belief that good must always conquer evil, adds dignity to this otherwise ludicrous ceremony.

On a second visit to Sirmione, Micky – still in uniform – went to see the custodian of the nearby *castello*. She had a letter to pass on to his son. The custodian thanked her and said that he had some Fascist soldiers imprisoned there. Would the Signora care to speak to them? Micky replied that she would take a look. She was shown into the cell. The prisoners, who were old and fat, were playing cards. 'They are expecting to be released – or shot – quite soon,' the custodian told her. On seeing Signora Micky enter, the men stood up and greeted her affectionately: 'I said: "What, no vino! Times have changed. Can't the custodian go out for some?"'

The custodian agreed to her request, but only on condition that she prevent the prisoners escaping. For several minutes, Micky – holding a service revolver – stood guard over the smiling card-players. One thinks inevitably again of Falstaff and his ramshackle recruits – Mouldy, Shadow, Wart, Feeble and Bullcalf – in *King Henry IV, Part Two*, as Micky points her gun at the obese, elderly former blackshirts, eagerly awaiting their promised wine.

In Milan, Micky renewed her friendship with Gina Cigna, who had paid for the upkeep of Casa Mickie during her absence. Gina Cigna was actually French, but her family was of Italian origin. The two operatic roles in which she excelled were Tosca, which she sang at Covent Garden in 1938 with Beniamino Gigli as Cavarodossi, under the baton of Vittorio Gui, and Turandot, which she sang 493 times. Micky was obviously in love with her, but whether that love was reciprocated physically has to be a matter of conjecture. Cigna, whose career was cut tragically short after the war as the result of a car accident – she survived, but with serious damage to her heart – was a woman of enormous spirit. She, too, was visited by the Germans, who demanded that she sing for them. She whispered in reply that she had a sore throat. They paid her a second visit, making the same demand. Her son, her *bambino*, was desperately sick. (He had a slight cold.) They came a third time. Cigna's mother (who was robustly healthy) was on the brink of death. She was sorry, but her voice had vanished because of all the strain and suffering she had experienced. She could only sing when she was happy. The Germans left, never to return, and Gina Cigna sang for joy.

In the autumn of 1945, Micky was in London, seeing Basil Dean, director of ENSA, which was soon to be disbanded. Dean was hated by many of the actors who had worked for him in peacetime, because of his habit of choosing a whipping-boy in each production and using bullying tactics to elicit stronger performances from players he considered inadequate. Micky quite approved of him, due to the fact that he had allocated her a private car and driver in Italy. As Micky entered his office, he told her to sit down and remarked 'So you don't think I've any sense of humour, do you?' Micky had made this criticism in her recent book *Me – in Wartime*.

'No, candidly, I don't.'

'Would you have a sense of humour if you'd been sitting in this bloody chair for five years?'

'Yes, I should, because I should have started off with a sense of humour, you didn't.'

Her answer was met with Dean's 'queer, barking laugh'. *Mind's Eye 1927–1972*, written eight years after her death, demonstrates a sense and appreciation of the ridiculous way beyond Micky's comprehension.

She did not enjoy her stay in London. This once passionate socialist and potential Labour Party candidate was now espousing her mother's Tory beliefs. It was her view that the British people had betrayed Winston Churchill, the man most responsible for the Allied victory. She did not understand that those same people were sick of jingoism, continuing poverty and the necessary hardships of war. She found shop assistants rude and indifferent to her demands. Taxi drivers were insolent. Pre-war deference to the customer had been relegated to history. She quickly decided, and never altered her opinion, that the cause of this hostility was Clement Attlee's government, which encouraged the contempt of the lower orders for the likes of Naomi Jacob, a woman accustomed to having her own way.

In 1946, the war and Micky's ENSA duties over, life at the villa returned to its old routine. She had two Pekinese dogs to replace the adored Sammy, and innumerable cats, including Catullus and the snooty Lesbia, with whom Micky liked to imagine he was enamoured. She was at her desk every day, producing yet more novels – *A Late Lark Singing*, *The Heart of the House*, *Antonia* – and more volumes of memoirs.

The prisoners she had drunk wine with the year before had been released and were now with their wives and families. Many people in the district were trying to pretend that Mussolini had never existed, despite the proximity of Salò, scene of some of the worst excesses of Fascism. Men whom she remembered as having worn black shirts on *festa* days now assured her they were never really true Fascists at heart. And although she does not name Gianina Signori, it's clearly the Catullo's owner Micky is referring to in this passage from *Robert, Nana and – Me*:

One woman who had told me before I left Italy, 'The Eengleesh are so stupid, signora, 'ow can t'ey 'ope to vanquish the great power of Gairmany, 'oo 'ave the finest and grreatest armie in the vorld! No, signora, zis time the Eengleesh veel be beaten!' Two years ago she said to me, 'Ah, signora, I 'ope now zis terrible var is over, zet you vill send all your Eengleesh friends to my hotel. So many years you 'ave sent so many peoples, and I 'ave always been so 'appy to 'ave them. I 'ave such admiration for zee Eenglish!'

I said 'Really – even though they won the war, signora?'

Yet Micky was of an essentially forgiving nature, and was generous with both money and food in the immediate post-war period. Like the infinitely more talented George Frederick Handel, she was a dedicated recycler of her own material. The same stories and anecdotes recur over and over again in virtually all the *Me* books, sometimes slightly altered for greater effect, and occasionally set in totally different places from the ones mentioned in earlier instalments. James Norbury hints that drink may have rendered her memory hazy. 'I know my faults as a writer very clearly,' she declares in *Me – Likes and Dislikes*.

I do not write faultless English, my punctuation is dreadful . . . I find it very difficult to stick to a subject, my mind leaps about, and I remember a hundred things I want to say! My novels – well, I don't read them. I correct them, and that is sufficient for me. I do pat myself on the back for one thing at least – I have never, and will never, write *dirt*.

In the meantime, Harold Lang was introducing the character of Micky Jacob to cultivated men and women who would face a firing squad rather than read her books. While travelling with her in Italy, he had studied her every gesture, her swaggering walk and her vocal inflections. He could become Micky on the instant, bawling out her inflexible opinions on any subject that occurred to her. Lang's wide coterie of friends – which included academics, psychiatrists, writers and critics, as well as his fellow actors – begged him to take on the role of Micky at dinner parties, when she would bang her 'maulies' (her term for 'fists') on the table to stress some particularly forceful point. Lang had noticed with what relish Micky employed the words 'woman' and 'women', licking her lips as she did so. One of his surreal Micky fantasies has the intrepid novelist striding into the sitting-room at Casa Mickie, opening a box on the sideboard, and turning on her quaking girlfriend with the menacing challenge: 'Sylve, there were a hundred women in here this morning, and now there's only three left. What have you done with them?'

Once, when Lang was engaged to play the Detective Inspector in J. B. Priestley's *An Inspector Calls* for a British Council tour of Turkey, his Micky studies actually came to his rescue. The director was in despair over Lang's characterization: 'You're a good actor, I know, but you're so bloody effete. It's too camp, Harold. For God's sake, can't you be a bit more butch? He's a tough North Country policeman.' As the opening night approached, Lang was in a state of total dejection. Then, one evening, his close friend Charles Laurence, who was playing Eric, suggested that they do the scene they shared with Micky Jacob as the Detective Inspector and the frightened Sylve as Eric. Within minutes, they were helpless with laughter. They said the lines as Micky and Sylve, and after a page they knew the Micky impersonation would work. The truth of it was,' Lang told the actor Nicholas Amer, 'I was a damn sight butcher imitating Micky than I was as myself.' At the next rehearsal, he came on as Micky, assuming her walk and her voice. The director and the entire company clapped their approval. He played the Inspector in this fashion throughout the run, to considerable success.

(Years later, watching the legendary, disastrous production by George Devine of *King Lear*, designed by the Japanese sculptor Isamu Noguchi and starring a perplexed John Gielgud, I was struck by the fact that Harold Lang, as Edmund, was the only person on stage speaking with a Yorkshire accent. I understand now that he had called Micky to his assistance yet again, since Edmund is lusty and virile, and not sensitive in any respect.)

Lang's acquaintances only knew of Micky from his increasingly elaborate fictions. (Inside her famous cane was secreted a special dildo from Asprey's, which she called Sir Roger de Coverley.) They had not encountered the cocky little woman, though they may have heard her on *Woman's Hour* complaining about London's laundries: 'I don't know if it's the water or the starch, but your shirts come back like a board.' Then, in the autumn of 1951, with the Conservative Party in power, she was in England giving a series of lectures. Derek Prouse, the film critic, was a keen disciple of Lang's Micky, and hearing that the real woman was in the country, he rushed round to Lang's flat in such a state of high excitement that he was barely able to speak the words 'She's here. In London. She's talking at St Pancras Town Hall.' Harold Lang immediately booked the first five rows of seats, and on the evening of the lecture they were occupied by some of the most distinguished artists in the capital. Behind them were women in plenty, who shrieked with anticipation as their hero, in tweeds, hobbled on to the stage with the aid of a walking stick. 'I'm sorry about this, darlings, but I've done my ankle in,' she explained to her fans.

Micky's subject was the history of the theatre. She praised Shakespeare, dismissed the playwrights of the Restoration as 'smutty', hadn't much to say in favour of Oscar Wilde, and then turned the full force of her intellect in the direction of Ibsen. It was at this point that everyone seated at the front realized that Harold Lang had not been exaggerating. The real Micky was just as preposterous as the artificial one. 'Ibsen? Ibsen?' she asked herself. 'Ibsen?' she asked again. '*The Wild Duck*. Just when you think the girl – Hilda, or some such – is going to shoot that blessed duck, she shoots herself instead. Ibsen? *The Wild Duck*. Quack, quack. That's what I think of Ibsen.' Lang and his party applauded this inspired outburst, as did the women at the rear.

Prior to the event, Lang had been nervous that Micky would not live up to the reputation he had created for her. His head was in his hands when she appeared. But after her dissection of *The Wild Duck*, he knew that she was giving of her awful best. Micky invited questions from the audience. A woman with a tremulous voice asked her why she didn't write plays any more. 'I can't. No. I can't. No. No. No,' she replied, dismissing the woman's suggestion that she produce a sequel to *Mary of Delight* with, 'No. No. I can't. That's that.' Another woman, a middle-aged American, called out, 'Tell everybody what you did for the girls in Italy during the war, Micky.' There were screams from the back of the hall. Micky smirked, wagged her finger, and muttered, 'If I come down there, I'll do you . . .' Her voice trailed away. The next thing she said was 'Rattling bedsteads' to more screams from the women and barely controlled hysteria in the front rows. Lang whispered 'Pearls from heaven' to Kenneth Tynan, who was seated beside him.

It was in 1951 that Micky advertised for a new secretary to replace Elsa Manley. A former Wren, Denise Martin, was the successful applicant. She would be known as Martino in Sirmione, where she fulfilled her duties with admirable efficiency. In that same year, Micky may have contacted Olivia

Etherington Smith, who was responsible for the acoustics in the newly built Royal Festival Hall.

Encouraged by the extraordinary performance in St Pancras, Harold Lang and Kenneth Tynan collaborated on a play with Micky in mind. They gave it the title *The Quest for Corbett: An Enquiry for Radio* and sent her a copy, with the invitation to play the leading role of Aphra Corbett. She declined at first, saying that she didn't understand a bloody word of this 'avant-garde tripe'. Lang flew to Italy, spent a day with her at Casa Mickie, and returned home with the news that Micky had agreed, with some reluctance, to star – though she didn't know it – as herself.

The Quest for Corbett, which was produced by Douglas Cleverdon, one of the pioneers of serious broadcasting, went out on the Third Programme, the predecessor of Radio 3, on 15 July 1956. It opens on a Yorkshire moor with two goatherds playing cards. They hear what they think is the evening train in the distance, but when the sound is repeated they suddenly become afraid. The tiny cough is coming from a mineshaft, from which a small creature is emerging. The first goatherd goes over to it and asks, 'What are you?', and the thing replies, 'A baby.' 'Ay, but a baby what?' the goatherd demands. 'A baby woman,' is Aphra's answer. The infant will grow to gigantic proportions, rivalling Moby Dick's, as the drama unfolds.

The piece is deeply silly. The novels Lang and Tynan attribute to Aphra might have dropped from the untiring pen of Micky herself. 'Books flowed from her like toothpaste,' observes the aesthete Dorset Loveless, played by Ernest Milton, whose strangled vowels marked him as one of the great eccentrics of the English stage. The judgements of appreciative reviewers are allowed to interrupt the action:

More than a Woman, Miss Corbett's remarkable study of taxidermy, is a chilling account of the havoc wrought by a woman who poisons and afterwards stuffs her two nieces. The squalor of the subject matter is brilliantly offset by the ironic gusto of Miss Corbett's style.

Nothing is said of *Red Cabbage*, a credible Micky title, but Aphra's next effusion is lauded thus:

The Ballad of Stansgate Dyke must be regarded as a major contribution to the literature of coastal erosion. In violent, almost pugnacious prose, it tells the story of a sturdy milkmaid who interposes her body between the village she loves and the fury of the sea.

The play's funniest line occurs when Aphra, who is taking New York by storm rather in the manner of King Kong, is asked by a journalist, 'Do you think the modern girl uses too many cosmetics?' Aphra's reply contains the essence of Micky: 'I never put anything on my face that you couldn't buy at a butcher's.'

The one surviving member of the original cast, Miriam Karlin, as the Romanian entrepreneuse Cuni Niculescu, found Micky completely frightening. She had not seen anyone like her before. The tweed suit, the starched shirt, the bow-tie, the cigar – all of these attested to a way of life she had not associated with a woman. She realized that she had had a sheltered upbringing.

In her last years, Micky was the centre of a *ménage à trois* once more. She and Martino had been joined by the Titian-haired Sara Turner. 'Sara fills my cup of happiness all the time until it is brimming over,' she told James Norbury, with whom she celebrated her seventy-sixth birthday at the Toucan Club, owned by Josie and May Adair, in London in 1960.

Raymond Savage, the agent who had worked so tirelessly on her behalf, had to impart the news that Hutchinson no

longer wished to publish her. She was furious. The friend and
adviser of thirty years was banished instantly. She did not listen
as he tried to explain that her sales had slumped and that her
mode of writing was considered out of date. He had failed
her, and she could not forgive him.

Micky's unwanted, and unexpected, removal from the
Hutchinson list inspired Harold Lang to invent the cleverest
of all his Micky fantasies. The Balaclava'd Micky, assisted by
two women with their faces similarly hidden by the woollen
helmet from the Crimean War, tie up the security guard at
Hutchinson & Company and plant water-resistant recording
devices in every toilet bowl in the Great Portland Street
building. They steal away, pleased with their fiendish plan.
The next day, the staff come to work as usual. An editor goes
to the lavatory, and while he is peeing Micky's voice comes up
from the water, chanting her titles like a mantra – *White Wool,
The Loaded Stick, Barren Metal*. The woman in charge of
publicity perches on the toilet seat and hears *A Passage Perilous*
and *Groping* from somewhere beneath her. Everyone in the
house of Hutchinson is driven to madness by the incorporeal
Micky, and there are those who suffer from more or less
permanent constipation, thanks to the subaquatic baritone
intoning *Me – Again, More about Me, Me and Mine*.

The small firm of William Kimber published *Me – and the
Stage* to coincide with her eightieth birthday on 1 July 1964.
She and Sara and Martino had moved out of Casa Mickie and
were living in a smaller house in Sirmione. She had a creamy
rice pudding for dinner and drank a little wine. She died two
weeks later, with Sara and Martino at her bedside. On the
Saturday after the funeral, a memorial party was held, attended
by all her friends in the town.

Naomi Jacob, *la scrittrice inglese*, lies at rest in Sirmione's cemetery, her grave marked with a photograph in which she is wearing a dinner jacket and a bow-tie and is smoking a cigarette. You'd think, if you didn't know to the contrary, that you were looking at an especially truculent man-about-town.

'What I want to do is capture in words the whole woman; the flesh and bone, the blood and sinew, the heart and brain, the stomach and entrails . . .' writes James Norbury in the Introduction to *The Seven Ages of 'Me'*. It has to be noted that he fails in his ambition, particularly in regard to Micky's entrails. He is no more illuminating on the subject of her many operations than she is.

It is the custom of lazy novelists, who tend to write for equally lazy readers, to make their characters instantly comprehensible in ways that differ from everyday experience. For all her prodigious industry – 'Wrote the usual novel before breakfast,' boasts Aphra Corbett – Micky was inherently idle, preferring to deal with the good and the bad, the ugly and the beautiful, the absolutely genuine and the completely bogus. The plot of *Four Generations* is not dissimilar to that of *Buddenbrooks*, Thomas Mann's great early novel. Plots belong to everyone, whereas insight into the subtle workings of human nature is the privilege of the few. Her autobiographies start promisingly before descending into chitchat. She always stops on the brink of true revelation. She never understood, on paper at least, what a complicated woman she was.

She left behind an Everest of verbiage, but only one of her books stands even half a chance of surviving. '*Our Marie*', her biography of Marie Lloyd, published in 1936, is severely flawed in terms of factual information. She is as cavalier with dates and places as ever. Yet she does give the reader something that Lloyd's latest biographer, Midge Gillies, in *Marie Lloyd: The One and Only* (1999), doesn't – a sense of what it was like to play to an audience that needed to be silenced and cajoled into appreciation. Micky had seen those rowdy audiences, been in the dingy dressing-rooms, watched great artistes succeed or 'die the death', and her book captures that peculiar combination of energy and vulgarity that kept the music hall alive for so long. Gillies accuses Micky, in a couple of sentences, of 'romanticizing' the music hall. The charge is accurate, in part. Micky knew and loved Marie Lloyd, and that affection prevents her from offering a balanced portrait. The painstaking Gillies supplies the facts, the dates, the information, but not the spirit of the age in which Marie Lloyd's genius flourished. Micky, almost by default, catches that spirit.

Micky adored the mother who abandoned her when she was fifteen, and hated her cultured father. We have to assume that Samuel Jacob was the monster she says he was in her later autobiographies. He died in poverty, but bequeathed her his handsome gold watch, which she instantly passed on to the priest in Sirmione, who was delighted to receive such an expensive gift. Micky shows Samuel no mercy or compassion, yet it's possible to believe that he possessed one or two virtues she chooses to ignore. Nana is presented almost without criticism, even when it is obvious that her behaviour is heartless and her opinions insufferably snobbish.

Micky does not reveal why she retained her father's 'common name' or why she called her favourite dog Sammy. Perhaps she didn't know why herself. Perhaps she was paying him subconscious homage.

3. 'The Portly Sunbeam'
Arthur Marshall (1910–1989)

I started reading the *New Statesman* when I was a schoolboy in the 1950s. Its books and arts pages were then without rival. A perfect issue would contain an essay by V. S. Pritchett on Henry James or Samuel Richardson, and reviews by D. J. Enright and the always contrary Geoffrey Grigson, among others. These serious and thought-provoking pieces would be followed by something altogether more light-hearted in tone by Arthur Marshall. Not for him the likes of Thomas Mann or Alain Robbe-Grillet. No, he was happiest with such storytellers as Nancy Moss, whom he hailed in 1954 as the true successor to Angela Brazil (pronounced to rhyme with 'frazzle') and Allen W. Seaby, whose *Blondel the Minstrel* took him into the 'world of white palfreys, frumenty, quilted overshirts, plague – purifications, baldrics, silken mutches and women called Adalberta'. He was equally at home with the autobiographies of the vainglorious, the pompous and the self-deluded: the millionaire-chasing Norah Docker in her gold Rolls-Royce; the dancer and choreographer Serge Lifar, who was nearly shot dead by one of Stalin's agents ('He opened his raincoat and showed me his weapon'); the eccentric Colonel Wintle, author of *The Last Englishman*, whose observation 'No Englishman is so happy as when he is astride a horse' elicited the response 'I would have news for the colonel were he not, alas, dead'; and Godfrey Winn who, in *The Positive Hour*, noted, 'I wonder if other authors have the feeling, which often assails me, that everyone else seems to write so much more arrestingly than oneself.' Marshall's reaction to this unconvincingly humble aside was 'Er, yes.'

Arthur Marshall began writing for the *New Statesman* in 1935, at the invitation of the literary editor, Raymond Mortimer, who was an admirer of his sketches involving headmistresses addressing the girls at end of term or a botany mistress taking her charges on nature rambles: 'There's ever such a dainty hellebore by your left plimsoll, Cynthia.' (The cry of 'Tits, lassies!' comes from *Prefects at Springdale* by Angela Brazil's only serious challenger, the felicitously named Dorita Fairlie Bruce.) Marshall, an avid reader of books for girls from childhood, had begun performing these short skits three years earlier for the benefit of friends. They were an immediate, and to him surprising, success. In 1934, a BBC producer asked him to appear on *Charlot's Hour*, a monthly late-night revue broadcast on the Home Service. Then, in 1935, he signed a contract with Columbia, and made five gramophone records on which he assumes a bosomy contralto for the head and a more melodious chirrup for the junior mistresses and girls. The word 'dear' is invariably elongated into 'deee-aaah' to indicate either disapproval or praise, depending on the sentiments expressed.

His brief at the *New Statesman* was to contribute an article each Christmas on the best books for girls published during the year. Angela Brazil, author of *At School with Rachel* and *A Patriotic Schoolgirl*, in which a German spy – Chrissie, who has a 'highly nervous organism' – is exposed by the plucky Marjorie at the eleventh hour, was coming to the end of her career, but Winifred Darch, May Wynne and Dorita Fairlie Bruce were still in their prime. This last specialized in unusual nomenclature, with girls called Isolt Kingsley, Fearnelith Macpherson, Desdemona Blackett, Ryllis Rutherford and Clemency Walton. In *Dinsie Intervenes*, Miss Fairlie Bruce has her hard-working headmistress point out, 'My dear, I am never off duty except when I'm in bed – and not always then.'

Arthur Marshall's odd and happy relationship with the *New*

Statesman ended in 1981, when he was sacked by the editor Bruce Page, who considered his weekly dispatches from his fictional country home 'Myrtlebank' too frivolous for such a serious and socially conscious magazine. His flippancy had been acceptable to Kingsley Martin, Paul Johnson and Anthony Howard, but Page was not amused by Marshall's cry of 'Coo-ee!' followed by 'Isn't Mrs Thatcher doing wonderfully well?' whenever he appeared at the office in Great Turnstile to deliver his copy and pick up the latest batch of ropey autobiographies.

Marshall wrote about bad books and writers with a stylishness and wit they scarcely merited. It is a matter of some sadness that he never set down his thoughts on Micky Jacob's rambling memoirs. His deep love of Balzac's novels, which he reread frequently, was known only to his closest acquaintances, as was his scholarly essay on the subject. 'I have made laughter my prime consideration in life,' he once remarked. He did not in the least resent the fact that some of his many friends treated him as their licensed, but unpaid, jester. 'Artie' was always in demand because he was unfailingly cheerful, even when he was enduring the misery of unrequited love. 'He learnt to laugh at his mother's knee,' Noël Annan observed at his memorial service in July 1989. 'Sitting in the dining-room of a Torquay hotel he and she became convulsed when two elderly ladies, famished and long neglected, called out, "Waitress, waitress, we are the two stuffed marrows."'

He was born on 10 May 1910, the second son of Charles Frederick Bertram (Bertie) Marshall and his wife Dorothy, née Lee. He was christened Charles Arthur Bertram. Mr Marshall was not a doting parent, though he wasn't unkind either. He did not care for the company of small children, and retreated to his study (which he called his 'den') or to a shed at the bottom of the garden behind the large family house in

the south-west London borough of Barnes. It was left to
Dorothy and the nanny to talk to Brian and Arthur, to read
to them at bedtime, to make sure they learnt to be polite.
Dorothy was a loving mother and 'provided a constant flow
of devoted support and comfort and encouragement', but she
did not spoil her sons. She took upon herself the sole parental
responsibility of disciplining Brian and Arthur when they
misbehaved or were petulant:

If, overexcited and jabbering, I went first through a doorway and
preceded some adult, I was dragged back and the whole process was
repeated . . . I was rather given to sullen moods and pouts and there
was an unfailing method of getting rid of a fit of the sulks: 'Go
straight up to your room, wash your face and hands, and don't come
down until you are looking altogether more attractive.'

Arthur heeded her words. Throughout his life he was
respectful of the feelings of others. For him, common courtesy
was an integral part of every-day discourse. Self-pity, self-regard
and, especially, self-aggrandisement he found insufferable. He
truly said goodbye to tantrums and pique in his boyhood.

Charles Marshall was a successful engineer, in charge of a
firm called the Pimlico Wheel Works. In his autobiography,
Life's Rich Pageant, published in 1984, Arthur writes regretfully
of his father's aloofness:

I saw other children perched happily on their fathers' knees but the
only time that I ever remember so perching was for professional
photographic purposes and when I was recovering from whooping-
cough in the healing ozone of Frinton . . . The photograph still
exists and shows no very contented percher.

Arthur was envious of those boys and girls he saw being
dandled or jogged up and down by their fathers. He makes

light in *Life's Rich Pageant* of the 'emotional imbalance', recording how he made a 'determined search' for what are now known as 'substitute father figures'. The search led him to a cousin, Willie Thomson, a soldier in a Highland regiment. 'There is a photograph of me applying to this handsome, smiling and kilted figure, which any all-in wrestler might envy, a head-lock with "submission" written all over it.'

There was also a man who came to the house every Sunday morning in order to clean Mr Marshall's boots and to polish the cutlery. He had been invalided out of the army and walked with a slight limp. Arthur 'counted the days to Sunday, hoping that the boots would get themselves muddier than usual so that Albert would have to stay longer'. He sat with Albert in an outhouse shed, looking at him raptly, admiring his moustache. In adult life, Arthur would often say that he liked a 'man with a 'tache'. He would always be attracted to strong-looking men with a military bearing. One of his longest attachments was to a doorman at one of London's smartest clubs, who was married. Dick sometimes told his wife he was going to do night duty at a newly opened club called Arthur's.

Another surrogate father was a steward at Roehampton Golf Club. On fine Sundays in summer, Charles would take Dorothy and the boys to the members' tea-room, where they would eat and drink while a three-piece orchestra played selections from *The Arcadians* and other musical shows of the period. The steward was a kindly man, 'suitably fatherlike', who sometimes invited Arthur behind the green baize door and chatted to him as he did the washing-up. On one such occasion, he gave the smiling little boy a box of chocolates. (In today's society, Cousin Willie, Albert and the steward would be viewed with the utmost suspicion. Such friendliness towards the young has assumed a sinister aspect.) Mr Marshall was not worried by the attention they paid to his younger son. Indeed, he was actually relieved that 'others had cheerfully' shouldered that part of a parent's duties that he couldn't find it in him to undertake.

Arthur's obsession with the theatre began at the age of four, when he was taken to see *Peter Pan* at the King's Theatre in Hammersmith. Peter was played by Madge Titheradge. Arthur was enchanted and enthralled. Then, at Christmas 1915, he went to his first pantomime, *Sinbad the Sailor*, at the same theatre. The Dame, Mrs Sinbad, was a man in drag, of course, and even late in life Arthur could remember 'her' saying goodbye to 'her' son and his boat, the *Saucy Sue*, while falling about on the quayside with the phrase, 'Drat them bollards'. He did not understand the vulgar jokes – 'I have no money but my aunt has piles' – but he relished the 'rather elderly' Sinbad singing 'There's a long, long trail a-winding into the land of my dreams'. It was explained to him that the reason why an older actor was cast as Sinbad was because all the younger performers were fighting at the Front.

The, following year, Arthur was enrolled at the kindergarten section of the Froebel Institute in Hammersmith. The bus taking him to this extraordinary school, where the pupils were encouraged to believe that learning is a pleasurable activity, passed the King's Theatre. Arthur could see and read the billboards announcing such treats as *The Scarlet Pimpernel*, which contained a line that always reduced him to helpless giggling: 'Hoity-toity, Citizeness, what fly stings you, pray?' There was *The Only Way*, an adaptation of *A Tale of Two Cities*, starring Sir John Martin Harvey, who was 'nobly assisted by his wife, Miss N. de Silva, a determinedly evergreen heroine who must hold the record for matronly Ophelias and who was still gamely hitting off that unfortunate girl at the good old age of 51'. Miss N. de Silva's feat was as nothing to that of the athletic Sir Frank Benson, who went on playing Hamlet into his seventies. Arthur does not disclose how Sir Frank coped with the mother and stepfather problem.

One of Arthur's new-found friends, an especially imaginative child, wondered if the combination of the foreign words 'kindergarten' and 'Froebel' might mean that the schoolmistresses were German spies. Arthur put him right. Since he was already an expert at the game L'Attaque, he knew that a spy was a 'black-suited male wearing a large and broadbrimmed hat, imperfectly concealed behind a tree'.

It was thanks to his father that Arthur became irretrievably stage-struck. One of Mr Marshall's employees at the Pimlico Wheel Works worked at night as a stage-hand at the Chiswick Empire, the thriving music hall, to supplement his income. Mr Marshall told the man about his son's fascination with everything theatrical, and the man said he would be delighted to show Arthur backstage during a performance:

I took instantly to that rather weird theatre smell – a mixture of greasepaint, powder, size, fusty clothes, biscuits, sweat, dirt and, I am afraid, cats. I snuffed it all joyfully up. Though the front of the house was nice enough, the stage itself was paradise. I stood at first in the prompt corner but was later allowed to climb a ladder into the flies and gaze down at the acts below on the brightly lit stage.

It has to be assumed that Brian did not share his brother's enthusiasm for the theatre, since Arthur makes no mention of him when he describes how his mother took him to matinées from 1918 and into the 20s. Arthur would remain in love with the frothy light comedies, the improbable melodramas, and – especially – the musicals and operettas he saw in his childhood and adolescence. The two great successes of the second decade of the twentieth century were *Chu Chin Chow* and *The Maid of the Mountains*, both of which had very long runs. While his parents enjoyed these and other operettas such as *The Merry Widow* and *The Balkan Princess* as pure escapism, Arthur was bemused by the absurdity of the plots and the dialogue. In *Life's Rich Pageant*, he makes fun of the average operetta, set in a ridiculously named Central or Eastern European country, in this case Boldonia:

I was always very fond of the scene, set well downstage to enable the glories of 'The Boldonian Market Square at Festa Time' to be erected and hung behind, in which the Grand Duchess Zaza, a lot of whose dialogue relied rather heavily on the letter 'z', summoned to her boudoir ('Zit down, *ma petite*') pretty little Melodie Metterling. A heroine has to be called something and the name Melodie alerted the public to the fact that she was, and quite soon, going to sing. One usually found that Melodie had rashly lost her heart to Igor, a penniless strolling musician (a prince in disguise) with a fine tenor voice and the two best numbers in the play, 'The Way of Man with Maid' and a robust drinking song, 'Drain We Our Bumpers'.

The Grand Duchess 'seeks to dissuade', as the programme note had it, Melodie with the sort of dialogue that went, 'Zis young man, Igor, vot do you know of eeem? Zese young men, zey are all the same. Zey lov you for a day, zey take vot you 'ave to give, and zen POUFFE, zey are gone.' Let me hastily explain that the explosive word POUFFE was constantly on the lips of Middle-European Grand Duchesses and was accepted as indicating somebody or something that had suddenly vanished in a cloud, or puff, of smoke. The Duchess then croaked out her only number, a rambling account of her own disastrous love life and called 'Zere is Nozzing Left', after which there was a partially successful black-out in which dim figures darted on and removed Zaza's chaise-longue. Then the lights came suddenly and excitingly up, and lo and behold, we were in the Market Square with crazed Boldonian villagers rushing in, singing violently and jigging vigorously up and down in a manner that could only be called unbridled. But it was, after all, Festa Time.

Arthur's addiction to tosh, nurtured in childhood, was unwavering. In old age, he became a devotee of ludicrous television soap operas, such as *Crossroads*, set in a motel in which the walls wobbled (he once appeared in an episode); *Dallas* (the recently dead Bobby's miraculous emergence from the shower was an event to cherish), and *Dynasty*, which featured a royal wedding designed to kill off most of the cast, who were shot down by crazed gunmen, leaving only Alexis Morell Carrington Colby Dexter Rowan, impersonated in all her finite variety by Joan Collins, alive. He shared Micky Jacob's opinion of Ibsen ('Not a fun one') and had little patience with high tragedy. He loathed 'that dread couple' Racine and Corneille with an equal passion, after studying their plays as an undergraduate at Cambridge. 'If Racine and Corneille knew any jokes, they kept them to themselves.'

The two years Arthur spent at the English branch of the Froebel Institute were 'an enchanted time'. The teachers created such a friendly and jovial atmosphere that the children were always absorbed in some creative activity, whether it was painting, making cardboard models, singing or acting scenes from *Hiawatha*.

From there he went to Ranelagh House, a co-educational school over-looking Barnes Common – 'the common itself becoming at dusk an educational eye-opener for the older student'. The forbidding headmistress, Miss Wright, taught him English, History, Latin, Geography and Scripture. Whenever he played a wrong note on the piano, she rapped him sharply on the knuckles with a pencil. A Madame Croxford was in charge of Gymnastics, Art and French. Under her guidance, Arthur learnt to execute a 'violent hornpipe dance', which he performed, 'to thunderous applause', at Barnes Town Hall. A lady gave him chocolates, and the vicar a 'playful nip'.

In the summer of 1920, Charles Marshall left the Pimlico Wheel Works and moved his family to Newbury in Berkshire.

He was now employed in the newly built paper mills in nearby Thatcham. Within days of arriving in Newbury, Arthur was whisked away to a preparatory boarding school, Stirling Court, on the Hampshire coast, where his brother was already a pupil. His removal there was a 'traumatic experience' for a ten-year-old. He suffered acute homesickness, but – thanks to his mother's training – he resisted the urge to cry until after lights out. The 'cheerless and outstandingly unsybaritic surroundings' depressed him deeply:

Macbeth who, when in the mood, could come out with some quite good things (thoughts on tomorrow, for instance) remarks on his very first entrance that he has never seen so fair and foul a day. Plainly he was not educated at Stirling Court. There, sharp and rapidly changing contrasts of grief and joy, sunshine and shadow, pain and pleasure were the pattern of our every waking moment.

The gloom at Stirling Court was soon lightened by the presence of a plump and cheerful boy named Williamson, whose sense of humour was as pronounced as Arthur's. Williamson asked the Scripture teacher questions he would have preferred not to answer:

As soon as, in Genesis, we reached the Cities of the Plain and Sodom in particular, Williamson's alert mind spotted that we were not being told All. The story, as watered down for our youthful ears, was feeble in the extreme. Everything hung on a secondary meaning of the verb 'to know'. This, we were told by a young and blushing Mr Sinclair, just meant 'getting to know you' and merely indicated a chummy approach – one imagined a sort of exchange of names and visiting cards ('I'm Uz, and this is my friend Obal'). But why then the fire and brimstone and why, most revealing of all, those blushes? Williamson kept up a fine barrage of 'But, sir . . .', Mr Sinclair countering strongly with 'Oh do shut up, Williamson!'

The determined and curious Williamson went to the school library after this frustrating lesson and looked up the verb 'to know' in the dictionary. He was pleased to find 'to have sexual commerce with' among the definitions. The following day, Williamson asked the embarrassed teacher, 'Please, sir, what does "commerce" mean?'

(The man who taught Religious Instruction in my own school three decades later was slightly, but only slightly, more direct than the confused Mr Sinclair. He told us that we had to know that 'to know' in the Bible was not 'to know' as we knew it. When the young and old males of Sodom demanded of Lot that he bring his visitors 'unto us, that we may know them', they had something more than a friendly handshake in mind. The scribe responsible for Chapter 19 of Genesis is annoyingly vague on the methods employed by Sodom's welcoming committee, and our teacher emulated his vagueness. We had to read between the lines.)

In his autobiographical essay 'The Crooked Bat', Arthur remembers Williamson as a remarkable boy, 'an even more improbable day-dreamer than I':

He liked to pretend that he was the king, *a* king, any old king, graciously living incognito among us, and firmly incognito he looked with his blazer and grey shorts and grubby knees. It was possible to make him happy for hours by suddenly popping out from behind a tree and yelling, 'Sire, Sire, I bring grievous news. Thirty of our stoutest bottoms have foundered off Gravesend.' There was half a minute's pause for silent laughter. No schoolboy of twelve in those unsophisticated days was proof against the word 'bottom', even when signifying a ship. Then Williamson would draw himself up to his full three foot eight and shriek in a piercing treble, 'Then go build ye fifty more, an' Sherwood Forest be stripped bare.'

On the football field, playing centre forward, Williamson

would pretend to be Henry V leading his troops to victory at Agincourt. The rest of the team would support him with cries of 'God for Harry, England, St George and Williamson!'

No boy at Stirling Court was allowed not to play cricket. Short-sighted boys were instructed to leave their glasses in the pavilion. (The contact lens had yet to be invented.) Players in the First and Second Eleven wore a surgical box to protect their genitals, but the less talented had to fend as best they could with only a bat to stop the oncoming ball. In the ultra-masculine ethos that prevailed at Stirling Court, the pupils were expected to be tough. English, French, History and Geography were taught, but the principal emphasis was on games – football, cricket, fives, rugby, boxing. Anyone discovered writing poetry could expect to be caned. The wicked Lord Byron was held up as an example of the bad effects of versifying.

(Something of this attitude still survived when I was a schoolboy, even though my English master encouraged me to learn poems by heart – a practice that has stayed with me. Kipling's 'If' was considered acceptable with its exhortation 'You'll be a man, my son', as were those rousing Victorian ballads honouring military or naval heroes, but Keats and Shelley and the Elizabethan lyricists were regarded as sissies.)

Arthur became acutely aware, in November 1920, of just how fortunate he was. There were boys in the school whose fathers, uncles and, in some cases, older brothers had been killed in the trenches of Flanders. On Armistice Day, during the two minutes' silence:

An overwrought boy whose father and uncle had both died had a bad fit of hysteria. Starting slowly, his wild and maniacal bellows of a sort of laughter gradually increased in speed and volume – a dreadful and horrifying sound that chilled the blood. The boys next to him edged nervously away . . .

The grief-stricken boy was sent home for a few days to his equally desolate mother.

The next school Arthur attended was altogether more congenial than Stirling Court. 'Here was freedom and spaciousness and a more liberal outlook,' he writes of Oundle in Northamptonshire, which he joined in the summer term of 1924. Two years earlier, he had been captivated by the charm of the headmaster, Dr Kenneth Fisher, when his parents had taken him to be interviewed for a place. (Fisher and his wife would become his lasting friends.) It was Fisher's great triumph that there was absolutely no bullying at Oundle, since it was made clear from the outset that it would not be tolerated. The teaching was of a consistently high standard. Arthur, who had been bored by History at Stirling Court – 'Day after day we sat solemnly at our desks and learnt dates. I defy anyone to get a crumb of comfort or intellectual stimulus from "English regain Madras (1749)" or "Siege of Danzig (1734)"' – now found the subject more involving, though it left him with a penchant for what he calls the 'mini-facts' of history, such as the visit paid by the Queen of Hawaii in 1889 to Lambeth Palace, where the lesbian wife of Archbishop Benson (and mother of his three queer sons) served her tea. The Queen had to be dissuaded from dunking her sponge cake in the teacup.

Arthur excelled at French and Mathematics, and was a member of the winning house rugger team in 1926. He enjoyed every class, it seems, except Scripture. His knowledge of the Bible – and the Old Testament, in particular – was as thorough as it was unwanted, since he had to listen to 'vast chunks' of it read out loud. The myriad beauties of the King James translation eluded him. He read and listened quizzically, from a rationalist point of view. A sentence such as 'Howl, ye ships of Tarshish' bewildered him.

When a dog-collared divine, clutching the lectern, let fly with 'Who
is this that cometh from Edom, with dyed garments from Bozrah?',
a rhetorical question for answer came there none, one was quite
frankly nonplussed, apart from noting the fact that the dye used
seemed to come from squashed grape skins, as far as one could
gather, and the garments would therefore be either Burgundy-red
or Beaujolais-purple rather than a dull Hock-white. And then,
where was Edom and where, as though one cared, was Bozrah? And
why was almost everybody in the Old Testament permanently ratty
and disagreeable, with God (whom we were constantly thanking for
this or that) by far the rattiest of the lot. It didn't make sense then
and, by golly, it makes a great deal less now.

Arthur gave expression to this long-festering resentment at
the age of seventy-four.

Arthur realized he was sexually wonky ('wonky' was among
his favourite, and most employed, words) at an early age. He
appears to have been free of guilt to a remarkable degree, at a
time when homosexuality was considered a diabolical wicked-
ness. Perhaps his loathing of the 'mirthless twaddle' in the Old
Testament rescued him from debilitating notions of sin.

Neither his parents nor his teachers told him what used to
be known as the facts of life. He discovered these for himself,
when interesting and unusual things began to happen to his
fourteen-year-old body. 'However involuntary and natural the
manifestations might seem, not to speak of the possibility of
them being, later on, advantageous, to talk about them to
anybody, or even to think about them, would have come under
the heading of "Smut", and Smut was harmful and to be
avoided.'

Yet, even before these startling physical changes, Arthur was
aware that certain adults had some pretty strange habits. One

summer's day in 1922, the boys at Stirling Court were taken by charabanc to Portsmouth to watch a professional cricket match in which the famous Philip Mead would be batting. They arrived at the ground and claimed their seats, then made for the lavatory, where an alarming sight awaited them:

In a corner, and facing outwards, an aged clergyman was standing, smiling encouragement and wildly waggling. At our fairly tender years this was a startling spectacle and one hardly knew where to look. Where not to look was plain to all. Subsequent visits found him, hope on hope ever, still there and still at it. Not a cricket lover, evidently.

On the return journey, the boys talked only of Mead's brilliant performance. Their thoughts on the 'muddled divine' were not given even mocking expression. Nor was the matter discussed with Matron at bedtime.

In 'The Crooked Bat', Arthur reveals that he was a clued-up and flirtatious schoolboy:

To be honest, it must be confessed that the incident with the wonky clergyman was not entirely surprising to some of us. Preparatory schools at that time seemed each to have its quota of unmarried masters who were still looking about for Miss Right. Although it was difficult for them to marry on their miserable salaries, that was not, for all of them, the problem. Some of them were by nature looking about for Miss Right rather less vigorously than others. Dedicated paedophiles stalked the linoleum-covered corridors and, seeing a non-frosty reception, pounced . . . The purpose of these ungainly gymnastics was lost on the more naive boys; they referred to the odd activities as 'romping', a verb which has since caught up with them. But I, an odious and knowing little giggling plumpness, was well aware of what was toward and realized that the merest show of cooperation would lead, sooner or later, in God's good time, somehow somewhere, to a sticky tribute. Bulls' eyes, for instance.

Arthur was a keen singer at Oundle, taking part in annual performances of *Elijah* and the *Messiah* and, most adventurously, Bach's Mass in B Minor with a fifty-piece orchestra that contained some professional musicians. Although he already regarded God as a 'disagreeable elderly gentleman', he relished the music that was dedicated to him. His music master encouraged him to apply for a choral scholarship at Caius College, Cambridge. There was no direct line from Oundle to Cambridge, so on his way there he had to change trains at a small station in a town called March. He went into the lavatory, 'primly obscured by laurels':

Here I found myself face to face with, though I didn't realize it at the time, my first specialized sexual graffito, fully visible in all its incomprehensibility. 'Why don't we form a So Club,' an excited hand had scratched on the wall, 'and meet here on Thursdays?' I was later to discover that the word 'so' when applied to male amatory abnormalities derived from the German phrase '*Er ist so*' and was the equivalent of the then fashionable 'He is one of those'. But at the time I merely wondered what the letters stood for. Sanitary orderlies? Station operatives? And why on earth choose such a whiffy trysting place, and what was so special about Thursdays (early closing day, perhaps)? No time was mentioned and so wouldn't they have to hang about (indeed) for hours?

Arthur was seventeen and relatively innocent, but he noted the message and found out its meaning. He failed his choral examination. He went on to Cambridge just the same, where he studied Modern Languages and became a leading member of the ADC, the prestigious amateur dramatic club, which had royal patronage.

★

Arthur's imaginative and inventive friend Williamson went to
a different public school, but the two met in the holidays.
Arthur often stayed with the Williamson family and was struck
by the 'regal way' in which the boy who liked to pretend to
be a king treated his parents. He addressed them as Percy and
Daisy, which shocked Arthur somewhat. Such familiarity was
contrary to every social grace Dorothy Marshall had drilled
into him. Williamson referred to them collectively as 'the
Williamsons'. He spoke of them, in their presence, with total
confidence that he would not be chastised: 'I'm afraid the
Williamsons are feeling a little bit out of it. We'd better
drag them into the conversation.' Percy and Daisy smiled
affectionately. He was their only child, and they cherished
him. Mr and Mrs Williamson sometimes accompanied the
boys to the cinema, but on one occasion their clever offspring
remarked as he and Arthur were going out of the front door:
'We're leaving the Williamsons at home for this one. It's a
German film called *Metropolis* and rather beyond your intellectual range, Daisy, so you and Percy can have a quiet little
evening *à deux*. Don't get into mischief.'

It was during the Cambridge vacations, when Arthur was
with his parents in Newbury, that he began to realize that his
father had become seriously eccentric. It was difficult to invite
his undergraduate friends to visit unless they travelled by train.
If they came by car, there was every certainty that Charles
Marshall would attack it physically if it was parked nearby. He
would remove the detachable lamps and drop them on the
gravel path. He would get into the driving seat and run
the battery down. It became necessary for Arthur to advise his
friends to leave their vehicles several streets away and arrive at
the house on foot. A more bewildering aspect of Charles's
eccentricity was his habit, prior to going on holiday, of closing
and locking the piano and pocketing the key.

This always struck me as hard luck on burglars who, after they had stuffed our silver and my mother's Persian coat into a large bag labelled SWAG, might want tunefully to celebrate their haul with a few Chopin études or, in more thoughtful and grateful vein, a keyboard setting of 'Bless This House'.

The three years Arthur spent at Cambridge, from 1928 to 1931, were among the happiest of his generally happy life. Miss Pernel Strachey, who lectured on Benjamin Constant and other French writers, and Professor Elsie Butler, who referred endearingly to 'poor old Goethe' and 'poor old Schiller', were stimulating teachers. Arthur, who had decided at Oundle, despite the mesmeric teaching methods of A. C. Bray, that Racine and Corneille were literally insufferable, now had to study their plays in detail. Bray was acting out *Phèdre* in class one day with such ferocity that his nose began to bleed. He lay on the floor to stop the flow but went on reciting the 'liquid lines'. Bray, who had a longish nose, was particularly fond of Edmond Rostand's *Cyrano de Bergerac*, and would invariably weep when he read out the last scene, where Roxane realizes that the dying Cyrano is the man she has really loved. Arthur, and the 'less hard-boiled' boys, wept with him.

Arthur was unlucky at Cambridge in only one respect, in that his tutor, a prematurely old man in his thirties and an expert on Ibsen, was entirely devoid of wit or humour. He called Arthur 'Mr Marshall' for three years and was a complete stickler for the college rules at Christ's. He was possessed not of *joie* but *douleur de vivre*.

Joining the ADC, of which Arthur would become president, more than compensated for the gloomy, punctilious tutor and the regular penance that was Racine and Corneille. Arthur and his Oundle friend Maurice Johnson were quickly accepted into the club, which boasted among its former presidents the Prince of Wales, who became Edward VII. The garish club tie, which Arthur wore with some embarrassment, was composed of the Prince's racing colours.

Arthur, at last, was in his element. Although his tutor discovered a college rule that prevented his playing Cordelia in *King Lear* for the Marlowe Society, he was allowed to appear as Elizabeth in Somerset Maugham's *The Circle* in 1929. Writing of the production in the *Cambridge Review,* George Rylands praised Arthur's ability to underact and show a 'peculiar modesty and taste' in a female role. He added: 'And ought not Mr Marshall's beautiful legs to be insured while he is a member of the ADC?'

George, known always as Dadie, Rylands was one of the brightest figures at Cambridge in the inter-war years. He was among the foremost Shakespeare scholars of the twentieth century, and put his scholarship to practical purposes. His work for the Marlowe Society led John Gielgud to invite him to direct *Hamlet* and *The Duchess of Malfi* at the Haymarket in 1944. This was Gielgud's last interpretation of Hamlet, and by many accounts the best. (Rylands later chose the excerpts from Shakespeare's plays and poetry for Gielgud's one-man show *The Ages of Man.*) T. S. Eliot considered Rylands's production of his *The Family Reunion* the finest he had seen, because Rylands was aware of the mordant comedy inherent in the play. Eliot was gratified to hear the audience laughing.

The friendship between Arthur and Dadie was established immediately in 1928 and endured into the 1950s, when Arthur tired of being reproached for his 'devotion to the trivialities of the professional theatre', as Noël Annan writes in his book *The Dons.* Rylands, who once remarked that 'no one had ever made him laugh more', teased him for his lack of seriousness. Outliving Arthur by ten years, he died blind and deaf at the age of ninety-six. His sexual life had been a fairly continuous misery to him. Unable to shake off the Christian guilt he inherited as a boy, he resorted to drink in middle age. When drunk, he cast off his inhibitions and became reckless. He escaped prosecution by a hair's breadth after an incident involving a soldier in a telephone box at Victoria Station. Recklessness was followed by shame and remorse. The happy-go-lucky Arthur, who must have had his share of rejections, enjoyed sex whenever he could. For Dadie Rylands, it was a curse. Arthur, exasperated by Dadie's high moral tone, said that 'friendship with Dadie was like being on an ocean liner from which one was hurled into the sea for a misdemeanour; as one surfaced one saw the heads of a dozen old friends bobbing in the waves'.

The last play in which Arthur appeared for the ADC was, in fact, directed by George Rylands. In Shaw's *Captain Brassbound's Conversion*, Michael Redgrave, in the title role, was 'acted off the stage by Arthur Marshall as Lady Cicely', according to Noël Annan. The spy-to-be Guy Burgess designed the sets. The production was praised by the London critics; Shaw came to see it and wrote Rylands a letter of thanks; the Duke of Kent brought a party of friends one night, and extra performances were staged to satisfy public demand. Arthur was now convinced that he might persuade his parents to support him in his patent desire to pursue a career in the theatre.

He was wrong. When he proposed to them that he descend on London, armed with his excellent press notices, the better to influence one of the major impresarios into engaging him, 'Bertie' Marshall 'looked doubtful and unhappy', but it was Dorothy who said what Arthur didn't want to hear: 'I do rather wonder, dear, what sort of welcome they would give to an amateur female impersonator. I think I'd keep rather quiet about it if I were you.'

They reminded him that Dr Fisher, three years earlier, had

more or less offered him a post as a teacher at Oundle, should he want it. And it was to Oundle he returned in 1931, as house tutor in a town house called Laundimer. (The boarding houses at Oundle were divided between field houses and town houses.) Laundimer, which had belonged to Lord Lyveden, had a pleasant rear garden and a tennis court. Arthur was given a small room on the ground floor, with a window that offered a view of North Street, along which lorries rumbled day and night en route to Peterborough and the brick fields. He had to share a lavatory with the house master, so coughing was essential to ensure privacy. He could only take a bath three times a week, at 6 p.m. precisely. He had to vacate the bathroom promptly, as Matron was scheduled for 6.30.

It says much for Arthur's wit and charm, and for Kenneth Fisher's tolerance and understanding, that he was to revolutionize the teaching of Scripture at Oundle by simply refusing to teach it. After conducting an initial class with twenty senior boys on the subject of St Matthew's Gospel, in which the students were encouraged to read the text out loud in order to make the hour pass quickly, he was then told to teach it again at seven the next morning.

Once more we started reading St Matthew, taking up where we had left off. Not even the Last Supper aroused interest and after about ten minutes I could bear it no more. 'Oh do please stop,' I cried, adding in the silence that fell, 'Isn't this all perfectly ghastly? What *are* we to do?' We closed our Bibles and just stared at each other for a time, the boys quite unaccustomed to such a candid approach. And then I said, 'I tell you what. If you promise not to spread it abroad that we've dropped St Matthew, we'll read something that ought to interest you more. We'll begin next lesson. Have any of you ever heard of Aldous Huxley?' And so then, and in the years to come with this particular subject and form, we had a lively series of readings.

They began with *Brave New World*. They went on to
H. G. Wells, whose books they enjoyed discussing. They read
Cold Comfort Farm, with Arthur no doubt explaining the
origins of the satire (principally the doom-laden, earthy sagas
of the thoroughly earnest Mary Webb). In the Scripture Higher
Certificate Examination, some of the boys failed to score
a single mark, and an examiner registered a complaint of
blasphemy. Other boys in other forms were studying the Acts
of the Apostles, but Arthur was permitted to continue teaching
contemporary fiction. It seems incredible that Dr Fisher should
have allowed him to do so, but allow him he did.

It was in the French lessons that Arthur was at his most
brilliant and original. And, indeed, inspiring, as one of his
pupils from that time, Gilbert Bradley, told me. Bradley left
Oundle a fluent French speaker, with absolute confidence in
his ability to communicate. Arthur did not ignore grammar,
but he was determined to show the boys they were dealing
with a living language. He invented short scenes for the boys
to act and improvise – 'a tremendous row in a greengrocer's,
say, about the cost of cabbages ("*Je refuse absolument de payer*")
or a scene in a doctor's consulting-room with a patient moaning
"*Ah, que je souffre*" and a spirited death or two ("*Allez chercher
le gendarme!*").'

Thus, when the time came to read the short stories of Guy
de Maupassant ('his less saucy tales in a purified *Contes Choisis:
Édition pour la Jeunesse*'), the boys already had a substantial
vocabulary. They also read Mérimée's *Colomba*, 'full of
Corsican feuds and vendettas', and acted the more powerful
bits, with Arthur assuming the title role, a fiery, humourless
lady, intent on murder. His falsetto screams and shrieks ensured
that the boys learnt more words. Laughter can be educative.

In the mid-1930s, there was one particular boy in the school
who was generous with his sexual favours. His name was
Shepherd-Smith. In chapel on Sundays, when 'The King of

Love My Shepherd Is' came to be sung, some of the naughtier choristers provided alternative words:

> The King of love is Shepherd-Smith,
> His bottom faileth never.
> I nothing lack if I have his,
> And he hath mine for ever.

It is impossible to imagine how Arthur could have won so many admirers in the theatre, and beyond, without the inspiration he gained from the works of Angela Brazil. Once he began to read them aloud, he instantly realized their comic potential – phrases such as 'It's a grizzly nuisance'; 'What a blossomy idea', 'What a frolicsome joke', 'Scootons-nous vite', 'Don't get raggy, old sport', and the now mysterious 'Miss Jones is a stunt, as jinky as you like' caused hilarity when spoken. Dr and Mrs Fisher were amused by his Brazil-based sketches, and permission to leave Oundle was granted whenever he was invited to perform them on radio or at dinner parties. In January 1938, he received an invitation from Ivor Novello to see his musical *Crest of the Wave* at Drury Lane and to join the maestro for a small supper party at his flat in the Aldwych. (Ivor Novello's flat could be located behind the first 'O' in a huge neon sign advertising DAEMORRHOIDS, the tablets much favoured by sufferers from piles.) The guests at supper included Leslie Henson, Beatrice Lillie, and the young Vivien Leigh and Laurence Olivier, who had recently fallen in love. Arthur performed as the games mistress, the botany mistress, as poor put-upon Mademoiselle uttering cries of fractured French, and as the headmistress herself, sternly bringing her wayward girls to heel. Encores were demanded. He became an irritated hostess and a *grande dame*. His heroes applauded him. He drove home in a 'cloud of bliss':

Those whose dreams have also come true will understand what follows. To be accepted as one of them and to be made much of by those whom I had so long admired was too great an emotional moment for me, and when I got into bed I was shaken by sobs and wept my heart out till dawn.

The next day, Arthur was in front of his class again, performing in a slightly more restrained manner. Teaching, he believed, is a form of acting and, as Gilbert Bradley remembers, Arthur's enthusiasm and vitality made him one of the most popular masters at Oundle. The young, with a few dull exceptions, take to people who make them laugh, who remind them of life's funnier aspects.

While Arthur was a pupil at Oundle, he witnessed with embarrassed horror an entertainment that was staged every two years or so in which masters and boys told jokes, sang rugby songs, and invited the audience of parents, school governors and local dignitaries to join in community singing. This biennial revue Dr Fisher now entrusted to his care. Under the title *Masterpieces* – 'we aimed high' – the show became infinitely more sophisticated:

A good idea for providing moments of glory was to have a Kenneth Clark-type lecturer discoursing on various famous pictures which were then posed for by performers suitably rigged up, in an empty frame, against a black background. 'The Anatomy Lesson' went well, and a rather timid physics master as the Mona Lisa ('Note the little half-smile. She seems to know what you are thinking, eh?') scored a great hit.

They put on a ballet, *La Tentation du Professeur*, in which Arthur was prima ballerina. He had to stress to his fellow dancers, all wearing 'specially constructed tutus', that they dance properly, or as well as they could, to achieve the required

comic effect. Cheap laughs – someone falling over, for example
– had to be eschewed. Arthur had learnt from the great
players he admired – Jack Buchanan, Gertrude Lawrence, Noël
Coward and Beatrice Lillie (who once executed, in both senses,
'The Dying Swan', in a riot of moulting feathers) – the
importance of timing and understatement.

Arthur and Dadie Rylands were now inseparable friends.
Arthur had bought an Austin Seven in which he drove to
London and Cambridge, so they met frequently. Rylands was
not the only academic to enjoy Arthur's company – another
was C. M. (Maurice) Bowra, the Warden of Wadham College,
Oxford. This deeply complex man, who supported the strikers
during the General Strike of 1926, loathed the prevailing class
system in England, had a profound knowledge and love of
Russian literature, especially the poetry of Pushkin. He translated from the Greek and wrote several books of criticism. His
talk was livelier than his prose, which is workmanlike but rarely
idiosyncratic or inspired. 'An hour with Bowra was like being
given a blood transfusion,' writes Noël Annan in *The Dons*.
He spoke his witticisms in a booming voice that carried for
yards, if not miles: 'He's the sort of man who would give you
a stab in the front', 'He gave me the warm shoulder', and
other such inversions. Once, when Arthur and Dadie Rylands
were present, he astonished some rather decorous students
who were also in the room by returning from the lavatory and
exclaiming loudly, '*Most* satisfactory.' Arthur felt honoured,
nothing less, that Bowra preferred to spend an evening with
him rather than with the many distinguished academics of his
acquaintance. Arthur made him laugh.

Noël Annan first met Arthur in 1935. Annan, who had
been educated at Stowe, was one of several Old Stoics who
were trying to put on a charity performance at the Rudolf
Steiner Hall to raise funds for a working-class boys' club called
the Pineapple Club because it was situated in a pub with that

name. A friend said, 'You must get Arthur Marshall to do one of his turns.' Since Stowe and Oundle regularly played each other at rugger, there was a connection of sorts. Annan went to see him, though he did not think for one moment that Arthur would accept. 'Of course Arthur was prepared to perform at the drop of a hat. He came, and was an immense success.'

Arthur and Noël Annan shared a flat in South Kensington in the 1940s. Arthur would sometimes visit the pub that Joe Ackerley patronized, not far from Knightsbridge Barracks.

The phoney war ended on 10 May 1940, which happened to be Arthur's thirtieth birthday. Because of his fluency in French and German, he had been enrolled in the Intelligence Corps in January and 'groomed for stardom' at Mytchett, a camp near Aldershot, where the men were told everything they needed to know about the security branch of the Intelligence Service. After weeks of indoctrination, he was given battledress and posted to northern France.

Arthur was disconcerted by the military top brass. It was the 'aura with which high rank seemed to hedge itself' that startled him. He soon found a way – a typically Artie way – of coping with the aloofness of the moustachioed generals:

However, and because of my admiration for Angela Brazil, I chose to imagine we were all in a vast girls' school: headmistress, Miss Gladys Gort; school colours, Khaki and black; school motto, Don't Look Back Or You Might See Something Nasty. All the Junior girls were dead nuts on that new and dashing little hockey mistress, Miss Brenda Montgomery, and with this phantasy, the tensions gradually eased.

His letters to friends at this time were sometimes signed Second Lieutenant Marigold Marshall. The soldiers who took instructions from him were given girls' names, which he chose carefully to suit their personalities. This was innocent, harmless fun, and the men seem to have treated it as such.

Arthur was in command of a field security section in Lille when he met Miss Brenda Montgomery. The section was small, consisting of a sergeant-major, some trained NCOs with motorcycles, and a Ford car. Its purpose was to 'thwart enemy attempts at espionage, sabotage and propaganda' and required the men to work with the French authorities. Arthur presented himself to the general, who asked him questions which he answered in detail while marvelling at the 'elegance and length' of Montgomery's nose.

On that fateful day in May, the 'fog of war swiftly descended and before long it became difficult to locate our formations and units'. Abandoned offices contained documents that had to be burnt in case they should get into enemy hands. Chaos reigned as the German army advanced into the region. On one occasion, Arthur and his men were driving along a highway near Oudenarde in Belgium when they 'became aware that shot and shell were passing rather close overhead' and that they made a 'target as splendidly visible as those ducks that judder by in a fair's shooting gallery'.

And on another:

Becoming aware of a swishing sound from behind, we turned and observed a German aeroplane gliding towards us, and although I emptied, as they say, my revolver into it, it kept right on, dropped two bombs, covered us with earth and stones and killed a cow.

With the ill-equipped and listless Belgian army on the verge of collapsing totally, a kind of insanity prevailed. The most unlikely people were suspected of being spies; even nuns were not excluded. (They were thought to be German officers in drag.)

There were three methods of dealing with a suspect. There was the British one, which was to question him and then, in our customary and just manner and for want of solid evidence, release him. There was the French method, which was to question the man and then shoot him. And there was the Belgian, which was the same as the French but without the questions.

A field security officer drove out of a side road one evening and joined a 'column of vehicles moving north-west' before realizing, after some minutes, that they were German. Fortunately for him there was another side road he could turn into, and to his surprise and relief, no one seemed to notice or care when he did.

Then something even more surreal happened. The French and Belgian authorities opened up all the prisons and mental institutions in the district and released the inmates. Murderers and thieves, pilfering when the opportunity presented itself, added to the general confusion, while the lunatics, instantly identifiable in green corduroy, laughed and howled. There was only one solution to this new problem. Within days, they were all arrested. Luis Buñuel and Eugène Ionesco could not have invented anything so bizarre.

Food was scarce, and drinking water unobtainable. (They drained the radiators in abandoned cars for the water.) As the German army closed in on Dunkirk, Arthur set off on a mission with his driver in a jeep. Both men were unarmed. 'What if you meet some Germans?' he was asked. 'I shall give them a very dirty look,' he replied.

Arthur was ordered to disband the unit and to make for Dunkirk, 'all too visible as it blazed away on the horizon'. The atmosphere there, after the pandemonium of the past few weeks, was alarmingly orderly, with the British navy 'radiating calm'. Arthur and his officers spent two nights sleeping in a sand dune. The troops who were waiting to be rowed out to the destroyers and other ships were patient and tired. There was one madman present, however, in the form of a 'very conscientious major'

who, disturbed by the scene of devastation on the seashore, with its littered stores and equipment and greatcoats (people swimming out to boats aren't going to be bothered to take such things with them), went round, in his own phrase, 'to tidy the place up a bit'. We gave him a hand, as it was something to do while waiting, and we made little piles of uniform here and little piles of webbing there, but I cannot think that the Germans (known to everyone as, and with surprisingly little hatred, 'Old Jerry') were deceived. '*That's* better,' said the major, giving a final look. But it wasn't.

   Back in England, Arthur spent three months with a security section on the Cumbrian coast before being sent – 'for reasons unvouchsafed to me by the War Office' – to Lisburn in Northern Ireland. Life there was relatively comfortable, with the army rations supplemented by goods from Eire. To begin with, Arthur had no idea what he was supposed to be doing, until the commander, Sir Henry Pownall, explained that everyone in the camp had Battle Experience. This was true of the other soldiers, but not of Arthur, who was 'long on Experience, but a bit short on Battle'. They were based in Lisburn to make forays into neutral Eire, which – rumour had it – was going to be invaded by the Germans. On these excursions they were required to measure roads and bridges and make plans for the imminent battle. It never took place.
   They practised firing revolvers at Germans in 'plywood

silhouette' and learnt how to throw live hand grenades. 'If you or your instructor dropped a grenade prematurely, they urged you not to wait or apologize or to cry a mocking "Butter-fingers" but to dart behind the buttress, where there was room, I hoped, for two.'

On leave, Arthur went to Dublin, saw plays at the Abbey and Gate Theatres and dined at Jammet's, where members of the German embassy staff were frequent customers. 'It was only military decorum and British dignity that prevented one from leaning towards them and startling them with a loud "BOO!", followed by "Who's losing the war?"'

In April 1942, Arthur was transferred to the London head-quarters of Combined Operations in Richmond Terrace, off Whitehall. He was made Security Officer (Military), SO(M). The 'M' was to distinguish him from his naval counterpart, SO(N) Lieutenant-Commander Gerald Williams. It was their task to ensure that news of forthcoming raids on enemy territory was restricted to those involved in the operations. A series of elaborate codes had to be instigated – so elaborate, in fact, that Arthur was occasionally confused.

Arthur had to report sometimes to Commander Lord Louis Mountbatten, who had an office on the premises:

I once had to spend twenty minutes with Mountbatten while we decided where the marine sentries could stand so that they would be out of a draught, although draughtless nooks and corners tended to mask their field of view and diminish their usefulness as sentries. We tried this place and that ('Stand over there, Marshall. Now, are you in a draught?'). The sentries looked on, nonplussed by this quite unusual care for their welfare.

A distinctly ratty commodore often called in at Richmond Terrace to find fault with Arthur and Gerald Williams. He was marginally polite to Williams, but always brusque and rude to

Arthur. One day, standing, next to the commodore in the canteen, Arthur adopted an ingratiating smile and said, 'I say, do stop being horrid.' The commodore, who could have charged him with insubordination for not using the word 'sir', was so taken aback that he managed to be less openly unpleasant thereafter.

Arthur was greatly amused on the day that Princess Marina of Kent, visiting Mountbatten, wandered into the MOST SECRET map-room by mistake, and had to be led out blindfolded by an officer. On another occasion, a duchess telephoned David Astor, who was press officer, asking him that if there was ever a raid on Le Touquet, 'would the raiders please bring back her golf clubs, left in locker 47. They can't miss it. It's got my name on it. *Too* kind.' This is a perfect example of what Arthur called Tumbril Talk, of which he was an avid collector.

It was thanks to Mountbatten, whom he hero-worshipped, that Arthur suffered one of the worst – perhaps *the* worst – social embarrassments he could recall. Ten members of the staff at Combined Operations were invited to dine at the Senior Army and Navy Club. Mountbatten was host. After dinner, Mountbatten and his guests moved to the large smoking-room for coffee. The room was filled with 'high-ranking officers busy digesting their food and reading newspapers'.

Mountbatten said, 'Now, Marshall, I hear you do comic turns on the wireless. Get up and do one for us.' Horrified at the dreadful suggestion, I protested vigorously, but no notice at all was taken of my objections. 'Nonsense. Up you get and start at once.' So there was nothing for it. Our little group responded merrily and loyally to my botany mistress taking her girls for a nature walk, complete with mild indecencies, and to mock chapters from Angela Brazil, but they could not see what I could, and all too clearly see, a look of total horror on the faces of generals and admirals scattered around. Only Mountbatten's presence and prestige prevented a public outcry.

One day, in 1943, Arthur received a call from a BBC radio producer, David Yates Mason, a close friend from Cambridge, asking him if he would stand in for a comedian named Richard Haydn, who was ill, in a comedy programme to be recorded the following Sunday. Mason suggested that Arthur impersonate a 'hearty and bossy nurse come from the hospital to report on Richard's condition'. Arthur agreed. 'Out of my way, dear' was Nurse Dugdale's opening cry, and so successful was his five-minute sketch that the BBC invited him to star in a series, which he and Mason wrote together. They wanted to call it *Nurse Dugdale's Doings*, but this was considered too risqué, so they settled for *A Date with Nurse Dugdale*.

Nurse Dugdale's sidekick was the dithering, virginal Sister Parkinson, played by Marjorie Westbury. Other characters included old Mrs Muirhead, who fused her electric blanket in every episode, and 'larky' Canon Baldwin, 'for whom the BBC dance programmes, relayed to the wards, proved too exciting and who was discovered "out of bed and locked in a frenzied beguine with one of the bronchials"', and a forbidding Matron whose voice was never heard but who frightened everyone to death (in some cases, literally). Jokes of the 'Oh dear, the tea urn's exploded all over Sir Timothy's agenda' kind were the norm.

Later that year, Arthur was among those who were moved from Combined Operations to Supreme Headquarters Allied Expeditionary Forces (SHAEF), based at Norfolk House in St James's Square. After the arrival of General Eisenhower (What was Arthur's name for him? Sadie, perhaps, or Betty – as in Grable and Hutton?), the headquarters was moved to Bushy Park, Twickenham, where the staff fed the Germans details of false invasions, which they accepted gullibly.

Hearing an air-raid warning one day, Arthur rushed into the nearest shelter. In the darkness, he made out another seated figure, who turned out to be Eisenhower. There was a long silence. Then the general spoke: 'Well, as long as I keep sitting here, they can't ask me to sign anything.'

In 1944, the hostilities nearly over, Arthur was forced to endure the command of a spectacularly humourless major. So dour was he that Arthur grew more and more determined to make him laugh:

On one occasion he gave me a deeply depressed look and said, 'Everybody in this outfit seems to be using Christian names. What's yours?' I have three initials and the first is 'C'. 'It's Cynthia,' I replied, wishful to lighten the gloom. '*Cynthia?* That's a bloody silly name for a man!' 'Yes, isn't it?' I said. However, for a week he called me Cynthia loudly and rather defiantly and until I had to beg him to stop. 'People,' I said, 'are talking,' but the little joke passed him by, alas, and he just thought me odder still.

At the end of the war, Arthur was part of a delegation from SHAEF sent to Flensburg, the Baltic port where the German high command finished up in ignominy. They were lodged on Hitler's 'commodious yacht', where 'courtesies were exchanged' with the crew. It was Arthur's job to discover Himmler's whereabouts. 'He was later caught by a Field Security Section and, thus saving everybody a lot of trouble, obligingly did away with himself.'

Arthur and an Oxford don, both in battledress, looking dishevelled, 'with bulgy blouses and dull boots', interview-ed four German officers of equivalent rank wearing their best uniforms. 'Everything that was supposed to shine, shone.'

I saw them staring at us with a look of total disbelief on their faces. Whatever is this riff-raff? they were thinking. What on earth went wrong? How could we possibly have lost the war? Thinking it over, I was as perplexed as they.

Meanwhile, in the yacht's dining saloon, some German naval personnel were 'engaged on a course of lectures on submarines and explosives', as if they were unaware of the Allies' victory.

On 19 July 1945, Lieutenant-Colonel Arthur Marshall wrote to his friend Noël Annan from Germany in the guise of M'Bonga, a dusky maiden:

Little Jungle Flower sends greetings and fifteen tribal gestures to dear Big Chief.

He then reverted to being Arthur briefly:

Spoke to Germans in the street – Odd as it may seem very pro-British – I found my German flowed quite easily.

But M'Bonga had more to impart:

M'Bonga is now off to Paris to make a few forgiving gestures. M'Bonga thanks Big Chief for two willow-bark communiqués which M'Bonga read with aid of white man specs, traded for $\frac{1}{2}$ dozen millet cakes. M'Bonga plenty pleased with Big Chief. White Man Wonder Bird.

Later that month, M'Bonga wrote to Annan again:

Big Chief sends early smoke signals to M'Bonga so M'Bonga catchum early news. M'Bonga inserting larger earthenware plate in lower lip to please Big Chief plenty. M'Bonga's supply poison darts OK.

At the beginning of August:

I am bringing you back an assegai, a millet cake, fifteen wolves, four yards of inner tubing, two coconuts and a gourd of wild honey. M'Bonga, Queen of the Night.

On 23 August, he was writing to the future provost of King's College, Cambridge, and vice-chancellor of London University as Edythe. Edythe, alias Arthur, had attended the first night of Noël Coward's revue *Sigh No More* at the Piccadilly Theatre:

In the interval Joyce Carey took me to Mr Coward's box where I had a drink with him and discussed the first half!! I was luckily sufficiently boozed up a) not to feel nervous and b) not to burst into tears with the excitement of the moment. I saw him again afterwards, had a gay chat with Miss Lillie . . . met Miss Grenfell, and left in a haze of happiness equal, in your particular world, from the pleasure you would get from an intellectual set-to with Sheila Kaye-Smith, Warwick Deeping, Storm Jameson and Daphne du Maurier.

Noël Annan was keenly aware that Arthur was extremely unhappy at this time. He had fallen in love with a man named Charlie, with whom he was having an on-and-off affair. There is only one reference to him in the long correspondence Arthur sustained with Annan. The year is 1946:

Charlie is now demobbed and starts work, after only a week's leave, on Thursday, in a factory doing brazing: he once explained to me what this was but I have unfortunately forgotten.

Arthur, who was now based in Christow, the Devonshire village where his widowed mother and cousin Madge were living, returned to Oundle in the summer term of the same year. His friend Dr Fisher had retired the year before, and had died almost immediately afterwards. The new headmaster,

Graham Stainforth, hid an 'acute sense of humour' behind a somewhat bleak exterior. Arthur was made a housemaster in 1947.

In November 1946, M'Bonga wrote to Big Chief Annan about the forthcoming rugby match at Twickenham:

M'Bonga humbly kiss Big Chief's toe.

M'Bonga velly sorry but M'Bonga have specially reserved seat in topmost date-palm for Thursday. M'Bonga only able to obtain seat by method not approved of by Big Chief. All seats now gone and M'Bonga quite unable to squeeze Big Chief in, wave pampas grass skirt how she may. If Big Chief dead nuts on seeing match, Big Chief must queue on Zambesi bank and maybe M'Bonga wave to him from date-palm. M'Bonga make up to Big Chief later and do special dug-dance for him in wigwam. M'Bonga mighty keen join Big Chief for rice cake and gourd of coconut wine after game. Big Chief no regret coming of M'Bonga; M'Bonga plenty friendly.

Fifteen nose-rubs from M'Bonga.

Arthur took his housemaster's duties seriously, meeting and writing to the parents about the progress of the boys in his charge. He once remarked, 'The boys are quite safe with me. It's their fathers I'm interested in.' On one occasion, he had to explain to a couple that if their son fell ill, he would send them a report every day. The mother said, 'Oh please don't bother about that. Just send us a postcard if he's dead.'

He remained at Oundle until 1954, when he decided that he did not wish to end his days as a half-blind Mr Chips scratching away on the blackboard. The financier and phil-anthropist Victor Rothschild had invited him to be his secretary, and Arthur had accepted. The job took him back to Cambridge, where he and Rothschild had met in the 1920s. He was given a little cottage near Merton Hall, which was not only Rothschild's home but the centre of his business.

Rothschild and his wife Tess were unfailingly kind to him, but he came to realize that he wasn't really ideal for the post.

Arthur's first book, *Nineteen to the Dozen*, which he dedicated to George Rylands, was published in 1953 by Hamish Hamilton, whose managing director was Roger Machell. Machell had played Lady Kitty in *The Circle* opposite Arthur's Elizabeth. 'Jamie' Hamilton, the publisher, was known for being strongly anti-queer, but he made an exception of Arthur, who – one need hardly say – made him laugh. *Nineteen to the Dozen* is a collection of Arthur's occasional writings for the *New Statesman* and the long-since defunct *Lilliput*. One piece, 'Advice for Operatic Heroines', has Artie (as he was known to his many friends) in the role of agony aunt, passing on her knowledge of men and their wicked ways to Mimi (Paris), Isolde (Cornwall), Cho-Cho San (Nagasaki), Elsa (Antwerp) and Brünnhilde (Valhalla). She also advises Don José (Seville) – 'You do not really belong on my page but your case has moved me' – to 'Leave this girl *at once.*'

Here is what she has to say to Mimi:

Mimi (Paris) – You are young, dear, and Bohemians can, of course, be fascinating, but the *quartier* you inhabit sounds altogether too *artistique*. Can you not move to more wholesome surroundings (I understand that St-Cloud is delightful) and sew your seams there? Your painter friends seem, I admit, a very cheery crowd but don't besot yourself with this Rudolf. If he truly loves you he will come to visit you wherever you are, and if he does not – well, there are plenty of other *poissons* in the *mer, n'est-pas*? Do do something about that cough; it may be only a tickle at present but just look what happened to Violetta! Luvivox Voice Pastilles are the very thing for your ailment: deliciously flavoured, they bring instant balm to – but you can read all about them on the tin.

And to that noted horsewoman, Brünnhilde, she writes:

Brünnhilde (*Valhalla*) – Yours, though worrying, seems to be largely a transportation problem, and of course it is galling for a girl of your spirit to be seen constantly lugging dead heroes about. Can you not catch Wotan in a good mood and point out that you and your steed (Grani, is it not?) are by no means as young as you were? Don't try to pull the wool over your father's eye as regards your age. Possibly, his sight being what it is, he has not noticed your exhaustion and you are to him still the 'girlie' of your early years. I do congratulate you, however, on keeping so cheerful at your work: 'Sing As You Go' is a grand motto. Now, settle down quietly somewhere (why not Shropshire?), and, if you feel that you don't want to get rusty, enter for an occasional point-to-point. I don't think that I should sing during any competitive riding: the other horses will not be accustomed to it and we don't want black looks in the unsaddling enclosure, do we? Do let me know when you are racing: I would love to venture a 'bob' or two. Good luck, dear, and keep those chins up.

But the book isn't all froth. It contains a short story, 'The Experience', about a woman in quiet hell with an unloved and unloving husband, that gives off a welcome whiff of melancholy. It's no masterpiece, but it is carefully constructed and elegantly written, and it is serious. It offers an insight into the kind of life Arthur feared living; into a dull and lasting pain that not even laughter can relieve.

Nineteen to the Dozen was reviewed glowingly by John Betjeman in the *Daily Telegraph*. Betjeman wrote: 'Like all the best humorists, he has a strong sense of pathos,' and the judgement seems right. Betjeman admired 'The Experience', describing it accurately as 'unsentimental'.

Arthur's next job was offered to him by Hugh (Binkie) Beaumont and his partner (in life and in business) John Perry, the former lover of John Gielgud. Beaumont was head of the company H. M. Tennent Ltd, which had almost total control over the West End theatre during the 1940s, 50s and 60s. Although Beaumont staged the occasional revival of a famous or forgotten classic – one thinks of Peter Brook's great production of Thomas Otway's *Venice Preserv'd* in 1953, with Gielgud and Paul Scofield – most of the stuff he put on was cosy, middlebrow pap. The plays of N. C. Hunter and Wynyard Browne needed resuscitating when they were first produced, but now they are beyond help. Under Beaumont, the English theatre took no notice of the huge social changes that were taking place in post-war Britain. On the London stage, people still came in through the french windows; were served drinks by the butler; had Cockney cautions (played by Kathleen Harrison) to do a bit of dusting and get a few laughs; and behaved, even as they suffered, with commendable restraint. Beaumont employed the finest actors – Edith Evans, Gielgud, Alec Guinness, Ralph Richardson, Irene Worth – and made a deal in the late 1950s with the newly formed Associated Television Company to provide plays in which they could star. Arthur became the script reader for Globe Productions, and in the five years he laboured in his office above the Queen's Theatre he discovered no new talent, though he did encourage writers – such as myself – with a long and generous letter. I should have known, even then, that the piece I submitted would never be put on by H. M. Tennent. It was about a group of old working-class men and women who were neither patronized nor depicted as comic stereotypes, and it ended on a dying fall. I was pleased enough that Arthur admired the dialogue.

It was during his time at Globe Productions that Arthur wrote *Season of Goodwill*, adapted from the novel *Every Third Thought* by the American writer Dorothea Malm. He was attracted to the story of two elderly sisters (played by Sybil Thorndike and Gwen Ffrangcon-Davies), living with their brother (Paul Rogers) in Minneapolis, who are visited each

Christmas by their despised great-niece and her husband. The sisters know that the young couple are after their money and tease them accordingly. Nothing much happens until the last scene, when someone is murdered.

Season of Goodwill opened in London in the autumn of 1964, and abruptly closed. (Its director, Vivian Matalon, had once been engaged to Georgina, the daughter of Lord Ward of Dudley, who was Aviation Minister in Harold Macmillan's government. Lord Ward summoned his future son-in-law to dinner at Claridge's. During the meal, his lordship stared at Matalon for a considerable time before remarking, 'You're Jewish, aren't you?', to which Matalon replied, 'Yes, I am.' There was a thoughtful silence, and then Lord Ward said, 'That's all right. We can cope with that. Having a Jew in the family is no worse than having a homosexual.' The impetuous and honest Matalon couldn't stop himself saying, 'Well, you've got two for the price of one.' The engagement was over.)

Arthur had more luck with his second theatrical venture, also presented by Binkie Beaumont. The comedy *Fleur de Cactus*, by Messieurs Barillet and Gredy, had been a huge success in Paris. Under the title *Cactus Flower*, rendered into American by Abe Burrows, it had also enjoyed a long run in New York. Arthur was asked to translate it from the original French, restoring the scenes Burrows had cut. Additional material that Burrows had inserted had to be de-Americanized. Arthur's version of *Cactus Flower* ran for seven months to packed houses at the Lyric Theatre, only closing because its star, Margaret Leighton, was previously contracted to appear in a Tennessee Williams revival in New York.

Arthur did not have a place of his own in London. He lived for six months in John Gielgud's house in Westminster, which was stuffed with treasures and theatrical bric-a-brac. John Perry warned him not to open any drawers, in case Ellen Terry's false teeth fell out. Then he moved in with the actress Coral

Browne and her then husband, the agent Philip Pearmain, who was homosexual. The story goes that Coral Browne, who was about to play Goneril, was reading *King Lear* in bed one night, when she turned to Pearmain, who was deep in a thriller, and said, 'I've found the perfect part for you, Philip. Act Five, Scene One. The British camp near Dover.'

Throughout the 1960s and 70s, a succession of terrible books came Arthur's way to review. There was Barbara Cartland's memoir of the 1920s, *We Danced All Night*, which he demolished memorably, describing the 'honey-packed . . . tireless purveyor of romance' as a 'gleaming telly-figure with a Niagara of jabber and the white and creamy look of an animated meringue'. The book, an 'indigestible feast of period gossip', contains such boastful sentences as 'Men wanted me. I had forty-nine proposals before I said "yes".'

Bewitching (it seems) Miss Cartland was placed upon a pedestal. 'The young men treated me as if I were made of Dresden china.' They did more:

> Men who loved me would stand outside my house late at night, on the evenings I did not go out with them, in a silent salute . . . They would write me poems, and there would be flowers. 'Good morning, darling,' one note read, 'I want these roses to see you.'
>
> An unexpected delight for the Gloire de Dijon, *n'est-ce pas*?

And then there were Godfrey Winn's two volumes of autobiography, with titles snatched from T. S. Eliot's *Four Quartets*: The Infirm Glory and *The Positive Hour*. Death, which is often so merciful to us, prevented the publication of a third volume.

Mr Winn's taste in words is immature. He has not advanced. Schoolmasters will reach for their red ink. A simple word alarms him, and so 'to marry' is 'to exchange vows', to meet is to encounter, to live is to dwell, very tired is utterly spent, a joke is a sally, London is the metropolis, and Fate is inscrutable. He refers, twice, to 'The whirligig of time', and not with a smile. There is a deplorable sentence that begins 'The sleeping landscape crystallized under the aurora of the untarnished moon'.

Nobody capable of any self-mockery could write such things and it must, alas, be said that when the good fairies were handing out humour, Godfrey Winn had been called to the telephone.

Arthur had met Godfrey Winn in the early 1930s, when his Cambridge contemporary the actor Geoffrey Toone took him to Winn's house in Ebury Street for drinks. Winn was still in the theatre, had tossed off a novel or two, but was just beginning to be famous as a journalist, 'producing articles', in Arthur's words, 'on such thoughtful subjects as "The daughter I would like to have", "Why the young are bad-tempered" and "Have we failed the dead?"' On arrival, Godfrey gave them sherry in 'glasses reminiscent of·acorn-cups and of the size from which one might imagine Pease-blossom and Mustard-seed sipping dew, though perhaps it wasn't quite the moment for letting the mind rest on midsummer fairies'.

While we two sipped, Godfrey twinkled to and fro and up and down and, eventually twinkling right out of the room, soon came twinkling back becomingly attired in two-piece cerise pyjamas, the top half of which had one of those flaps which fold across the chest and are secured by a button high up in the neck and look vaguely Russian. Oh, I thought. He then made a tour of the room, showing off various possessions . . . After that he produced a folder containing several photographs of himself taken by the then fashionable Paul Tanqueray. We were invited to peer and admire. 'I told Paul to make me look eighteen.' 'Oh,' we ventured, though I was longing to say, 'What went wrong?' We escaped after an hour or so and as I was far less censorious in those days, I merely thought our host a little peculiar. But I would now supply, for it had really been too much in the field of egomania, an unkinder adjective.

(Godfrey was still twinkling, if in a rather lacklustre fashion, thirty years later. In the late 1950s, he was a television agony aunt in a show called *As Others See Us*. Each instalment contained three problems, to which Godfrey, seated in a book-lined study, offered solutions. Each problem was dramatized. I was nineteen when I appeared in *As Others See Us*, acting the part of a fresh-faced student who becomes – on Godfrey's advice – the surrogate son for a grief-stricken mother whose boy has been killed in a road accident. We rehearsed for a week without Godfrey, who turned up at the studio on the day of the live transmission. At the afternoon rehearsal, he was wearing a pale blue cashmere sweater that did not hide a copious belly. Then, in the evening, he wore a dark suit, and the belly was safely tucked inside a corset as he uttered his gems of wisdom. The director sat in the control room weeping with laughter whenever Godfrey spoke. Godfrey had trouble with the letters 'l' and 'r', and his script was generously laced with both. 'I some-times wonder,' he mused, 'what is in the minds of young girls who accept lifts from lorry drivers on lonely roads late at night.'

Godfrey, like Arthur, was a keen tennis player. He was playing doubles on the day he died, in the second set of a match he and his partner were losing. After his body had been taken off, the three men went back to his Brighton home, where they were quick to invade the drinks cabinet. Since Godfrey was notoriously stingy with drink (hence those acorn-cups), the friends opened bottle after bottle while they leafed through Godfrey's address book and phoned all his acquaint-ances with the sad news. Late at night, one of the trio, now seriously drunk, put a call through to Noël Coward at his villa in Switzerland. The phone rang and rang, and then the unmistakable voice, sounding rattled, said 'Yes?' The tearful mourner asked, 'Is that Sir Noël Coward?' 'Yes,' was the crisp reply. 'I think you ought to know that Godfrey Winn is dead.' 'Good,' snapped Coward, slamming down the receiver.)

Perhaps the funniest of Arthur's reviews for the *New Statesman* is the one devoted to *Ma Vie*, the autobiography of the preposterously egotistical Serge Lifar, translated by James Holman Mason:

The translator has finely caught the spirit of the thing and has come across with gem after gem. Diaghilev sends a parcel ('What could it be? Some knick-knacks?'); Diaghilev becomes chummy ('Our two souls met together in an upsurge towards the Beautiful'); Lifar becomes practical ('I shook off my musings').

About his abilities as a dancer, the Paris-based Russian is not in any way *shy*. Tributes flow ('Bravo, Lifar') and Diaghilev is pleased ('Thank you, Lifar'). Lifar criticizes Pavlova for being unenterprising ('It's possible, Lifar'), takes over the choreography of *Prométhée* ('Upon my word, Lifar'), and a tiff follows ('Calm down, Lifar').

(Lifar's ridiculous vanity was still intact when I saw him dance *L'après-midi d'un faune* at Covent Garden. He was pushing sixty, plump and far from nimble. On the posters outside, some wag had crossed out 'faune' and substituted 'éléphant'.)

Arthur's writing for the *New Statesman* was not confined to book reviewing. In 1970, he produced an amusing spoof involving a couple of blackmailers, Eleanor and Gervase Hartwycke. Eleanor's letters to Gertrude, Queen of Denmark and Lady Macbeth were discovered by a 'National Trust representative in a walled-up tiring room at Holdingham Hall, Suffolk', the Hartwycke family seat. The cache of documents, finely preserved, were entrusted to the editorship of Professor J. de B. Hambrill of London University. Lady Eleanor was in the habit of keeping 'fayre copies' of every epistle she dispatched, and two of these are quoted in full in Arthur's 'An Important Find'.

The letter to Gertrude opens thus:

What a heavenly weekend! The time just flew and Gervase and I hated having to dash down to the docks before the theatricals began but, as it was, we only just caught our packet.

She goes on to mention 'Ophelia's impromptu cabaret' and the excitement of 'Hamlet's unofficial engagement (no, no, *not one word*, I promise)' and Ophelia's 'wildflower collection' and 'well-stocked herbarium':

I think you are well advised to postpone her swimming lessons until after she is safely married. A snuffly cold at the altar creates an unfortunate effect on that Day of Days.

It is then that the blackmailing begins in earnest:

As to the armoured apparition that appeared in our room on the stroke of midnight and started jabbering nineteen to the dozen about some orchard picnic party that had gone wrong (and who, this weather, can hope to stop flummery curdling?), I think your explanation must be the right one. It was a nightmare caused by indigestion – *no* reflection, dearest Gertie, on your tasty *smorgasbord*! At all events, we hardly heard what he said, being entirely occupied with trying to puzzle out how he had managed to come straight in through the wall. Gervase *thinks* he remembers what was said but I have told him he is wrong. Quite quite wrong.

But the '*pfennig*' did not drop with Gertrude ('not the world's brightest lady, and kept in the dark anyhow, and too drowsy with sex to be over-percipient'). The trip to Inverness proved far more successful for the Hartwyckes. Lady Macbeth got Eleanor's drift straight away. Gervase saw something in the corridor. Or did he?

Next morning, Maggie brought up our breakfast as usual (ummmm! your *baps!*), told us the very unexpected news about the King's death (a *real* test for a hostess and you came through it *superbly*), and then the moment Maggie had gone, out it all came! I shall not even *begin* to tell you what Gervase thought he saw in the passage. Not one word of it shall ever pass *my* lips! He didn't see either of you, really he didn't, and if he did you were both quite EMPTY-HANDED. And if you *weren't* completely empty-handed, we think you must have been helping to clear away after that *delicious* dinner.

The money to restore the West Wing of Holdingham Hall reached Eleanor by return of post.

In January 1979, one of Arthur's readers sent him a photocopy of a page from a nineteenth-century acting edition of *Macbeth*, complete with stage directions, two of which he found particularly diverting:

Enter Lady Macbeth with a candle right upper entrance.

and

Exit Lady Macbeth with a candle left upper entrance.

Arthur was always happy to perform his sketches for friends. He was staying with Alfred Lunt and Lynn Fontanne (two peerless light-comedy players who were at their peak in the 1930s, when they starred with Noël Coward in *Design for Living* on Broadway), when he added another eccentric lady to his repertoire. This last of his impersonations was a novelist of a certain age who produces a surprise bestseller entitled *Lust is Silent*. The voice he assumed was very much like that of his friend Rose Macaulay (author of *The Towers of Trebizond*). Dame Rose, a frequent broadcaster, had an intrusive 'h' in her speech, so that *Lust is Silent* became *Lusht ish Shilent*.

In the last fifteen years of his life, Arthur lived in Christow with Peter Kelland, a former schoolmaster. It was a perfect relationship. Their home, Pound Cottage, is the 'Myrtlebank' from which Arthur sent hilarious dispatches first in the *New Statesman* and then in the *Sunday Telegraph*. Archdeacon Ward, in his address at Arthur's funeral, described them accurately as 'beautifully manicured vignettes . . . all about very little, but which always left one with a chuckle'.

One aspect of village life which did not get into 'News from Myrtlebank', is recorded in a letter signed by Edythe to Noël Annan on 7 April 1987:

The arrival in the village of the AIDS LEAFLET has caused problems, especially the injunction not to CHANGE PARTNERS, for here there is at least one whist drive a week, where the whole point is to switch after each round. We are also wondering what Elsie (a neighbour and friend, then in her 80s) would do with a FREE CONDOM if they are ever delivered . . .

Arthur wrote often to his friend James Bernard, signing his letters Mélodie, in deference to Bernard's career as a composer of film music. 'Jimmy' was a connoisseur of Arthur's 'tumbrils'. Here are two examples:

An extremely grand and titled lady of the manor, on hearing that the son of her humble rector had won a scholarship to a public school, summoned him for a congratulatory glass of sherry and said,

'I hear that your boy has won a scholarship.' 'Yes, indeed.' 'And to which school, may I ask?' 'Well, actually, it's to Eton.' To which Lady X said, '*Eton*! Not *our* Eton?'

and:

Last weekend Peter and I were at Chatsworth [a tumbril sentence in itself!] and our hostess [the Duchess of Devonshire] told us that her mother-in-law liked staying in hotels and always insisted on taking four dogs with her and in preparing their meals, with her own foodstuffs, in the hotel kitchen. And she was doing this once in a hotel kitchen and in front of a very bolshie and anti-duchess collection of maids and cooks and she was heard to say loudly, 'Now, I must try to remember which of the dogs it is that doesn't like grouse.'

Arthur became relatively famous in old age, after a lifetime on the periphery of the theatre. His naturalness as a performer, his limitless good humour and unfailing sense of the ridiculous, made him a lovable figure on radio and television. In the programme *Call My Bluff*, in which two teams are given three obscure or arcane words to define, Arthur's team invariably lost. For Arthur, the definitions themselves were the real treat, especially when they came from his opposing team leader, Frank Muir. When Arthur laughed, which he did frequently, at least four chins wobbled. No wonder Frank Muir called him a 'portly sunbeam'.

He was constantly commuting from Devon – opening fêtes, taking part in fund-raising events for charity, giving out prizes in schools, and being a very talkative guest on television chat shows. On one such, the late Russell Harty tried to find out if there was a serious man behind the merry exterior. As Arthur related it afterwards to Frank Muir: 'I briskly threw away the frivolous mask and, speaking in all sincerity and from the heart, said to Mr Harty, "I regard myself as the Jeanette MacDonald of the prose world."'

In the final year of his life, when he was dying of cancer, Frank Muir wrote him a long letter every week to keep him entertained. The letters are stuffed with witty digressions, quotations from books Muir had been reading, much genuinely scurrilous gossip and the odd anecdote. In one of them, he talks about Suza, a Spanish woman who worked for Muir and his wife, Polly:

Suza came bursting into the room where Polly was entertaining a couple of very old ladies to give her some good news about a Spanish lad who had volunteered to service her car. 'Mrs Mewer,' she shouted into the room, 'Jesus will change your oil on Thursday afternoon – cash.'

The other remark, somewhat more embarrassing, was passed by Suza's husband, Jaime, a smallish, rather furtive-looking but very nice man in his late fifties. Jaime is Portuguese and has only lived in England for twenty years so speaks English so badly that it is almost impossible to understand what he says. One of his tricks is to shorten words, i.e. 'weather' comes out as 'weath', butcher as 'butch'. Polly and I were talking to some stuffy and no-fun-at-all neighbours at the gate, listened to by Jaime. We were telling these bores about a walnut tree we used to have from which we made pickled walnuts when Jaime suddenly thought he might contribute a little interesting information to the discussion. 'In my cunt,' he said affably, 'we grow four kinds of olive.'

One can hear Arthur's laughter. 'From an early age I liked to laugh,' he writes in *Life's Rich Pageant* (a phrase he coined in a sketch recorded by Columbia.) In his last years, he read in bed every night a few pages of P. G. Wodehouse, so that if he died in his sleep it would be with a smile on his face.

Peter Kelland was with him when he died on 27 January 1989.

Afterword

Fred Barnes and Naomi Jacob were famous for a time but are now forgotten, and Arthur Marshall's books are unlikely to endure. Of the three, Fred was the only one to flaunt his sexuality, during a period in history when it was dangerous to do so. Perhaps his very outrageousness – the fancy clothes, the heavy make-up – afforded him a kind of protection. Besides, he was on the stage, and people who were on the stage were allowed to be different, even in 1910.

Micky Jacob looked like a man, and a decidedly masculine one at that. She was also part-Jewish. You only have to read the popular (and, in some cases, the seriously literary) fiction of the 1920s and 30s to appreciate the role anti-Semitism played in British culture. She therefore had two battles to fight. She could not hide the very obvious fact that she was homosexual and the name Jacob (which her mother wanted her to change) was clearly not Anglo-Saxon. No photographs of her father Samuel survive, and I suspect that Micky destroyed them, but it is fair to assume that she inherited his looks. Micky turned herself into a 'character', as so many people do, to keep a certain protective distance from the ordinary world.

Arthur's penchant for impersonating schoolmistresses ensured that he would be regarded as an eccentric. The English adore eccentrics, and Arthur was a particularly adorable one, no more so than in his genial old age. He alone lived on into the era of gay rights, which he never espoused. Demonstrating for one's freedom to be queer would not have been, for him, the done thing – to use one of those slightly dated expressions of which he was so fond. It is revealing that he doesn't mention

Anthony Blunt in his autobiography, which was published after the spy had been exposed. He had known, and been friends with, Blunt for half a century. But Arthur was patriotic, and had fought hard for his country in the Second World War (under Gladys and Brenda), and such betrayal could not be countenanced. Arthur shared Anthony Powell's dislike of W. H. Auden and Christopher Isherwood, a dislike that had nothing to do with their being gay. (The homosexuals in Powell's novels are not stereotypes or caricatures.) It was founded solely on the fact that they took themselves off to America when Germany was warming up to conquer Europe. Their going, too, was a betrayal, and not to be forgiven. There was one matter that Arthur was always very serious about: if you had enjoyed the privileges of living in a democracy, then you should be expected to defend them when they come under enemy attack.

My own queer life began in the age of extreme bigotry and continues into the time of Aids. I have made no secret of my homosexual nature, which I have never flaunted, since 1972, when I referred to it casually in a book review for the *New Statesman*. In that same year, I fell hopelessly in love with a bisexual man (he subsequently married) and began an affair that had anguish etched all over it in large letters. Such is our human lot. Whenever I am described as a gay novelist, I reply that I am a novelist who happens to be gay. What's more, I don't function in that ubiquitous 'gay community' beloved of politicians and the media. I live in a community composed of varied men and women. I live among, and write about, human beings.

Prejudice persists, in spite of the advance in knowledge and tolerance. (The arrival of Aids in the 1980s had the Bible-thumpers shrieking of God's vengeance on perverts.) I could not help smiling when a noted lecher (now a peer), who treated his mistress contemptibly, declared on a radio programme that he considered homosexuality an 'abomination'. And when the tireless Baroness Young defends her opposition to the lowering of the age of consent for homosexuals with the self-aggrandizing observation that she is 'protecting the young', she has it on my authority that she is doing no such necessary thing. At the age of sixteen, I needed to be protected from queer-bashers, from clerics who thundered on about the sins of the cities of the plain, from neighbours who talked of 'pansy boys' in much the same way they talked of 'Jew boys'. This sensitive, working-class youth would have welcomed the protection of someone he trusted, someone – man or woman – who could have told him his feelings were natural. You protect the young by kind and considerate example. I had to find my own normality, slowly and painfully.

The pedant in me refuses to use that odd coinage 'homo-phobia', which, in the Greek sense, means 'hatred of sameness', and in the Latin 'hatred of mankind'. I'm happier with 'queer-hating', coarse as it is. The queer-haters are among us still, and will be there always. The saddest of them are those who adhere to the men are men and women are women principle and are blind to the surprising and subtle gradations of human sexuality. The worst of them are those intellectuals who justify rank prejudice with argument and reason. In his *British Writers of the Thirties* – published as recently as 1988 – Professor Valentine Cunningham calls male homosexuals 'youthies', Auden and Isherwood 'bourgeois buggers' and their love affair 'perverse'. The sneering doesn't stop there. Auden's marriage to Erika Mann, to enable her to flee Nazi Germany with a genuine passport, is described as 'typical of the Old Boys' relish for a practical joke'. The real joke is that the professor, safe in the cloisters of Oxford, cannot recognize an act of decency when it ought to be staring him in the face. The 'Old Boys' are the 'youthies', Cunningham's own quaint term for 'queers'. So it goes.

I can no longer bear to listen to Judy Garland, or indeed any of the other, less talented, fag hags of the 1950s and 60s. I prefer Peggy Lee or Billie Holiday. And if I need to read a gay poet, I turn to Cavafy and Frank O'Hara, whose witty and life-enhancing art was stopped in full flow when he died, tragically young, in an accident. I have to say that Henrik Ibsen, so maligned by Micky and Arthur, is among my heroes. Ibsen was, and is, the enemy of bourgeois complacency and entrenched thinking – the best kind of enemy there is.

I could have written about three other queer lives, more serious ones perhaps. There are enough to choose from. But Fred appealed to me, and so did the often monstrous Micky, as did the sometimes relentlessly jolly Arthur.

Requiescat in pace Fred, Micky, Arthur and all those thousands of now-anonymous queers who lived, laughed, loved and suffered.

Books Consulted

Fred Barnes

There are references to Fred Barnes in Harry Daley's *This Small Cloud* (1986) and in *Sex, Death and Punishment* by Richard Davenport-Hines (1990). He is mentioned in *Sweet Saturday Night* by Colin MacInnes (1967). He also features in Naomi Jacob's *Our Marie* (1936) and in at least two of her many volumes of autobiography. Tony Barker's essay on Fred Barnes in the magazine *Music Hall* is the nearest thing to a biography to date.

Naomi Jacob

The Seven Ages of Me by James Norbury (1965) is the only biography of Naomi Jacob. Norbury was the knitting correspondent for *Woman's Own* and similar magazines. A high Tory homosexual, Norbury dismisses Micky's involvement with the Labour Party as a youthful folly.

Me: A Chronicle about Other People (1933) is the first of Micky's autobiographies. Later volumes are often at variance with it, especially in regard to places lived in or visited. The most detailed account of her childhood can be fond in *Robert, Nana and – Me* (1952). From her vast output of fiction, only the novels concerned with the Gollantz family can be recommended with any confidence. Few English novelists of the 1920s and 30s were writing about Jewish life in London and the north of England, and these books – whatever their stylistic failings – do contain some interesting and unusual social detail.

Arthur Marshall

Arthur Marshall's autobiography, *Life's Rich Pageant* (1984), is very amusing, especially about his time as a pupil and then as a teacher at Oundle. His first book, *Nineteen to the Dozen* (1953), shows him in more serious vein. *Girls will be Girls* (1974) is a collection of his reviews and articles for the *New Statesman*. He is remembered affectionately in *The Dons* by Noël Annan (1999).